The Magicians

The Magicians

An Investigation of a Group Practicing BLACK MAGIC

Gini Graham Scott Ph.D.

ASJA Press
New York   Lincoln   Shanghai

The Magicians
An Investigation of a Group Practicing BLACK MAGIC

ASJA Press
an imprint of iUniverse, Inc.

iUniverse books may be ordered through booksellers or by contacting:

iUniverse
2021 Pine Lake Road, Suite 100
Lincoln, NE 68512
www.iuniverse.com
1-800-Authors (1-800-288-4677)

Originally published by Irvington

The views expressed in this work are solely those of the author and do not necessarily reflect the views of the publisher, and the publisher hereby disclaims any responsibility for them.

(except for brief quotations in critical articles or reviews)

ISBN-13: 978-0-595-43362-9
ISBN-10: 0-595-43362-6

Printed in the United States of America

Contents

CONTENTS

Acknowledgments

I wish to thank the many people who helped me in preparing
this book. First, many individuals in the groups I studied
provided me with information and advice.

Secondly, I received much help and encouragement from
many sociologists and anthropologists. In particular, I
should like to thank George DeVos, who worked with me
closely on the manuscript, and Marcello Truzzi, Eugene
Hammel, and Joseph Tamney, who offered their comments and
support.

Introduction

Modern society has prided itself on its rationalism and enlightenment and on the power of science and technology. Yet, in recent years, growing numbers of people of all classes have turned to a belief in magic—the use of supernatural forces to manipulate events—to increase their feelings of power and control.[1] Perhaps several hundred thousand believe, for the scale and complexity of modern society is overwhelming to many of all social classes, and they find magical thinking and practice a simple uncomplicated way to attain what otherwise might seem like distant and unreachable goals.

Many non-believers consider this shift frightening, since it suggests a return to irrational thought. Yet believers are attracted to magic by its non-rational qualities. They believe that the intuitive mind has untapped powers they can develop and use to get what they want.

This interest in acquiring power has a long history, since from the beginnings of human development, humans have sought all kinds of power—physical, economic, political, and social—to achieve various goals, including overcoming the natural environment, altering restrictive social customs and institutions, and going beyond the limitations of the physical self. Rosinski calls the process one of "self-transformation, self-conquest, and self-surpassing."[2] The result has been continual physical, social, and cultural change and progress, culminating in the high tech world of today.

Nevertheless, throughout history, this outward manipulation of power has never been enough, for humans have wanted to _feel_ powerful as well. At times, too, they have wanted more than they have been able to achieve through ordinary types of power. Thus, when doubting their ability

to use ordinary power, or when feeling this power was not
strong enough, they have turned to the supernatural realm.
In doing so, they have accepted its reality on faith, because it is an unknown, unseeable world—at least to
ordinary vision—and there is no way to prove or disprove
its existence. But believers have from the beginning
appealed to this world for personal and group power and
have developed elaborate magical and religious systems to
contact and use supernatural power for desired ends.
Through magic, believers have sought to manipulate spiritual power for particular goals by actively directing their
will or using objects of power to gain those ends. Through
religion, they have used supplication, prayer, and worship
to gain the spiritual assistance of a higher being. [3]

Traditionally, social scientists have claimed that the
believer sought supernatural power through magic because he
experienced a lack of knowledge, power, or security; felt
weak, frustrated, uncertain or deprived; and wanted to feel
more secure, powerful, and in control. [4]

They have based this argument on the assumption that
magic is not an effective means to practical ends, but a
delusionary system used when other power techniques fail. [5]
Therefore, with increased knowledge or power, believers
should have less need to believe and less interest in magic.
By this argument, one might expect interest in magic or in
magically based religious systems to decline due to the
massive expansion of knowledge, science and personal resources
in modern post-industrial society, since individuals can
turn to more scientific and effective techniques. Yet,
there are numerous indications this has not happened.
Rather, in spite of steady technical progress in the West
since the Middle Ages, a continuous magical tradition has
thrived, though it has gone through periods of greater and
lesser interest and openness. Also, sporadic periods of
religious revival have occurred which have attracted
believers by the promise of attaining goals through renewed
spiritual belief.

Historically, these movements have been especially
appealing to the downtrodden and powerless, although some
of the most knowledgeable and literate people of the times
have studied magic or participated in magical groups since
the Middle Ages, including Medieval monks, Humanist
scholars, and Romantic poets. Even Ben Franklin and Thomas
Jefferson were active in magical fraternities, and this
tradition of the scholar involved in magic continues today.

Much of the modern revival dates from the spiritual
growth movement of the 1970's, which spawned numerous off-
shoots that have continued strong into the '80's, such as
quasi-religious and therapeutic groups like est and more
secular self-improvement and prosperity-consciousness
groups. While many new religious groups have featured
explicitly magical belief systems, such as Satanists and
Witches, many other groups have incorporated elements of
magical thinking, but generally avoid the term "magic,"
because of its occult and Witchcraft connotations. These
magical thinking techniques include methods such as developing the will and visualizing to obtain a desired goal.

The popular press has widely chronicled these modern
developments. Other indications of the growing interest in
this area are the popularity of books on positive thinking,
the growing literature describing magical techniques, and
the expanding field of parapsychology. Some parapsychologists have been conducting studies on psychokinesis to show
that the mind can influence matter—a basic principle of
magical thinking.

Predictably, a growing number of critics and skeptics,
such as the Committee for the Scientific Investigation of
the Paranormal, have responded with alarm to what they
consider a revival of discredited irrational and magical
thinking, among not only the downtrodden and powerless, but
among all social classes.

The question is why is this happening? Why should
people who seem to have both knowledge and power in the
real world seek additional power through magical practice?
What do they gain from their beliefs, and what are the
effects of pursuing such practices? And how does believing
in and practicing magic change the believer's behavior,
patterns of social interaction, and lifestyle?

The Magicians explores these and other issues by
focusing on a magical-religious group composed of mostly
middle-class, well-educated individuals, which I call the
Church of Hu to protect its identity. The group describes
itself as an elite society of magicians involved in practicing black magic. I was a participant and observer in
this group for six months. For comparative purposes I
spent three months in a suburban white Witchcraft group, I
call the Church of Empowerment.

Classically, the distinction between white and black
magic is based on the intention of the practitioner in
using magical power. The white magician uses magic for

good ends, such as helping or healing others, while the
black magician uses magic for evil purposes, such as hurt-
ing or destroying someone.

However, the Hutians define black magic differently.
They claim black magic involves transcending or going
outside the natural order to achieve personal objectives,
and they believe they can do this. In their view, intent
does not matter, for magical power is neutral and can be
used to either help or harm. What distinguishes black from
white is that the white magician cannot step outside the
natural order to exercise his power over it, but can only
prod or bend it, whereas the black magician can direct and
control it from outside or above it. Conversely, numerous
practitioners of white magic would vehemently disagree, on
the grounds that they too can influence the natural order
to get what they want, though they use different terms and
symbols.

Holding these beliefs has very real and dramatic
effects on the values, behavioral patterns, relationships,
and lifestyles of believers, as I show by highlighting the
Hutians and presenting some parallels in the Church of
Empowerment.

To provide a background for this discussion, Part I
describes the relationship between religion, magic, and
personal power and the pervasiveness of magical thinking in
Western Society. Readers already familiar with the history
and role of magic in society may wish to skip this section.

Then, Part II describes the Hutians at length, and
discusses their beliefs, social backgrounds, use of ritual,
group organization, and the effect of magical practice on
their everyday lives.

Part III begins with a consideration of how the focus
on power produces some of the same group dynamics in the
Church of Empowerment as among the Hutians. Then it
features a discussion of how the search for power through
magic fulfills key psychological needs and affects the
believer's perception of reality.

I have written this book to appeal to the intelligent
lay reader and college student, although the serious scholar
should find it of interest, too.

PART I:

THE NATURE OF MAGIC AND POWER

1

Magic and Religion as a Source of Power
in Primitive and Modern Society

Since the origins of the social sciences in the late
1800's, anthropologists, sociologists, and psychologists
have examined the role of magic and religion in society.
The traditional point of view has been that magic—the
pragmatic manipulation of supernatural powers to achieve
specific goals—represents a response to feelings of
powerlessness and helplessness in the face of events the
individual can't control. Although social scientists still
recognize that individuals may turn to magic for this
reason, in the last two decades many researchers have
studied magic as a symbolic system or system of meaning
and claim that magical practice does change the individual's perception and experience of the situation. Also
it creates new shared meanings which influence how he acts
and interacts with others. Regardless of his original
motivation for turning to magic, the magical world view
restructures his experiential world and creates a new
reality.[1]
        Magical thought is based on two key principles of
thought, first stated by Sir James Frazer in 1922—the law
of similarity and the law of contact or contagion. The
magician uses practices based on one or both of these laws
to achieve the results he wants.[2]
        According to the law of similarity, he imitates the
desired result in his ceremonies on the premise that by
performing an action symbolically on one thing standing for
something else, he will similarly affect the thing sym-
bolized. For example, in image magic, he makes or obtains
an image of a real person, object, or situation, and acts
on it in some way. Or he performs motions which represent

something he wants to affect.

The history of magic is replete with such examples. A hunter draws a picture of a deer on a cave wall and strikes it so he can successfully kill the deer; a witch makes a doll image of someone she dislikes and destroys it so the symbolized victim will die; an Indian tribe performs a rain-dance in which participants imitate the motions of the falling rain to bring rain. In each case, an image, object, or motion stands for a real person, object, or event, and since it is similar, believers think the action taken against the one will correspondingly affect the other. [3]

In the case of the law of contagion, the magician acts upon a material object previously in contact with the person he wants to affect, on the assumption that whatever he does to the object will affect the person, because they were once in contact. For example, a magician gathers up some human waste products, like hair combings or nail clippings, or he takes a person's clothing and uses these in a rite to hurt or harm the person. To harm him, the magician might burn his hair combings or smash his nail clippings; to help him, he might hang up his clothing and use it to direct héaling energy to him.

Anthropologists have described how primitive tribes have used these principles, and magical practitioners in modern societies still use these principles today. However, as Frazer and other empirically-oriented social scientists studying magic claim, these principles are based on faulty assumptions about natural law and cause and effect, which incorrectly presume that humans can control the supernatural world as they do the natural one. [4] Not only can't they control it, but many social scientists assert there is no supernatural world, and hence nothing to control.

According to anthropologist George DeVos, these magical ideas about cause and effect actually represent a form of pre-causal thinking, as conceptualized by Jean Piaget in his scheme of the stages of cognitive development from infancy to adulthood. This type of thinking, DeVos asserts, is akin to the way the child views the world before he develops adult ideas about mechanical cause and effect. Stuck in the precausal phase, the individual believes real power to affect the external world derives from his personal intention or from the intention of a greater supernatural being. Then, being with others who believe the same way, he gets group validation and support for his beliefs. [5] In addition, when

he performs magical rituals in a group, he gains a sense of
participation in a power greater than himself, for the group
is a source of power, and he gains his power from it, as
Durkheim has proposed. [6]

The dispute about whether these magical beliefs and
practices create a valid new reality or faulty one is not
one that is easily resolved. But whether the reality is
true or not, these beliefs are deeply rooted. From the
first, primitives used their magic to help them kill
animals, plant crops, make objects, and achieve other ends.
As society developed, these beliefs about cause and effect
survived in religious and magical systems, and modern
believers continue to believe.

The reason these beliefs have hung on is because they
seem to work, either because the results are produced due
to non-magical causes or because the symbolic power of
magical ritual does indeed have some effect. In the first
instance, the believer may think he destroyed an enemy by
injuring his image or cured an illness by imitating the
desired healthy state. But in reality, the enemy was already embarked on a self-destructive course, and the ill
person was beginning to recuperate. However, the magician
does not want to accept a non-magical explanation, for by
believing in the efficacy of his magic, he can maintain a
sense of power and control. [7]

On the other hand, when the believer conducts a healing ceremony, he may find that the ceremony itself contributed to the cure, despite the possibility of other
explanations, perhaps by mobilizing the patient's conviction
he will be cured. Or possibly some energy produced in the
ceremony itself influenced the cure.

The reason why magic appears to work is still unclear.
But since it does seem to have this power, the believer seeks
to obtain it for several reasons. First, using magic gives
him confidence in a situation where he is uncertain he will
succeed and helps him feel protected when he fears bad luck
may adversely affect his efforts. Even though he may be
aware of natural causes, and may have sought to achieve the
desired results through his own best mental and physical
efforts, he may still fear failure or unfavorable supernatural intervention. [8]

This is the position Malinowski took after making his
classic study of magic among the Trobrianders, a Melanesian
people of the South Seas. As he observed, the Trobrianders
used magic when they lacked knowledge or certainty about an

outcome, but tended to use it less or not at all when they
did have knowledge and when chance results were less likely.
For instance, they took care of their gardens by using
their knowledge to select the soil carefully and plant and
weed as necessary, but used magical rites to protect themselves against the uncertain natural adversities, such as
droughts. Similarly, when they built canoes, they used
magical rites to complement their craftsmanship; and when
they fished on the open seas where the fishing was more
dangerous and the catch uncertain, they used magic for protection. However, when they fished in the inner lagoons,
they did not find magic necessary, since they already had
sufficient knowledge and confidence in their method. In
short, Malinowski found the Trobrianders used their
practical knowledge and work skills to deal with natural
forces, and magic to deal with supernatural power or the
unknown.[9]

When Evans-Pritchard studied the Azande, an African
people, he likewise found they used magic to fill in for
gaps in their knowledge. He noticed that they took pragmatic steps to multiply their crops, succeed in hunting,
smelt and forge iron, protect their property from theft,
and perform well in love-making. But they also used magic
when they performed these and other activities to protect
themselves from the evil powers of witchcraft which might
be operating in spite of any practical precautions.[10]

Tribal peoples are not the only ones to suffer
problems of uncertainty, powerlessness, and scarcity leading to a belief in magic. For modern humans, despite their
increased technical prowess, are still subject to the uncertainty of personal accidents, illness, and other
unexpected dangers, as well as the threat of scarcity, war,
blight, and other catastrophies.[11] So some of the anxiety-
producing factors contributing to magical thinking in
primitive society are still part of social life today, and
some people still use magic to cope with real and potential
dangers, as well as fill in for gaps in their knowledge.
They find it helps alleviate anxiety by offering them some
reassurance that they will overcome a threat or problem.
It helps them prepare to meet anticipated dangers by confronting it first symbolically through ritual, and it helps
increase their confidence so they can better deal with the
difficulty.[12]

Individuals and groups use magic to increase their
confidence and success in dangerous situations in numerous

ways. For example, tribal peoples in India use rituals
during childbirth to help the mother give birth and assure
a successful delivery. Sea-going peoples typically perform
rituals before setting off to sea. Modern sports figures
frequently use charms and personal rituals before entering
the sports arena. And some believers use prayer in a
magical way to give them strength and confidence to deal
with a crisis or achieve a goal. [13]

Performing magic also enables the individual to feel
he can attain a goal if he believes hard enough he will
get it and concentrates intensively enough on achieving it.
This quality of willing is basic to all forms of magic, and
it can be combined with both imitative and contagious
practices and used in any situation. Whatever the circumstances, the practitioner concentrates and directs his will
to raise power to obtain a desired result or prevent an
undesired one from occurring. [14] This is what modern magicians mean by "bending" the natural order or "speeding up"
the natural process to achieve their ends.

Magical practice can also bring the practitioner
personal benefits, such as prestige, political power, and
material goods through his claimed relationship to the
sacred. In primitive societies and folk cultures, the
tribal magician or shaman has traditionally been a figure
of high esteem. Today native clients still come from
hundreds of miles to be healed by noted South American
Indian healers. In the modern West, the magician is no
longer honored by society as a whole; but he gets recognition for his skill by other magical believers.

Finally, magic provides a system of meaning for
believers, through which they can pinpoint a responsible
agent or explain events in terms of ultimate causes apart from
ordinary cause and effect. Evans-Pritchard noticed the
Azande used magic in this way when they employed witchcraft
to explain every unfortunate happening, even though they
understood the other causes affecting the event. For
instance, if a granary collapsed on someone, they recognized
the physical causes causing it to fall (such as termites
eating away the supports). But they used witchcraft to
explain why it fell at the moment it did and killed the
particular man sitting under it. [15] The modern believer acts
similarly in attributing poor luck at a particular time to
bad karma or to magic directed against him by someone else.

The Functions of Magic as Part
of a Religious System

Though magical practitioners can practice magic outside of a religious system, more typically magic is
incorporated in a religious system involving a belief in
supernatural beings and forces, celebration, communal
expression, and worship. As part of such a system, magic
has additional functions.

First, when the believer performs magic as part of a
religious ceremony, he feels more power through belonging
to a group. Secondly, he gains extra emotional support
through believing in a spiritual world of powerful helpful
forces or beings and sharing this belief with others. As
Durkheim once observed, believing in the sacred exhalts the
believer and raises him above himself, while sharing in its
power helps him feel a greater force within. [16] In turn,
having such support helps him overcome feelings of aloneness
and alienation and increases his assurance and self-esteem,
so he can better deal with a sometimes hostile, uncertain
world.

Thirdly, the religious context gives the magical practitioner a system of meaning and order in a world that might
otherwise appear chaotic. [17] For example, without such a
system, events may appear randomly linked, making him feel
uncertain and helpless. But if he believes these events are
connected through a cosmic order of which he is part, this
makes them seem meaningful and he gains a feeling of power
and control. Likewise, when he performs a ritual couched in
a supporting system of religious myth, he can feel he is
part of a larger whole transcending his private existence
and therefore part of a greater system of meaning. [18]

In sum, the magician who practices magic as part of a
religious belief system or community not only feels power
through his magic, but from his religious belief and participation. His belief helps him feel raised above the human
condition and gives him a system of meaning and order,
while his participation links him with fellow believers in
a network of mutual emotional support. In turn, these feelings of power and support give him a sense of well-being,
which becomes a sign his belief system is effective and
thereby reinforces his belief. Thus, in effect, his belief
system produces the feeling of satisfaction which supports
his beliefs.

The Belief in Magic and Religion as a
Response to Personal Lacks

Although believers may gain strength and well-being
through their beliefs, some social scientists, such as
Freud, Alfred Adler, and Charles Glock, claim this sense
of strength and well-being is false, since religious and
magical beliefs are "illusions" or forms of compensation
arising out of personal weakness. They argue that the
believer believes to compensate for personal lacks.

Freud has pointed out the illusionary qualities of
religion particularly forcefully, and his arguments against
religion seem equally applicable to magic, since much magic
is practiced in a religious context. He contended that
religion is an illusion, since it is based largely on wish-
fulfillment, and is not related to reality. The individual
seeks fulfillment through religion because he is basically
helpless, defenseless, lacks self-esteem, and wants to
overcome this condition. Yet he remains helpless, because
his religious ideas are ultimately unfounded.[19]

Similarly, the psychologist, Alfred Adler, viewed the
human drive for power as a reaction to a deep, pervasive
sense of inferiority from which all humans suffer, leading
them to strive for some type of power.[20]

Sociologist Charles Glock suggests that the individual
may find social and psychic gains through joining a religious group, but is motivated to seek these gains, because
he is deprived in some way. His arguments are equally
applicable to an individual joining a magical group with a
religious belief system.

According to Glock's theory, individuals embrace new
belief systems in response to five types of deprivation—
economic, social, physical, ethical, and psychic. They are
poor and disinherited or feel they do not have enough; have
problems in relating to others or feel a lack of prestige,
power, status, or social participation; suffer from physical handicaps; are dissatisfied with the economic and social
rewards of life or the efforts required to obtain them; or
are simply dissatisfied with their situation. By joining a
religious group the individual seeks to eliminate his feelings of deprivation, and does so by gaining renewed personal
power and esteem through the group.[21]

Although many who turn to religion or magic do feel
especially deprived, the problem with these compensation
and deprivation theories is that feeling deprived seems

characteristic of the human condition; for virtually everyone may feel deprived in some way relative to someone else
or feel helpless or insecure, given the uncertainties and
difficulties of the modern world.

Thus, these psychological and social psychological needs
might be viewed as "pushes" leading an individual to seek an
outside source of power because he feels weak or deprived in
some way. Magic or religion can be one such source.

The Source of Magical Power

Regardless of why the believer seeks power through
magic, the increased power he experiences through it comes
from a variety of sources. These are conceived differently
in different magical systems. In some systems, the believer may feel his power comes from animate other-worldly
beings, who own or control this power, and can direct it to
help him if he communicates his wishes to them properly.
In other systems, he may believe in an unattached, inani-
mate power, which he can draw on if he knows the appropriate
techniques.´ In still other cases, he may appeal to a ·
personalized entity to obtain his power. But once he .
acquires it, he may use it as an impersonal force or object.

As Norbeck summarizes it, the magician can draw on
three types of power:
- a personalized power, which takes the form of
  human-like beings who influence supernatural power
  and events according to their personal wishes, will,
  or judgment.
- an impersonal supernatural power existing throughout
  the universe, which the individual may manipulate
  himself once he gains access to it or learns the
  mechanical procedures for controlling it.
- a supernatural power, which the individual creates
  by initiating certain sequences of activity that
  result in a particular cause and effect.

Each of these types of power represents a form of in-
tentional power located in the individual, in a supernatural being, or in the cosmos as a whole. It is a type
of power which exists apart from mechanical, social,
political, economic or other mundane forms of power.

Examples of each type of power can be found at all
levels of society. As an example of personalized power,
primitive and tribal groups believe in animal deities or

human-like gods who possess a variety of character traits.
In classical civilizations, such as Greece and Rome,
believers honored and conducted rituals to appeal to particular gods, like Diana, the moon goddess. Today, many
magical practitioners call on these ancient gods for aid.

An example of impersonal power is the notion of
"mana," which refers to a depersonalized force that exists
independently of specific supernatural beings and can be
used to charge persons and things.[23] Through magical
ritual, the practitioner captures and uses this force.
Originally, Malinowski developed this concept from his
studies of the Melanesian belief system. But the idea of
impersonal power is quite widespread, though called by
different names—wakan by the Sioux, njomm by the African
Ekoi, and zemi by the West Indians. Among literate
societies, the Greeks had their notion of dynamis and the
Indians the idea of brahma.[24] However, while belief in
this force is nearly universal, believers claim that only
certain classes of people or beings can possess or use it,
such as divinities, heroes, or sorcerers, and that only
certain objects can be imbued with it, such as sacred
fetishes or idols.[25]

The magician works with this depersonalized force
differently than with personalized beings. While he can
appeal to these beings as conscious entities aware of and
influenced by human behavior, he cannot appeal to impersonal forces or try to please them, since they cannot
perceive human activities. Instead, he seeks to acquire or
control those powers that seem useful to him and to avoid
those that appear dangerous.[26] For instance, a magician
might recite a spell to draw the impersonal powers into
him. Then, forcefully mobilizing his emotions and will,
he might direct those powers to achieve a desired end, such
as healing someone who is ill.

While some groups believe in either personal or impersonal power, some believe both impersonal power and
supernatural beings exist. In their view, these beings
have more of this power and can use it better than humans.
Thus, a practitioner may productively ask them to help him
in using this power.[27] As an example, some modern Pagans, a
group that follows a nature-oriented religion, believe in both
an abstract spiritual force and in a pantheon of deities.
They claim these deities have been created in primitive and
classical societies and have been empowered through generations of belief. When they perform magical rituals, they

call on these ancient deities to help them gain access to
the impersonal power so they can direct it to some goal.[28]
    In contrast, some modern magicians believe all the
power they raise comes from within and that they can train
themselves to develop this internal power. The Hutians
believe this way, as do other Pagans.
    Still other modern magicians view themselves as a
channel for a power which lies outside themselves, either
in a personal or impersonal form. That power, they believe, comes from a divine source or god.[29]

Techniques of Using
Magical Power

    Whatever the source of magical power—personal, im-
personal, external, or internal—believers seek ways to use
it. They employ a variety of formulas and techniques to
gain access to this power, mobilize it, and direct it.
    Those who believe the power resides in powerful spiri-
tual beings use techniques to appeal to them, such as
supplication or sacrifice, and often express awe and
humbleness in their presence. Believing these beings will
satisfy their demands if they have the right attitude, they
approach much like the religious devotee who humbly prays
to his god or gods. However, whereas the devotee entreats
the deities and hopes his prayers may be effective if the
gods are willing, the magician seeks to manipulate the gods
to do his bidding through his magical techniques.
    In contrast, those who believe in an impersonal ab-
stract power seek to affect the natural world by using the
correct magical gestures, spells, charms, or rituals, or by
focusing and mobilizing the powers of the will. Although
in ritual they may call on spiritual beings to help them
deploy this power, they believe the magician's ability to
manipulate power lies within or depends on using the correct
techniques.
    Notions about how to use techniques vary widely, too.
In some systems, believers think success depends on speaking the proper words, using the correct spells or herbs, or
exactly replicating rituals culled from ancient texts, and
they feel the successful magician must be highly trained.
But other magicians believe that this power is available to
anyone and that the magician can develop his own magical
rituals.[30]

An example of the first type of believer is the late
19th century secret English magic society, the Order of the
Golden Dawn. Members of this group believed the individual
required a long period of training to become a magician and
must learn certain spells by heart. Conversely, many
modern teachers of magic claim everyone is psychic and can
readily learn to concentrate and use his mental powers to
get what he wants

The types of techniques magicians use to acquire or
employ power are extremely varied. For instance, they call
on many different kinds of entities for direct or indirect
assistance. Cultures worldwide have created such entities,
and the modern magician draws from the deities and beings
once worshipped by other cultures, including the ancient
Celts, Greeks, Romans, Egyptians, and American Indians.
Some of these beings are identified with human qualities
or activities, like love, strength, or war; with natural
forces; with plants or animals; and with objects or places,
such as stones or mountains. Many deities represent a
composite of characteristics. [31]

Magical objects are also used in virtually all magical
systems to increase power. The magician finds or creates
them, and unless he thinks they are already charged, he
charges them with supernatural power. Frequently, these
objects are unusual, such as an oddly shaped stone; sometimes rare, like a precious mineral; sometimes very
beautiful, like a rock crystal or piece of obsidian; and
sometimes very large and impressive, like a massive rock
formation or towering mountain peak.

In literate cultures, such as Egypt and Greece, written
symbols and formulas have often become ritual objects. To
gain access to their power, the magician writes them down,
says the appropriate names, or repeats the formula a given
number of times.

Magicians also use divination to gain knowledge about
the intention of spiritual beings, so they can predict the
future or explain past events. In divination, the magician
performs an action with a number of chance outcomes; then
he reads and interprets the results to understand what
might happen. For instance in one type of divination, he
casts a horoscope to gain information from the stars; in
another, he tosses the I Ching coins; in a third, he reads
Tarot cards or tea leaves. The value of divination is that
once the magician knows about present and future possibilities, he can employ other techniques, such as prayer,
spells, offerings, or sacrifice, to change the situation.

For example, he can use divination to diagnose illness and propose cures, to determine the best time and place for an activity, and to confirm whether a tentative decision is a good one.[32]

Visions, trance, and other altered states of consciousness are another traditional source of magical insight. As an example, the Plains Indians used to deprive themselves of food and use self-torture when they went alone into the wilderness to induce a vision which they interpreted as a sign of attaining power.[33]   In South America, traditionally and today, Indian healers have used hallucinogens, such as the vine *ayuahuasca*, to gain information on the patient's illness and acquire the power to heal.

Magicians may gain direct knowledge or understanding through an altered state, and many go into this state to communicate with spiritual beings and ask their help, as occurs among the South and North American Indian shamans.[34] Mystics, in the tradition of Christianity, Judaism, and Islam, have used the altered state as a channel to contact and merge with a single god.[35]

Other aids to magical knowledge are amulets, talismans, and power objects, used to increase the magician's power or protect him or his clients against malevolent spiritual forces. These can be found stones, unusually shaped roots, carved wood, painted parchment—almost anything considered a power source.

Magicians also use purification techniques, such as bathing or cleansing rituals, to make themselves more open to receiving power, help them separate themselves from the mundane world, and make them more acceptable to the spiritual beings they hope to contact in ritual. Then, they can better work with these beings and forces.[36]

Spells are another important source of power. In traditional magic, practitioners believe the words of the spell have power, because they are inherently powerful or have acquired power through use. As a result, they have transmitted spells from one practitioner to the next. Less traditional magicians, by contrast, believe the specific words of spells have no inherent power, for the emotions and feelings produced by the spell have the power. Thus, they create their own informal spells to express what they feel, and vary which ones they use from ceremony to ceremony depending on their mood.

In some cases, groups are extremely secretive and rigid about magical practice to preserve their control

over the magic. Malinowski found this among the Trobrianders, and modern Satanists and black magicians are like
this, too. But other groups are more informal and believe
anyone can have access to magical power or transfer magical
knowledge to someone else, as is the case for the Azande
and many modern Witches. [37]

Once a practitioner gains magical power through whatever means, he can mobilize it to achieve his goals, such
as gaining insights or influencing others. Other magicians
in turn will judge his magical prowess by his success in
attaining these ends. The greater his apparent success,
the greater his presumed power.

Yet there are limits on how much power he can use and
how he can use it, for all systems, modern and traditional,
not only have laws of magic stating what acts the magician
must perform to be effective. They also include taboos or
rules prohibiting certain actions. The theory behind these
do's and don'ts is that they represent a natural law the
magician cannot disobey, for if he does, he will have a
negative result or his magic will rebound against him. [38]

In tribal societies, these taboos usually refer to
specific acts which lead to negative consequences, such as
a rule that a man should not sit cross-legged when his wife
is pregnant, since he may make her delivery more difficult.
However, modern magicians typically express taboos in a
more general form, whereby they claim that any inappropriate
or injurious act will rebound against the practitioner and
cause him injury or difficulty in the near or distant
future. In modern cults influenced by Eastern ideas, the
theory is that negative acts cause the individual to build
up negative "karma" or personal destiny leading to problems
in this life—or in the next.

In sum, many magicians believe that the magician who
follows the laws of magic and avoids taboos will use magic
successfully to gain supernatural power.

They maintain this belief by pointing to examples of
magical success, such as a magical ritual followed by the
desired result. Believers see these examples of magical
cause and effect as sufficient proof that magic works, although scientists dispute their claims on the grounds that
believers use faulty logic in that they selectively ignore
negative evidence and only use positive evidence of success. Also, they charge, a magician may claim success when
he could have achieved a result due to other factors,
because magicians frequently use magical techniques along

with other strategies or at a time when the desired event
is likely to occur. For instance, he may treat an illness
with both magical rites and natural remedies or perform a
ritual when the individual is starting to get well.[39]

Believers, of course, would disagree and would claim
that without the spell the event would not occur or would
be delayed. Moreover, they consider it reasonable to use
magic with other techniques or at an optimal time for
success, since this gives the magic a better chance to work
by increasing the probability of pushing or bending the
natural order.

Magicians also have ways to explain failure and continue to believe in their magical system, though the
scientist sees such explanations as rationalizations of
failure which maintain belief in an ineffective system.
For example, after a failed ritual, a magician can claim
his original magic wasn't strong enough and use stronger
magic, decide he didn't perform the spell properly and do
it again, or think he was doomed to failure by counter-
magic, and use other magic to reverse this.[40] To the
magician these are valid excuses involving mistakes in
applying the system or an outside influence interfering
with its operation.

Thus, both the traditional and modern magician can
continue to believe despite some experiences of failure.
In turn, this continued belief disturbs many empirically-
oriented social scientists and other non-believers, who
can understand how the ancients maintained their beliefs
without the benefit of modern scientific knowledge. But
they find it difficult to comprehend how modern magicians
familiar with the scientific method and the findings of
modern science can still believe and reconcile magical
beliefs with scientific knowledge.

Yet, modern magicians do. Though they draw on the
ancient magical tradition, they accept the principles of
modern science. They believe the two can be reconciled,
for they believe that magic is a natural process operating
by its own natural laws using forces that lie hidden to the
non-magician or non-believer. When used correctly, these
forces enable the magician to increase his power and
thereby achieve his goals.

The Pervasiveness of Magical Thinking

Magical thinking and practice have been pervasive throughout
Western Society. Even during the Englightenment, when a
spirit of rationalism replaced the medieval outlook based
on faith, groups of intellectuals continued to study magic.
Today, this interest in magic still seems widespread at all
levels of society, and it shaped the groups I studied.
This pervasiveness can be seen in:
* the history of the Western magical tradition
* the rise of the new religions
* the popularity of positive thinking
* the techniques of modern magic
* the scientific efforts by parapsychologists to
  support magical beliefs

The Magical Tradition in
Western Society

In Western society, a relatively continuous magical
tradition has passed from generation to generation and gone
through periods of greater and lesser popularity and public
awareness. This continuity has occurred because magical
thinkers have valued past wisdom highly, and have continually looked back to the past for wisdom. As a result, they
have retained in the tradition many older ideas about the
nature of the world, such as astrological concepts of the
Babylonians, despite changing ideas of science. Some
modern magicians even look back to what they believe were
the practices of the late paleolithic and earliest neolithic peoples who used magic to help them hunt or grow
plants.

Thus, traced back, modern magic has its roots in the
dawn of man when the first Homo sapiens appeared about
40,000 years ago and used magic to help them survive and
understand an often incomprehensible natural order. At
first, the whole band may have participated in these rites,
but gradually the shaman-priest emerged as a magic special-
ist who had greater knowledge of the spiritual world and
greater access to its power.[1]

Then, to skip ahead thousands of years, more special-
ized practitioners appeared in the neolithic agricultural
villages, which first appeared around 8-10,000 B.C. These
magicians participated in fertility cults and performed
rites to promote agricultural growth; studied the skies to
draw conclusions about heavenly influences on earth; and
put up shrines to mark sacred spots or honor deities. When
succeeding conquerors took over the territories where these
sites were located, they rebuilt these shrines on a larger
scale. As these shrines grew in size and the population
under one ruler increased, the power of the priest-magicians
associated with each shrine expanded, too.[2]

Eventually, as large urban centers developed, some of
these shrines became the sites of temples and large
magical-religious complexes designed to glorify the state,
and even more priest-magicians were needed to oversee these
temples and conduct rituals. To provide the priests with
the necessary training, the rulers founded temple mystery
schools, in which the priests learned a mixture of traditional beliefs, practical knowledge, magical rites, and new
scientific ideas.[3]

The development of writing in these early cities contributed to the growth of the magical tradition, too, for
the priests began to record their magical beliefs and
practices and could now pass them on systematically to
future generations. The endurance of these practices is
shown in the elaborate systems of astrology, alchemy, ceremonial magic, and pantheons of gods dating from this period,
which are incorporated into some magical practices today.
In turn, these practices have endured, since many magician-
scholars from the Middle Ages to the present have regarded
the magical ideas of these ancient civilizations as a high
point in the development of magic and have continued to
draw on their beliefs, deities, and magical formulas.

When the ancient empires began to break up between
about 1000 B.C. and 300 A.D., the state religions and
centralized schools declined. In their place numerous

small religious and magical sects flowered throughout the
Roman Empire, which drew on the older Egyptian and Baby-
lonian magical ideas. Later the beliefs of the more
successful sects, such as the Kabbalists, a group of Jewish
mystics, became part of the magical tradition.[4]

The Roman state religion absorbed many of these older
magical ideas, but when the Christians gained power in the
4th century, they opposed traditional magic and sought to
stamp out infidels and witches. In response, the magical
tradition went underground and for about 800 years was
confined to isolated rural pockets in the Roman Empire
and to the libraries of the non-Christian Arab world.

Then, in the 12th century, Christian monks began to
revive the teachings of the ancient mystery schools when
they discovered and translated long forgotten works of
magic, contained in the Arab books brought back by the
Crusaders, who had captured Arab territories in their cam-
paign to conquer infidels.[5] In addition, some monks added
their own ideas by conducting experiments to validate
ancient claims. For instance, Roger Bacon, a Franciscan
friar, did experiments in the middle of the 13th century to
prove the stars influence events on Earth.[6] Others tried
to reconcile magic and Christianity by suggesting that the
alchemical transformation of base metals into silver and
gold was like the regeneration of the soul through a belief
in Christ.[7]

Through these efforts, medieval Churchmen made magic
respectable again, and Renaissance philosophers and
scholars continued to investigate, experiment, and combine
magical principles with the new scientific knowledge. As
an example, the Renaissance physician Parcelsus used
magical principles to cure disease when he claimed a plant's
medicinal value was based on its external form.

Magic's growing respectability was also reflected in
its acceptance in the schools and courts. By the time of
late Middle Ages and Renaissance, astrological doctrines
were taught in the schools, and several state rulers, including Catherine de Medici and Queen Elizabeth of England,
invited magicians, astrologers, and prophets to court for
their advice. Wealthy families sought magical counsel,
too.[8]

With the rise of rationalism in the 17th century, the
natural scientists, doctors, and rationalist scholars
gained more power, and official reliance on magic began to
decline. However, magical thinking survived in secret

societies, such as the Freemasons and Rosicrucians, organized in England and the Continent to pursue magical study.
Also, independent thinkers on the fringes of established
religion and science, such as Emanuel Swedenborg and Anton
Mesmer, continued to explore occult ideas.

Then, in the mid-19th century, the romantics rebelled
against rationalism, and some romantic intellectuals and
bohemians in Paris and London gave the magical tradition
new life by joining new secret societies to practice ceremonial magic. Most noted of these was the Order of the
Golden Dawn, founded by MacGregor Mathers, an English
theologian. The well-known poet, Yeats, was a member.
Meanwhile, in America, Spiritualism became a new craze, and
popular enthusiasm embraced phrenology and palmistry.
Madame Blavatsky founded the Theosophical Society, which
introduced esoteric Hindu and Buddhist ideas from the East
to the West.

Like previous generations of magical practitioners,
the romantics, spiritualists, and other contributors to
this revival drew on earlier magical traditions. Later,
the writings of major 19th and early 20th century figures,
such as Aleister Crowley, Arthur Edward Waite, and Eliphas
Levi influenced 20th century groups.

This revival continued through the 1920's. Then, with
the Depression, World War, and period of materialism and
affluence which followed, broad popular interest in the
occult declined, although occult societies like the
Rosicrucians and Theosophists continued, and an occasional
medium, such as Edgar Cayce or Arthur Ford, generated
popular excitement.

Then, in the 1960's, with the emergence of the counterculture, interest in magic and the occult mushroomed again.
Hundreds of new groups emerged embracing magical and spiritual principles. Older groups gained an influx of members.
Occult books zoomed in popularity, and new magazines and
bookstores appeared. Psychic fairs and conferences became
popular. These developments gave magical practitioners a
new aura of respectability, and social scientists began
studying this phenomenon.[9]

While many groups were influenced by the Eastern medi-
tative tradition and stressed religious rather than magical
ideas, others, such as the Church of Satan, focused on
magic and drew on the old magical tradition. As an example,
the Satanists used ideas from medieval Christian magic in
their rituals, though they reversed the symbolism, and they

read heavily in the writings of the 19th and early 20th
century magicians, particularly Crowley, who gained
notoriety for his blatant use of drugs, alcohol, and sex in
conjunction with magical practice.

In sum, the magical tradition has a long history in
the West, and each generation of magicians has looked to
the past for ideas, while adding some of its own. The
Hutians and Church of Empowerment are both part of this
tradition.

The Rise of the New Religions

The new religious groups which developed in the mid-
60's are the immediate predecessors of the black magic and
Witchcraft groups which emerged in the 1970's. Understanding why these new groups emerged helps to better understand
the development of these successor magical groups, since
members of the latter joined for some of the same reasons.

These 60's groups formed due to a number of factors.
First, members joined in reaction to the sterility, impersonality, anonomity, lack of emotionalism, and emphasis on
efficiency and instrumental values characterizing modern
urban, technological society. They had not found fulfillment in education and affluence, resented the strain caused
by pressures to achieve, and were no longer willing to
sacrifice present satisfaction for status or a career.
Thus, they experienced a crisis of meaning, since they no
longer thought there was any point in striving for mainstream goals. So they looked to groups which rejected
materialism, the success ethic, and rationalism, for a new
set of values which gave priority to nature, social relations, and personal feelings.[10]

Many also questioned the legitimacy of American
institutions, when they found these institutions could not
cope with a variety of social problems they thought the
government could solve, such as poverty, racism, and the
Vietnam War. Then, when they found the social upheavals of
the late 60's which attacked virtually all American institutions did not solve the problems either, many became
demoralized, concluded it was hopeless to seek broad scale
social solutions, and retreated into more individual means
of finding personal fulfillment through religious groups.[11]

Thousands were also inspired to join because they had
had powerful spiritual and religious experiences when they

were part of the mid-60's drug culture and wanted to develop
further spiritually. Hence, they turned to the teachings
of the Eastern spiritual masters and to the Western magical
traditions, which offered ecstatic, immediate, powerful,
and deep religious experiences or powerful charismatic
leaders with direct insight to the divine. But they avoided
the traditional churches, since these had become secular-
ized and rationalized. Then, as the new religious movements grew, the relentless media brought many newcomers
into the movement.

By the mid-70's, this upsurge of interest peaked, in
part because of the decline of the counterculture and because the declining economy led to a renewed concern with
achievement and making money to survive. As a result, most
of the spiritual growth groups with a contemplative, other-
worldly, or inner orientation, such as the Divine Light
Mission, lost members. In contrast, action-oriented groups
centered around magical practice or thinking continued to
thrive, since magic is results oriented. Typically, these
groups did not use the term "magic" to describe their
beliefs or practices to avoid the negative connotations of
magic in modern society, such as superstition, false
belief, and anti-Christian ideas. Yet these groups did
employ some of the same principles found in magic, such as
the concept of using positive will-power to achieve material aims, which the prosperity and success groups like est,
Actualizations and Lifespring claim is possible.

Frequently, members of these action-oriented groups
were in the counterculture or in an anti-materialistic
religious group. But in response to social change, their
own values changed. They continued to want direct, ecstatic personal experience, but now they wanted to achieve
success or other goals, too.

In some groups, such as the Hutians, members are still
rebelling against the qualities and institutions of modern
society like the believers of the 60's, and are also concerned with experiencing present satisfactions. But unlike
the 60's, 80's believers don't want to drop out into placid
contemplative religions. Instead, they want to act prag-
matically, to change themselves or their immediate environment, regardless of conditions elsewhere. It is as if they
have adopted a "that's how it is" attitude, so they feel
free to seek success, using their personal powers to get
what they want.

Secondly, whereas believers in the 60's thought seeking

status or a career meant sacrificing present satisfactions, those in the successor groups of the 80's view the process of willing and achieving success as a source of present satisfaction and enjoyment in itself. This is reflected in both the prosperity and magical groups in the way members share proudly about how they have successfully performed visualizations or rituals to achieve their aim and how they have enjoyed the process.

In short, the believers in the new magical groups of the 80's seem to be pragmatists who have joined groups and embraced beliefs which help them survive by enhancing and using their own power. Group members may variously call what they are doing practicing magic, positive thinking, prosperity consciousness, or self-actualizing, but their focus is similar—achieving personal goals in a world offering little personal or emotional support.

To reach these goals, members draw on techniques derived from the tradition of positive thinking or the practice of magic; and they use the research of the parapsychologists on psi and altered states of consciousness to support their belief that magical power is real.

The Popularity of Positive Thinking

The tradition of positive thinking is based on the assumption that one can get ahead and be successful with the right positive attitude. It reflects the get-ahead optimism of capitalism.

Although the term "positive thinking" dates back to the 1950's, when Norman Vincent Peale wrote The Power of Positive Thinking, the attitude has long been part of American enterprise. Its continued appeal is attested to by the popularity of books on success techniques like Power by Michael Korda and Looking Out for Number 1 by Robert Ringer. And salesmen and entrepreneurs typify this positive-think approach in their conviction they can sell their product or make things happen.

Modern magical groups accept the underlying premise behind positive thinking—that one can ultimately succeed if he sees himself succeeding and believes he can do it. In The Power of Positive Thinking, Peale claims this process works due to prayer power—a three-step process akin to magical willing which involves praying or communicating with God to decide what to do, picturing the

determined goal, and working to achieve it. Modern magicians use a similar process, though they describe it
differently—as divining, willing, and manifesting. Like
positive thinkers, they claim that the process depends on
"belief" to work, because believing mobilizes a universal
energy or force which sets in motion the events needed to
make the goal occur. Much like Peale, who believes "all of
the universe is vibration...When you send out a prayer...
you employ the force inherent in a spiritual universe,"
they believe directing the will releases a spiritual energy
that can be used to attract good things to oneself.[12]
     Since Peale, the literature on positive thinking has
become a flood. In TNT: The Power Within You, Claude M.
Bristol and Harold Sherman claim you can "get what you
want" by picturing it clearly and confidently and persis-
tently enough. Then, your inner magnetic creative force
will attract it to you, since like attracts like.[13]   In
The Magic of Thinking Big, David Schwartz urges readers to
think big to attain big results.[14]   In The Miracle of Universal Psychic Power: How to Pyramid Your Way to Prosperity,
Al Manning observes that "what the mind can conceive, man
can achieve."[15]   The techniques in these books are designed
to help the reader train his mind so he can direct it to
achieve these "miraculous" results.
     Besides such books, the modern positive-think movement
is fueled by hundreds of conventions, meetings, workshops,
and groups which promote positive thinking as a way of
life. Dale Carnegie pioneered this approach in the early
1900's with seminars appealing to the middle-class mainstream, and since the late 60's and 70's, numerous other
positive-think oriented groups have emerged, such as Silva
Mind Control, est, and Actualizations, which emphasize
developing mind power and improving the self to achieve
personal goals. Since the late 70's and early 80's,
several dozen groups have emerged which focus on training
members to mobilize their mind power for personal prosperity and career success through workshops with names like:
"Prosperity Consciousness" and "The Fundamentals of
Prosperity."
     Although these books and groups have a mainstream
appeal and avoid any occult, mystic, or supernatural associations, the ideas they advance are a form of magical
thinking. They are based on key magical beliefs, such as
the law of attraction, which states that one will attract
back to himself what he puts out. Also, many of the

suggested techniques involve activities used in magical
practice, such as visualizing, making affirmations, con-
centrating and chanting to achieve a desired goal. In
turn, modern magicians have adopted many ideas from these
positive-think groups and advocates by taking their workshops or reading their literature.

In addition, these modern magicians draw on ideas
about the power of thinking advanced by metaphysical
writers who claim a person can develop his psychic abilities to accomplish feats which the average untrained
person cannot do. For instance, in Psychic Perception:
The Magic of Extrasensory Power, Joseph Murphy asserts that
the individual's extraordinary powers of mind transcend the
five senses, so that he can learn to see and hear psychically and travel out of his body. Then, he can "see beyond
walls, locate lost friends or relatives, receive wealth and
abundance, visualize future events, receive a spiritual
healing, and more."[16]

Other magical and metaphysical writers, such as Sylvan
Muldoon, Hereward Carrington, Dion Fortune, A.E. Powell,
and Anna Kennedy Winner, detail methods the individual can
use to train his psychic powers for astral travel, psychic
defense, past life awareness, spiritual healing, and future
prediction. And some writers make even greater claims for
these powers, such as G.I. Gurdjieff and Peter Ouspensky,
who believe the person's psychic or supraconscious part can
be trained so humankind will evolve to a higher state. In
The Psychology of Man's Evolution, Ouspensky suggests this
will happen because every person is normally in a state of
sleep or waking consciousness, but has occasional glimpses
of self-consciousness, so he knows this higher state is
possible. With the right methods, including applying will
and action, Ouspensky believes the individual can control
his consciousness, become fully self-conscious, and know
the full truth about himself. Then, he can advance to the
highest state of objective consciousness, where he can know
the full truth about everything, control all states of consciousness within himself, achieve a state of free will,
and become immortal.[17]

                    The Techniques of Modern Magic

Modern magicians incorporate the premises and practices
of positive thinking into the magical techniques they use

by combining them with spells, formulas, and symbolism derived from the magical tradition. They also believe, along
with some authors, that the mind has special intuitive or
psychic powers which go beyond positive thinking. Colin
Wilson expresses this view in The Occult when he suggests
that the mind possesses a special intuitive faculty called
"Faculty X," which enables the individual to have a deep
insight into the nature of reality. Potentially, all individuals have this faculty to some degree, but they must
develop it for it to work well. Then it will open powerful
new doors for them. As Wilson conceives it: "Faculty X is
the key to all poetic and mystical experience; when it
awakens, life suddenly takes on a new poignant quality...
Faculty X is simply that latent power beings possess to
reach beyond the present...Faculty X is a sense of reality,
the reality of other places and other times...It is the
power to grasp reality, and it unites the two halves of
man's mind, conscious and subconscious."[18]

These premises about intuitive and psychic powers are
incorporated into three major magical traditons—ceremonial
white magic, black magic, and Witchcraft. Although there
is much overlap in practices and beliefs in these traditions in that individual Witches may practice ceremonial or
black magic while individual magicians may adopt Witchcraft
beliefs, in general, magicians and Witches use different
symbols in their magical practices. White magicians and
black magicians also differ, in that white magicians use a
symbolism oriented around the powers of light and goodness,
black magicians around the powers of dark and evil.

For the most part, the ideas of modern ceremonial magic,
both black and white, derive from a synthesis of beliefs
and practices developed by the Hermetic Order of the Golden
Dawn, a magical society of several dozen members, which
flourished in England in the late 1800's and early 1900's.
The society is especially noteworthy for its cast of highly
educated, well-connected members, which included the poet
Yeats and the magician Aleister Crowley, known as the
"evilest man in the world," because of his exploration of
the powers of darkness and his debaucheries with sex and
drugs. While the group lasted, its members studied and
practiced the magical arts drawn from a number of different
sources: medieval Christian literature, Egyptian theology,
Greek philosophy, the Jewish Kabbala, the European Tarot,
and the Chinese I Ching. Some members of this society,
like Crowley, were quite prolific in writing about magic,

and the modern popular manuals on magic include much of this
earlier material.

According to one popular manual of magical techniques,
Principles of High Magic by King and Skinner, there are
three main principles: 1) total reality consists of both a
material world and spiritual world divided into several
planes; 2) the human will can be concentrated and trained
to affect the environment when directed by the imagination;
and 3) the magician can use the ordered system of correspondences in the universe to achieve his own purposes,
whether for good or ill.[19]

In working magic, modern magicians strive to make
their will powerful by learning to focus and project their
consciousness. Then, with their focused will, they invoke
or call on various entities from the spiritual realm, such
as archangels, elementals, and astral beings, using a
variety of magical techniques to create a suitable magical
environment for better invoking these spirits and strengthening and directing the will.

The magician's tools are employed in ritual to create
a magical setting. He uses the athame (or knife) and the
censer (or incense burner) to cast the circle, the bell to
call on the spirits, and the wand or sword to symbolize and
strengthen his will. Also, he usually adopts a magical
name to symbolize the qualities and powers he possesses
when acting in the role of the magician.

To prepare for a ritual, the magician first places his
magical tools on the altar. Next, he casts the circle and
invokes the entities he wants to assist. Then, using
candles, spells, chanting, talismans, visualization, and
other magical objects or techniques, he directs his will to
his goal.

In some magical systems, these procedures and objects
are extremely elaborate. For example, the magician may use
a system of correspondences whereby he selects certain
colored candles, plants, metals, gems, and incenses, depending on the season, time of day, planetary arrangement,
or the ritual's purpose. Magicians believe that using
these correspondences can make the ritual more effective,
because certain magical activities or objects have specific
magical properties and because the associations increase
the ritual's emotional intensity. Thus, the magician can
better project his will and get results.

For instance, suppose a magician wants to do a ritual
to obtain wealth. According to one system, outlined by

David Conway in Magic: An Occult Primer, he might use the
rite of Jupiter, since this planet is associated with increase, and employ the colors, metals, plants, incenses,
and gems associated with Jupiter: respectively blue; tin;
leaves of oak, poplar, narcissus, or agrimony; the spices
of nutmeg, cinnamon, cloves, aloes wood, or balm; and the
gems amethyst or sapphire. He might also call on the Greek
or Roman gods associated with that planet—Poseidon, Zeus,
or Jupiter, or on the animals or objects linked to it: the
eagle, unicorn, lion, dragon, bull, peacock, or sword.
Also, he might ask assistance from the archangel and
guardian angel associated with this rite—Zadkiel and
Chasmalim respectively.[20]

These procedures may sound intricate enough, but some
magicians complicate them even further by following additional rules and guidelines. For example, to determine the
best time to perform a rite, a magician might consider
relevant astrological data such as where the ruling planet
of his subject's birth sign is located in the zodiac, so he
can perform the ritual when this planet is in an auspicious
zodiac sign. Further, he might increase the associations
with his ritual even more by selecting objects or symbols
corresponding with this sign. For instance, if he conducted the rite of Jupiter when his subject's ruling planet
was in Leo, he might add these items indicated on his table
of correspondences: some gold, an opal or zircon, a sun-
flower, and a greenish yellow object.[21] In addition, for
even more assistance, he might call on various names of
power, such as the most high names of God—Jehovah, Tetra-
grammaton, Adonay, and Helim—or on the names of selected
angels and demons. Finally, he might use some traditional
magic words and charms, such as palindromes or word squares
which read the same forwards and backwards.[22]

To a non-magician, following these numerous correspondences may sound like nonsense. But the believer who
practices traditional magic thinks it makes sense to do so,
since each corresponding object or symbol has qualities
associated with the type of rite used or with the person
for whom the rite is done. Therefore, each one reinforces
the ritual's purpose and further focuses his will.

In contrast to these traditionalists, other magicians
believe it is not necessary to employ traditional correspondences or schedule the ritual according to the planets.
Instead, they believe they can perform effective magic by
choosing any imagery or symbols with personal meaning, and

selecting any time that feels right to them. For example,
to do a ritual to increase wealth, a non-traditional
magician might simply choose a convenient time and place
some objects on the altar which have meaning to him, such
as some coins or bills and a green candle symbolizing the
money he hopes to get.

Magicians frequently work alone, and traditionally,
Western magicians have been individual practitioners. But
sometimes modern magicians join together more or less
formally in small circles or lodges for particular workings
or occasions. One may conduct the ceremony or they may
split up the magical functions. In the latter case, one
usually acts as the principal official and leads the chanting, while others represent the four quarters of the circle
and lead certain parts of the ritual.[23]

When Witches practice magic, they adhere to similar
principles, except they are more likely to practice in a
group called a coven, and they use different symbols derived
from the old religions pre-dating Christianity. Their
central belief is that there is one basic spiritual energy,
divided into two polar male and female forces, which are
manifested as the mother goddess and male god, though they
give primacy to the goddess. Thus, whereas magicians
generally call on archangels, angelic spirits and demons
drawn from the Judeo-Christian tradition, Witches typically
seek assistance from nature spirits or deities representing
the power of the goddess.[24] Witches also use spells which
have more female imagery in contrast to the male-oriented
symbols of traditional Western magic.

The Scientific Supports for
Modern Magical Thinking

Even though one reason for turning to magic is a lack
of knowledge, modern practitioners, particularly group
leaders, are often well-educated with college and advanced
degrees. Some have scientific backgrounds, most notably in
computer programming, engineering, and physics. And even
those without college or scientific training have been influenced by the recent popular interest in science in
America since the late 1970's, reflected in the rise of a
half-dozen new popular science magazines, including Science
80, Nova, Discovery, and Omni, and several popular television series, such as Cosmos.

This climate of sophistication and scientism has, in turn, led modern magicians to look to science to legitimate their magical activities and their belief that magic works. Most notably, they have drawn on the findings of parapsychologists, transpersonal psychologists, and consciousness researchers.

All of these disciplines are relatively new and experimental, and mainstream scientists have questioned the validity of their findings and methods. But this is not the place to consider scientific merit. What is important is that modern magicians believe these findings provide scientific support for their own practices, and bolster their case by pointing to signs that these fields are gaining acceptance, such as the decision of the American Association for the Advancement of Science to include parapsychology in the organization in 1969.

They claim that parapsychological studies show that the forces magicians work with do exist and can be manipulated to achieve desired goals. They believe the transpersonal and consciousness research provides data on the altered state of consciousness in which these powers operate. And many cite research findings to support the skills they consider necessary to practice magic effectively—such as exercising ESP (which includes telepathy, clairvoyance, and precognition) and demonstrating psychokinesis or PK (which involves using an unknown force of mind to move objects or heal tissue). Through reading pop psychology, parapsychology, and transpersonal psychology, discussing findings, sharing ideas at conferences, and experimenting informally with tests of ESP and PK, modern magicians find scientific back-up for their beliefs.

Despite the controversy in the scientific community over some of these findings and whether these research fields are truly scientific, magicians point to a variety of experimental results as evidence of the effectiveness of ESP, divination, foretelling the future, and various mind over matter activities. The type of evidence used includes the ESP card tests performed by J. B. Rhine, who claimed his subjects made more right choices than they would by chance;[25] the random number tests for psychokinesis by Charles Tart, who claimed that his subjects were able to influence the numbers that turned up in that the chosen numbers occurred at a greater than chance rate;[26] and the studies of precognition and prediction by G. H. Soal, who found card guessers had a high rate of success in predicting the card the sender was going to send next.[27]

Likewise, some believers claim the remote viewing experiments of Harold Putoff and Russell Targ at S.R.I. support their beliefs about clairvoyance, since Uri Geller, isolated in a double-walled steel room, drew pictures of most of the target pictures sent to him, and other subjects described the characteristics and activities occurring at a site when a team of experimenters secretly visited it.[28]

They have used still other research to support their belief that the mind exists independently of the body and can be directed to leave the body to influence objects, obtain information, heal, or perform other acts. An example of this type of research is Tart's investigations of out of the body experiences (OOBEs), where he found that a few subjects hooked up to his lab equipment were able to identify a target number located on a high shelf, while having an out-of-body experience.[29]

Magicians have also found research to support their belief that personal energy fields or auras surround the body and give information on a person's mental and emotional state. In this case, some support comes from the Kirlian photography research of Thelma Moss and others in which photo images have suggested that the energy field around the hands expands when a person thinks positive thoughts or when a healer heals, and that a transfer of energy may occur from the patient to the healer.[30]

Additionally, they have used research on acupuncture and healing to support their belief in chakras or energy centers in the body; studies on subjects who can reputedly move small objects, such as the Russian housewife Nina Kulgina, to support their belief that the mind can influence and move matter; and the lab experiments with healers, such as Olga Worrall, who have increased wound healing and enzyme activity, to support their belief that the mind can heal another person.[31] Similarly, they have used the reports on life after death experiences, described by Charles Moody, Elizabeth Kubler-Ross, and others, to support their belief in reincarnation and soul survival after death.

Finally, they have found support for their belief that the magician becomes more powerful in the altered state produced by ritual in the consciousness research by investigators like Charles Tart, who claims that the individual in an altered state becomes more receptive to ESP and better able to exercise PK.[32]

In short, many modern magicians use ideas from

parapsychology research, transpersonal psychology, and
studies of consciousness to support their belief that magic
works, since the findings, though still preliminary and
controversial, appear to legitimate their claims.

PART II:

THE USE OF POWER IN A BLACK MAGIC SOCIETY

Introduction

The search for power through magic can lead believers to two types of magical practice—black magic and white magic. Depending on how believers define it, black magic involves working outside the natural order or using magic to achieve an evil intention, while white magic merely bends or prods the natural order and is used with a good intention. Some believe they can use either type of magic, since power itself is neutral, but can be directed for different purposes.

Becoming a magical practitioner, in turn, has a major impact on the believer's behavior, life experiences, attitudes, and personality structure, since the magical belief system offers a world view that differs from the non-magical way of regarding the world. Everything that happens becomes fraught with meaning; events are no longer simply coincidences or chance occurrences. Instead the magician sees them as omens or magically caused by himself. Likewise, his desire for power leads him to see his own actions and interactions with others as indicators of his level of personal power. While individuals with certain types of values, personality characteristics, and social attributes may be attracted to magic, the magical experience acts on these qualities to shape and mold the believer's behavior, life experiences, attitudes and personality structure.

This section explores the way this process works in a black magic group, which I call the Church of Hu. I have changed the name of the group and the identities of members to protect them, but otherwise this discussion accurately describes events and processes occurring in the group.

3

Introducing the Church of Hu

The Church of Hu is a California-based secret magical
society which emerged in the mid-1970's. I have called it
the Church of Hu to reflect its Egyptian orientation, while
protecting its identity. In the classical Egyptian religion, the term "hu" signifies the divine creative power,
and since the group's primary focus is honing the will to
achieve personal power and direct it to desired ends, this
name seems quite appropriate.
    The Church was organized in 1975 as an offshoot of the
Church of Satan, which was founded by the well-known San
Francisco magician and former circus trainer, Anton LaVey,
who gained notoriety in the 60's and 70's for his Satanic
wedding ceremonies, baptisms, and pet lion, Togar, whose
roars frequently unnerved the neighbors. The Church consists of approximately 40 members, about 30 of them in
California, led by a high priest and administrative head,
called respectively the Magus and the Ipsissimus. This
division into religious and secular leadership is designed
to reflect a similar division in classical Egypt. A
council of nine members, aptly called the Council of Nine,
assists in making policy decisions and carrying out the
wishes of the Magus and Ipsissimus.
    The group views itself as an elite secret society
devoted to personal development through magic, and members
consider themselves part of an elect. The group's activities and hierarchical structure are designed to help members
develop their power through personal growth and further
their sense of being special and powerful. In turn, being
part of the group helps members feel they are better than
others, who they regard as "mere humans," and reassures
them that as an elect, only they will survive the coming

annihilation of humanity, which they are certain is only a
matter of time.

   According to the Church's philosophy, the Hutians are
an elect who will survive because they have chosen to revive
the cult and learn the wisdom of the Egyptian deity, Hu,
whom they regard as the prince of darkness and the earliest
known deity. A key principle of this wisdom, Hutians believe, is that personal power comes from properly developing
and strengthening the will through a long process of personal growth and then directing it to desired goals. They
also believe they must communicate with and gain the assistance of Hu to develop and exercise the will properly. However, they don't worship him; rather they consider him a
friend and guide, who will help them grow and achieve their
ends.

   In the group's chronology, Hu first appeared in the
modern world in 1904 as HarWer, his opposite self, when the
English magician Aleister Crowley announced the beginning
of a new Aeon and proclaimed himself Magus of this Aeon.
This period marked a time of purification characterized by
a focus on developing the will. Presumably this purification would end the stasis humans were experiencing because
they incorrectly believed in and accepted the reign of the
"death gods," and would prepare them for what would follow.

   Then, in 1966, year one in the group's canon, another
highly significant event occurred—the founding of the
Church of Satan by Anton LaVey, which marked the beginning
of the Age of Satan. According to the Church, LaVey
announced that the watchword of this age was indulgence,
and proclaimed an end to the hypocrisy of mainstream religion, thereby marking a new Aeon and taking a further step
in the liberation of the human spirit. Furthermore, Hutians
consider the age a major turning point, because they believe that HarWer and Hu now became fused together as one
composite being. This fusion, they believe, was like a
bridge between the preceding Aeon ruled by HarWer, and the
coming one, to be ruled by Hu. It was a means to prepare
the way for the coming Aeon of Hu which would be even
greater, for Hu would manifest in all his glory.

   Presumably, this latest Aeon got underway with the
founding of the Church. This occurred when about half the
members of the present Church, who belonged to the Church
of Satan left it in mid-1975, because they became dissatisfied with some of LaVey's policies, notably his decision to
sell church memberships and degrees to virtually all who

applied. Although LaVey decided to sell memberships because he needed money for the Church and considered the
degrees a meaningless symbol which could be used for
aggrandizement and manipulation, those who split away felt
his act made the Church's degree system worthless and made
the recognition of their efforts to develop as powerful
magicians meaningless. In their view, the degree system,
describing five levels of development from novice magician,
to adept, to priest, to master of the temple, to magus,
reflected each individual's level of achievement attained
through years of reading and magical practice. But if the
degrees were sold, anyone could rise in the Church, regardless of knowledge. He would merely have to pay for his
degree.

As a result, led by their present Ipsissimus or secular
head, whom I will call Ipsissimus Andrews, then a Magus or
Fourth Degree in the Satanic Church, they defected. Since
Andrews was the editor of the Satanic newsletter, he had
access to the mailing list and he wrote to the Satanists to
advise them of his plans to continue the Satanic Church in
a purified form, for at first he merely intended to purify
the existing Church. But during a fall equinox ritual, he
had an experience in which Hu manifested through him and
dictated a short book, I will call The Book of Emergence
Out of Darkness. He took this event as a mandate to
announce the beginning of a new age, the Aeon of Hu and
create the new Church.

According to this document, Hu revealed himself in his
majesty and designated Andrews the Magus of the new Aeon.
Also, Hu mandated Andrews to recreate and reconsecrate the
Church of Hu, which had existed in Egyptian times before
the cult of Osiris destroyed it, and to restore its rightful
priesthood. Those who sought the knowledge of Hu would be
called Hutians, but only the elect could obtain this knowledge, because the rest of mankind would be annihilated.
Though Hu could not preserve his elect, he would give them
guidance in strengthening their will so that no creature in
the universe could withstand it. Then they would be protected against the coming dangers.

This document also revealed that the way to develop
will was through personal growth or becoming as expressed
in the word "Xeper," which means become and derives from
the name of the Egyptian beetle god Khepri, god of the rising sun. Finally, the document instructed the Hutian to
speak directly to Hu at night as a friend and Prince of

Darkness, using a pentagram as a gate to contact Hu. Then, through this process, the individual could "Xeper" or grow.

But soon the question arose: "Become what?", and two years later, the present Magus, Kel, then a Master of the Church, spoke the word "Xem," referring to "the absolute" or "higher man," when he and a half-dozen Hutians were conducting a ritual. A year later when Andrews became its Ipsissimus, he passed the mantle of the Magus or Priest to Kel, who had first spoken the word "Xem." As a result, the group focused its practices around the phrase "Xepher Ir Xem"—become by working to evolve to higher man. The way to evolve, of course, was to develop the will and therefore one's magical powers.

Given the milieu of the 70's, with its emphasis on personal growth and the emergence of thousands of growth groups ranging from spiritual movements to personal therapy-type groups, it is not surprising that a magical group arose with a similar focus. But the Hutians differed from the others in their emphasis on developing oneself not only spiritually and psychologically, but as a magical being with a powerful will who could transcend the natural order and direct his will to achieve whatever he wished. Such an individual, to use group terminology, would have success-fully "Xephered" to "Xem."

But Xephering, as Hutians conceive it, is not an easy process, for it takes much commitment and discipline to look within and develop magically. To Xepher, group members must engage in two essential practices: they must regularly take part in individual and group rituals, and they must adopt and use a magical name representing the desired personal qualities. Hutians consider these practices essential, because they enable the individual to leave his mundane self behind and enter the magical realm where he can direct his will to affect the natural order and thereby achieve power over himself and the natural world. Although Hutians believe this development may be long and difficult, they feel it necessary and worthwhile, since at the end comes total self-mastery leading to complete freedom without limitations.

Of the group's approximately 40 active members in mid-1980, about half are males and half females. About one-third are married, about half of these to other Hutians. Although many are scattered around the country, the core of the group, about 25 members, is in California. Here, they are loosely organized into two groups called pylons—the

Horus Pylon in San Francisco, composed of about a dozen
members, and the Hathor Pylon in Los Angeles, consisting of
nine members in L.A. and three in Santa Barbara. Officially,
most Priests and higher status Hutians are not pylon members, since individual Priests organize these pylons to
instruct the lower level members, and higher status members
get together informally to perform rituals or study magic
on their own. But the pylons do form a focus of regular
group activity, and higher status members appear occasionally to assist the Priest or Priestess heading the pylon.
Since at the time of the study, several East Coast and
Santa Barbara members planned to move to San Francisco in
late 1980 or early 1981, increasingly the group is becoming
centered in the San Francisco Bay Area.

The group's leadership is provided by the priesthood,
which consists of members who have achieved Third Degree
status or higher, representing an advanced level of spiritual and magical growth. Currently, about half the membership—18 individuals—are at this level, with the bulk of
these—14 members—previously members or priests in the
Church of Satan. The lay members, called First Degrees
(Level I) or Adepts (Level II), are in training. While
First Degrees are in trial status, Adepts, who are considered accomplished ceremonial magicians, have permanent
status in the Church.

So who becomes a Hutian and why do people join? What
happens in a ritual? What do members believe about Hu and
how do they relate to him? How does the philosophy and
structure of the Church affect how group members perceive
and relate to members of the larger society and to each
other? And how do group members use the magical power they
claim to have?

In the following chapters, I consider these and other
issues. However, before doing so, a few remarks on how I
studied this group.

I joined the San Francisco Pylon as a full member in
January 1980 and was a member for six months, until I was
advised that I was not growing properly and was therefore
not of the elect. To join, I had to indicate that I was
sincerely interested in my personal growth and wished to
develop my will as a magical being. Also, I needed a personal invitation since the group is extremely secretive and
all new members must be sponsored by present members.

Thus, it took me some time to be invited to join. My
first contact occurred after I took a magic class with the

Priestess heading the San Francisco Pylon in the summer of
1979. But during the class, she never mentioned the group,
so I was not aware of her involvement. Then, about six
months later, I encountered a former acquaintance who
described himself as a practicing magician, and I referred
him to the Priestess. This referral led me to talk to her
again, and this time, when I mentioned my interest in getting involved in a magical group, she told me about the
Church. A major reason for her openness now was my contacting her about the referral, because she felt my chance meeting with my acquaintance and the subsequent chain of events
did not occur by chance, since she believed there is no
coincidence, but happened in order to lead me back to her.

However, even though she told me about the group, I
still had to prove I was sincerely interested by insisting
on my interest repeatedly, until convinced, she gave me a
brochure describing the Church's philosophy. Then after
reading it, I had to again reaffirm my interest to her.
Finally I had to send $37 and a letter to the Church's
Executive Director explaining why I wished to join and
indicating that the Priestess was sponsoring me.

About a week later, I was invited to attend my first
Pylon study group, designed to help the group's lay members,
consisting of three others beside myself, learn about the
Church and its teachings. In the next six months I attended
six of these study sessions, six regular Pylon meetings,
and the group's Annual Conclave. In addition, I socialized
about three times a month with Church members and read
several hundred pages of Church literature.

4

Who Are the Hutians?

Hutians come from a wide variety of backgrounds, although
there are certain commonalities since they share similar
motives for joining a group stressing the development of
power and the possession of elect status.

The concept of status deprivation is a useful one for
understanding why Hutians join. As sociologist Charles
Glock has observed, members of new religious groups tend to
be attracted because they feel deprived in status due to
economic, physical, social, ethical or psychic reasons. In
response, they seek out a group that makes them feel good
by giving them a sense of power, which they gain from their
new identity as a group member and from the support and
validation other members give them.

The dynamics behind joining the Church of Hu are no
exception. The image of being in an elect, elitist group
is a powerful one, and as a Hutian each member can feel part
of that elite. Then, any feelings of deprivation can melt
away through the affirmation of self in the group.

The idea of developing personal power can also be
appealing to someone who feels a lack of it in daily life
in two key ways. First, the group can help the member feel
more confident, so he becomes more effective in meeting
daily challenges. Secondly, it can provide him with an
explanation or rationale, so he feels more comfortable
about his lack of power in the everyday world. For instance, the group can claim that magical or spiritual power
is more important than worldly power, so the member can
feel he is a powerful being, despite experiences outside
the group which suggest otherwise.

The backgrounds of the Hutians and their motivations
for joining suggest these factors are operating, since

overall they do lack worldly power and show other characteristics fitting in with Glock's deprivation theory.
First, Hutians are characterized by a high level of intelligence, which might be expected in a group stressing
extensive reading and research on magic. Two members of
the group have doctorates or are getting them; two have
M.A.'s. Three members are in Mensa, an organization of
people scoring in the top 2% of the population in I.Q.
Several others have been to college or had some post gradu-
ate training. Yet, even so, most group members haven't
gone beyond high school, despite extensive study on the
occult and magic.

Occupationally, the majority of Hutians are in blue
collar or lower white collar occupations, including some of
the following: policeman, bartender, cook, salesperson,
hairdresser, word processor, secretary, unemployment clerk,
and government clerical worker. Although most are stably
employed, they do not generally find the world of work
interesting. It is boring, restricting, and not physically
fulfilling. A few have had trouble keeping jobs and have
moved from job to job. For example, one male moved from
one poorly paying sales job to another and frequently had
trouble paying the rent.

Those in higher level positions tend to work with
things or numbers rather than people. For example, two
members are computer programmers, and three members have
financial positions as a bank teller, accountant, and stock
broker. A few women are in lower level authority positions
as teachers and a high school principal.

Within the group, members who don't like their positions or everyday status can put them aside, since the
Church is oriented to the magical spiritual realm and not
to the mundane. Thus, outside occupational status doesn't
count for much within the group. In fact, group members
tend to avoid talking about their backgrounds, in part because they have limited interest in their low status jobs
and in part because they consider a discussion of mundane
topics a distraction from the group's focus on magical
growth. Thus, though some Hutians do occasional rituals to
improve their job situation, in general Hutians feel growth
should be directed at inward development, not external
success. In fact, as Hutians rise in status, they tend to
put more and more energy into their magical evolution rather
than into mundane activities, and may disengage themselves
from regular full-time jobs to gain more time for magical

study and growth.

Although most members exhibit this split between dull
mundane jobs and the magical world, for some members the
search for power within the group is paralleled by an interest in power outside it. As an example, several members
have engaged in military or intelligence work, and a few
are active as military reserve officers. The two members
who have or are working for doctorates are studying political science—another indication of their interest in power.

Religiously, most Hutians are deeply alientated from
conventional religion and even openly hostile. In fact,
many talk of turning to the Church as the "religion of last
resort," so disgusted are they with other religions. One
woman raised in New England as a Southern Baptist felt her
parents put her down as a child whenever she questioned her
religious tradition, and their attitude led her to doubt.
her religious beliefs, since she thought a fear of questions
suggested a weakness in the faith. When she learned about
the Church of Satan soon after it was organized, she joined
eagerly, for its philosophy of indulgence and an end to
hypocrisy expressed exactly how she felt. Then, when the
Satanic Church proved to be inactive, she joined the Hutians.

Another man originally wavered between being an agnostic
or an atheist, and as a teenager turned to fundamentalist
Christianity to gain group support. However, he soon became
hostile to Christian ethical precepts, because he felt they
emphasized suffering and supported a person being a "loser"
now, since he could gain salvation in a future life. Also,
he thought the faith was weak because it didn't require a
person to do anything, only believe. After he read Ann
Rand's philosophy of individualism, he rejected his past
beliefs, and when he heard about the Church of Hu from a
friend at work, he joined, since it supported his indivi-
dualistic anti-Christian beliefs.

These examples are characteristic, since most Hutians
have rejected Christian backgrounds, although three newer
members are Jewish. About half of the Christians have had
Catholic backgrounds, and they have been particularly
hostile to Catholic dogma and restrictions. For example,
one East Coast Master was born into a middle-class religious
Italian family and dropped away from the Catholic Church
because he disagreed with its creeds and emphasis on absti-
nence. Further, he blamed the Church and organized religion
for most of the problems in the modern world. In response,
he turned to the Church of Satan and later the Church of Hu,

because it set forth no inhibitions, which enabled him to
pursue the pleasures he liked without feeling the guilt
fostered by organized religion. Another female Master
abandoned her Catholic faith, since she considered it
"ignorant" and filled with narrow hatreds.

Others rejected Protestantism. In one case, a Priest
had converted to Catholicism in his early years after finding nothing in Protestantism and even studied to become a
religious brother. But after he failed to discover Christ
and the Host in himself and experienced only silence, he
concluded Christianity was a sham and sought something real.
At first he found this in the Satanic Church, since he felt
the presence of Satan, but joined the dissidents in founding the Church of Hu.

In other cases, members have explored alternative
religions in California prior to joining the group. One
Priestess who was formerly an atheist explored TM and Silva
Mind Control during the upsurge of interest in Eastern
religion, decided these groups offered only techniques, and
wanted something more. Another female Adept who had been a
Witch for 11 years got involved since she wanted something
to help her cope with a major life crisis—a suicide of a
close friend—which she didn't understand. After his death,
she found Witchcraft no longer seemed to hold the answers
for her, and she felt by delving deep within herself she
might better understand.

Besides being alienated from conventional religions,
most Hutians are alienated from society in other ways—some
because they have made lifestyle choices setting them apart
from the mainstream; some because they have personal
characteristics making them appear "different" or "weird."
Hutians frequently comment on this "weirdness," but in the
group it becomes a source of pride and a mark of their
specialness as a member of the elect.

This differentness is reflected in a number of ways.
About half the Hutians look quite distinctive: several
women are extremely heavy; one woman looks very masculine,
though she isn't gay; a few men are relatively short—5'7"
or less, and two are extremely tall—over 6'6". A few men
have grown beards or wear their hair in a distinctive
clipped way to look sinister or "Satanic;" some women wear
black lipstick or nail polish at times. In addition, four
senior members are gay. A few women are very pushy and
aggressive. Several members are socially inept, and have
difficulty relating successfully to members of the opposite

sex. And a few Hutians tend to avoid social contact. For example, one woman virtually never left her apartment except to go to work and to occasional group functions. And when she was home, she often kept her apartment dark, except for a few dim candles.

In short, by mainstream standards about half the members stand apart. In turn, this distinctiveness is often emphasized and becomes a point of pride within the group—so much so that Hutians frequently comment on the unusual reactions of outsiders who notice them or share examples of how people moved away from them when they have gone somewhere by themselves or in a group. For instance, one Priestess noted that people often moved away from her at parties; several others reported that people frequently cleared out when they went to restaurants; and a Hutian who had been at the first group gathering in Michigan in 1979 observed that people would come out of their rooms, see a group of Hutians in the hall, and go back inside.

While some people might find this kind of social reaction a disturbing sign of rejection, Hutians glory in it, as if the power and will they have developed acts to push others away. Thus, they interpret rejection as another sign of election and of being not only different but better than non-Hutians or "mere humans."

Ironically, before becoming Hutians, many members did not have or display this feeling of superiority, for they confronted assorted personal problems and some questioned their own worth. For example, one Priestess struggled with alcoholism, which she was able to overcome in the group; another Priestess previously felt insecure about whether she was a worthwhile human being, but realized after she became a Hutian that she had much to offer.

Others turned to the group to gain a sense of power and control over others which they lacked in daily life. For instance, one Adept joined both the Church of Satan and Hutians because he wanted to gain power to get others to do his will. In particular, he hoped to attract women and improve his financial position through lust rituals and rituals to bring success, because in the past he hadn't been very successful in either area. Another Adept claimed the group helped him become more focused and directed, so he could better know what he wanted and go after it.

Still others have been attracted by the idea of becoming part of an elect. One Hutian who hated her boring job spent several months thinking about whether to join, while

dating one of the Priests. At first, she was uncertain if
her interest was sincere or whether she was doing it for
him. But as she read and learned more, she concluded she
was indeed a member of the elect and should therefore join.
She felt even more sure of her decision, because when she
made it, she had temporarily broken up with the Priest.
Then, once she joined, they began dating again.

Finally, all members have been drawn to the group by
its focus on self-discovery, since they find appealing the
chance to look deep within to determine who they really are
underneath their external or "functional" personality, as
group members refer to the outer self. By looking within,
members claim they can peel through their outer layers, like
unwrapping an onion, to discover their core-self. Then,
they can draw on the powers within to project the will, the
source of all magical power, to evolve to higher man.

This focus on the self and being part of an elect
group in turn affects the way members relate to the external
world and the qualities they bring to the group. First,
since members are mainly concerned with self-development to
attain personal power, they have little concern with non-
members who are not of the elect. Secondly, since they
have a limited concern with others, most members tend not
to work in occupations involving personal service or care
and tend not to pursue such activities in their free time.

In summary, Hutians value responsibility to the self
and to the group, since they believe that only members will
survive the coming annihilation. Others, "mere humans,"
will not be saved. But then, the Hutians aren't disturbed
by this and consider their looming destruction just, since
they consider "humans" to be "annoying, often degenerate
pests, who are corrupt, untruthful, stupid, and generally
unfit to survive." Unlike the evolving Hutians, who have
tapped their magical powers and are in the process of becoming higher man, mere humans lack such powers and are
thus unworthy beings.

5

What the Hutians Believe

The beliefs of the Hutians are designed to reinforce the
central focus of the group—increasing power through personal growth and developing the will. There are five key
beliefs: 1) that the entity, Hu, exists; 2) that the
pentagram opens the door to communication with Hu; 3) that
self-growth through looking within is vital because it is
the path to becoming higher man; 4) that the use of magical names promotes communication with Hu and personal
growth; and 5) that personal and group ritual are necessary
since they provide a channel to another dimension, where
one can direct the will to get what one wants. This chapter discusses the first four beliefs; ritual is considered
in the next.

The Belief in Hu

The group's belief in Hu dates back to the night when
Andrews, the founder of the Church, claimed Hu revealed his
existence to him through a document called The Book of The
Emergence Out of Darkness. Supposedly, Hu announced his
presence to Andrews, indicated he had returned to mankind
again after a long period of being forgotten, and dictated
the document which proclaimed that it was time for Hu's
glory to live again and for Hutians to glorify his name.
Aside from these claims of revelation, the group justifies having Hu as its central deity on the grounds that Hu
is the most ancient recorded deity known to humans, dating
back to at least 3400 BC in Egypt. Initially, Hutians say,
the Egyptians honored Hu as a deity residing in the stars,
and considered him a counterpart to the god Horus. However,

with the rise of the cults of Osiris and Isis, those in
power portrayed him as an evil god, and the cult of Hu fell
into disrepute. Then, during the 11th and 12th dynasties,
the Hu cult had a brief revival lasting until about 700 BC
and the 15th dynasty, when the Osirians again squelched the
group.

But their action didn't destroy the belief in Hu,
Hutians claim, because the Hebrews took the conception of
Hu with them when they left Egypt, although they caricatured
him as Satan and the embodiment of evil, expressed in the
image of the Judeo-Christian Devil. But this imagery is
wrong, Hutians argue, because they regard Satan as a symbol
of freedom from repression. In their view, repression
stifles the human spirit, and when humans gain freedom,
their genius is revealed.

In 1971, Andrews, then a Satanist, elaborated upon
these ideas in a document called the Diabolicon, which he
"received" while serving in Vietnam. In this document he
recounted the battles of Satan against a repressive Christian god, who instilled in mankind a religion of fear. To
describe these battles Andrews used "statements" from the
demons Satan, Lucifer, Belial, Beezlebub, and a few others,
detailing how they fought against God's realm of order to
create regions of darkness and disorder where man could be
free. In these regions they worked with the power of the
black flame, representing the inner will, to create Hell—
a world beyond God's realm where all wills were equal and
freedom was absolute.

Then, after creating this realm, Hutians believe,
Satan and several other demons from Hell—Beezlebub, Azazel,
Abaddon, Asmodeus, Astaroth, Belial, and Leviathan—came to
earth to save man from godly ignorance by giving him intelligence and power as symbolized by the black flame, so he
could again use his will to achieve mastery of all things,
including control of the universe. Also, these demons came
to teach man that he could train his mind and will, so he
could create his own order in which he could subject all
behavior to his will rather than to natural and mechanical
laws.

According to Hutian philosophy, the Church of Satan
was created to help mankind use this black flame to get all
he wanted by will alone and thereby obtain perfect freedom.
But when the Church of Satan succumbed to worldly pressures
and began selling its degrees, its mission, watched over by
the spirit of Satan, ended. Instead, Hu became the guiding

deity of the new Aeon. Hutians characterize him as a
creature of night and the "prince of darkness."

Although the Priesthood and most Hutians recognize Hu
as a divine entity, they engage in extensive debate about
his nature, the extent of his powers, and how Hutians
should relate to him. Some Hutians see him as a friend and
helper who will help those who communicate with him but will
ignore others. Other Hutians see him as a powerful god who
can offer magical assistance. Still others are uncertain
about who or what he is. Frequently these debates are
played out in the group newsletter, which I will call The
Papyrus. For instance, in one article, an Adept observed
that as he wrote, he did not believe in Hu, since there is
no scientific evidence for Hu's existence. Yet, even so,
at another time when he sat by his one black candle, he
knew Hu existed, for he could gaze at him through his pentagram, was aware of Hu watching him, and could sense Hu's
pleasure or displeasure in response to his own actions and
thoughts.

This expression of doubt by the laity is common, and
members of the priesthood accept it, since they do not
require the laity to believe in Hu to be Hutians, although
some laity do believe. Instead, Hutians are free to question and doubt. In this spirit, one Hutian freely argued
at the Second Annual Hutian Conclave that: "One should
question everything, even the premises on which the Church
of Hu is based. And you don't necessarily need a belief in
Hu to work magic, for Hu is just a symbol." Then, after
implying he was a non-believer, he added cryptically: "But
this doesn't mean I don't believe in Hu."

For the priesthood there is less freedom, however,
since Hutians at this level are expected to not only recognize Hu's reality, but to have the experience of Hu descend-
ing to and through them. Hutians call this experience
"Getting the gift of Hu."

Before getting the gift the novice Hutian may believe
or not and may consider Hu an intellectual construct or a
symbol when he invokes him in ritual. But if he remains in
the group, he is expected to gradually come to regard Hu as
a real being. Then, as he stands at the threshold of becoming a Priest, he is expected to achieve a major break-
through in which Hu comes to him with such force that he
knows Hu exists as a real divine entity. When this happens,
Hu gives him the black flame which gives him the power to
use his will to transcend and break the natural order.

Obtaining this gift and experiencing this transformation is vital, Hutians believe, because before it happens
the novice or Adept can only nudge or bend this order. But
once the Hutian establishes a close personal relationship
with Hu and receives the flame, he becomes a full-fledged
black magician. Then, as soon as the group recognizes
this, he will advance to Priest.

Although Hutians consider Hu divine, they do not worship him, since worship would detract from the individual's
power to exercise his own will. Instead, they believe the
magician can call him down from his residence in the stars
and use Hu's presence to strengthen his own powers. Also,
the magician can ask Hu for advice, assistance and guidance.

Thus, when Hutians look at the pentagram in ritual,
raise one hand upward, and chant loudly: "Hail, Hu," they
are not worshipping him. Instead, they are honoring his
divinity, much as they honor the divinity of their High
Priest and other Hutians by raising their hands and hailing
them.

The Belief in the Power
of the Pentagram

Hutians consider the pentagram the channel through
which the believer communicates with Hu. Andrews designed
this symbol by modifying the pentagram symbol of the Church
of Satan: a five-pointed inverse star with the point down-
ward on which the image of a goat or baphomet representing
Satan was superimposed. According to Church doctrine,
Andrews made this modification after Hu revealed through
The Book of Emergence Out of Darkness that the new pentagram was to be pure, to signify that the corruptions of the
Age of Satan were eliminated.

The resultant image is an inverse pentagram set against
a circular field. The reason for using an inverse pentagram
rather than a regular one with the point up is because it
symbolizes change and movement rather than rest and preservation, since the other four points of the pentagram seem to
teeter on a single point. The pentagram is unbounded in a
circular field to indicate the Hutian is working outside of
the natural order. And it is surrounded by a ring of silver because silver is the traditonal color of change and
power and is associated with the night.

Hutians use this image for numerous purposes. They

use it as the seal of the Church on all official documents
and Church correspondence. Also, Hutians wear it as an
insignia. All of them wear a small medallion with this
pentagram on a chain around their necks to show they are
Hutians, and the color field around the pentagram indicates
their status in the Church: white for the First Degree or
Novice, red for the Adept, black for the Priest, blue for
the Master of the Church, and purple for the Magus. Some
additionally wear pentagram rings, pins, or tie-clips.

In ritual, they use a large pentagram mounted on a
board as a focus for invoking Hu and moving into another
dimension. Typically, the Hutian makes this pentagram from
a large piece of painted wood, usually circular, and uses
silver charting tape to form the star and circle. Then,
when he performs a ritual, he places the pentagram on or
slightly above the altar and gazes at it.

In some cases, Hutians make these pentagrams into
permanent altar fixtures if they have a room they can use
as a ritual chamber or are in a situation where it doesn't
matter if non-Hutians see the altar. But other Hutians who
lack privacy or don't wish to let others know their beliefs
keep their pentagrams hidden until ready to use them.

This secrecy surrounding the pentagram at times is
strictly pragmatic—to protect the believer from nonbelievers
if necessary, since there is nothing sacred about the pentagram itself. Whereas the Hutians charge their other ritual
tools with power, they view the pentagram as merely a door
or channel to the spiritual realm which has no special
power in and of itself.

Once the pentagram is set up, the Hutian seeks to contact Hu by gazing at it in a dark room where there is only
enough light to see. Then, as he looks into it, he hopes
to feel the gates open to the other world, which Hutians
describe as a timeless, spaceless magical dimension, and to
feel the presence of Hu. The first indication that something psychical is happening, according to Hutians, is that
the image of the pentagram begins to move or change. For
example, as Hutians watch, the pentagram may begin to whirl.
Others report seeing eyes in the pentagram staring at them.
Some see its points vibrate. Sometimes, the image dis-
appears. Hutians look for these changes and consider them
a sign of ritual effectiveness. Also they look for the
feeling that another energy is with them, since this is a
sign they are in contact with Hu. Typically, the experience of changes in the pentagram comes first. Then, after

working with the system for a while, the Hutian may sense
the presence of Hu.

Hutians find these changes in the pentagram very exciting and talk about what they see frequently, particularly
in the early stages of membership when these phenomena first
occur. Later, they become more blasé and take it for
granted that the pentagram will move. In some cases,
Hutians use what they see in the pentagram as a form of
one-upmanship when they compare their visions with others
and make their own sound more exciting or dramatic. Occasionally, a Hutian doesn't see anything, though he has been
working with the pentagram for several months or even
longer; and this long-term failure to see is a cause for
concern, because it suggests that the Hutian may not be in
touch with Hu. One example of this occurred when an Adept
was under fire for not being magical enough and confessed
to the Priestess of his pylon that he hadn't seen anything
in the pentagram for almost two years other than the symbol
of Baphomet when he concentrated on seeing it. The
Priestess reacted with great surprise and concern and took
his admission as one more indication that he shouldn't
remain at Adept status.

The Belief in the Importance o
Personal Growth and Evolution

The Hutians' belief that the individual can evolve
through personal growth to higher man is expressed in the
phrase: Xepher Ir Xem, become of the Gods. Hutians consider this growth process crucial, for it is the only way one
can develop his will and express his magical being.

To grow, Hutians believe they must use their pentagrams, communicate with Hu, use their magical names, and
perform rituals regularly to develop their inner or magical
being. Also, they must report on their growth to higher ups
and share their experiences with others on the same level.
This sharing is designed to help the individual grow by
providing feedback, and it gives Church officers a means of
checking on his progress to be sure he is growing in the
right direction. If not, he will be demoted or asked to
leave the Church, since Hutians value change and growth
above all else and charge anyone not growing with the terri-
ble crime of standing still.

The only problem with this emphasis on change and

growth is that Church leaders are not exactly clear on what
this process of becoming should be or what the idea of becoming higher man or of the gods really means. Thus, they
are constantly revising and refining their notions of the
meaning of xephering and xem. Nevertheless, while they
attempt to clarify these terms, all Hutians must work on
looking within to grow, and each must determine for himself
how to do it.

Despite this freedom and lack of clarity, the priesthood has promulgated some general guidelines. One central
idea is that there is a core self representing the essence
of the individual's being. By identifying with a magical
entity and choosing a magical name to express this, the
individual can cut through the outer layers of his functional personality, characterized by the roles he plays in
everyday life, to get in touch with his core self. Then,
by working with this inner essence, he can develop his will
and project it outward to achieve his goals.

Another key belief is that humans have a tremendous
growth potential since they only use about 10-20% of their
available brainpower. Hutians believe humans have this
potential, since they claim the human brain did not develop
solely through evolutionary processes, but was the result
of deliberate genetic engineering by a intelligent entity
who already existed free from the restrictions of nature
and God and could conceive of and create advanced brain
cells. This entity, Hutians claim, was Hu. As they argue,
the human brain is too sophisticated an accomplishment to
have developed through an accident of evolution. Instead,
Hu created it, with the result that man's great intelligence
puts him outside of nature. This apartness, in turn, gives
him the potential to further his own evolution and thereby
overcome the limitations of the physical world.

However, if he is to surpass these limits and develop
to full potential, Hutians believe he must realize he is a
machine, as P. D. Ouspensky writes in The Psychology of Man's
Possible Evolution. Only then can he rise beyond his
machine-like qualities and the ordinary states of sleep and
waking to achieve the state of self-consciousness in which
he perceives the full truth about himself. Finally, with
more work he can move beyond self-consciousness to objective
consciousness. At this final stage, he knows the full
truth about everything and can develop a permanent "I" and
free will, so he can control all of his states of consciousness and become at last an immortal, fully evolved being.

Hutians believe this growth process is an ongoing one, and they continually look within to gain new insights about themselves and to observe changes. Then they share their discoveries with others by letter, phone or in person. As an example, one Priestess wrote me that she felt the process helped her strengthen her will, so she could always choose correctly and do what is right, and it led her to gain extreme confidence in herself and her abilities. As a result, she claimed there was now nothing she could not accomplish, including controlling people to do her wishes, although in her pre-Hutian days she could not do so. In another case, an Adept excitedly informed his Priest he had just made a personal discovery when he realized that forming an image of what he wanted and focusing on it was a way to obtain his goal. Often Hutians talk about being more focused and directed, feeling more balanced, or having a greater sense of discipline and control from this process of growth.

This sharing occurs voluntarily and frequently at all levels, and Hutians are encouraged to share their experiences with each other and with higher-ups to aid the growth process.

However, this process isn't always easy, as Hutians recognize, since growth and change bring struggle, but they feel the effort is worthwhile. This is because, as one Priest wrote me, the end of the process is characterized by "joys and mysteries that you would never have believed possible for a person to experience; knowledge that is truly esoteric; a bond with other Hutians that is uncanny in its love; and an understanding that is deeper and absolute, and goes far beyond what a person could learn in conventional schools."

To promote the process, Hutians use ritual—both formal and personal—in which they look within themselves and talk to Hu about what they are feeling. They find the process especially valuable in times of difficulty, for they can communicate with Hu about possible alternatives and solutions. For example, when one Priest wasn't sure whether to take a job, he asked Hu and discussed the pros and cons with him.

Beginning Hutians often use this growth process to deal with mundane or worldly matters, although as Hutians advance in their growth, they are expected to focus on less trivial everyday concerns and stress developing as more magical powerful beings. Supposedly, Hutians will know when

they become more magically powerful, and more highly developed Hutians will recognize this. But what this more
powerful magical state involves exactly is not clear,
since higher degree Hutians claim it is not something that
can be explained to lower degrees, for there is no language
to explain it. Rather, higher ups describe it as a feeling
or realization which "you will know when you are there."
But they have no way or do not wish to tell anyone who
hasn't experienced this evolution what it is.

This lack of clarity, in turn, helps reinforce group
structure, since an upper level Hutian can always tell a
lower level one that he doesn't understand something because he has not yet reached that level of growth. Also,
this lack of clarity provides the priesthood with a fertile
field for extensive discussion about what growth is, what
it should be, what signs are indicative of growth, who is
growing, and how well.

Although Hutians aren't sure how to identify growth,
they agree that the purpose in growing is to become evolved
transcended man, who has become immortal and like a god,
through successfully completing the process and thereby
undergoing a transformation or metamorphosis, which Hutians
call a "Hutamorphosis." Unfortunately, Hutians are not
fully certain how to know when this evolution has occurred.
So, once again, this is a topic the priesthood continually
discusses.

Generally they agree that the individual who achieves
this state will attain the absolute expression of his own
potential and will have perfect freedom without limitations,
so he is totally unbound by the natural order and can get
whatever he wants. But they are not sure how to tell when
the individual has achieved his full potential. And they
are not certain how transcending the natural order at this
higher level will differ from their understanding that the
priesthood has the power to transcend the natural order.
So the debate continues, and as the High Priest and members
formulate and reformulate doctrines, they report them in
various Church publications which are available to members
according to their level of development, so they can understand the teachings. Presumably, lower status Hutians will
not understand the higher teachings until they have further
evolved.

The Belief in the Use
of Magical Names

Hutians also believe that using a magical name is a
key to growth. In their view, this name identifies the
individual's magical self, which he currently possesses or
wants to achieve and enables him to acquire the qualities
associated with that name. For example, if he chooses a
name of a powerful deity or royal figure, he can acquire
its attributes by working with that name and its qualities
in ritual.

These qualities don't have to be ones the Hutian
already possesses; they can be ones he wishes to attain. In
fact, Hutians think it ideal to choose the name of a being
with desired qualities as a magical name, since the individual is evolving and this name becomes a "talismic" image
or symbol to which he can aspire. One Priestess described
this process of name selection as "putting the self ahead
of the self."

Then, as the individual evolves and acquires the
qualities of the selected name, a Hutian believes he can
advance his growth by giving up that name and assuming
another representing an even higher level of growth. As a
result of this view, most Hutians occasionally change their
magical names, although a few have kept the same name since
being involved in the group. They don't make this change
by whim, for they believe it is a serious matter. At one
time, the priesthood believed a Hutian could select another
name after due consideration when he felt ready. But more
recently they decided that the individual should play a
passive intuitive role in the process and let the entity
with the name choose him by appearing to him in ritual and
in effect possessing him.

This kind of possession occurred to one woman who became Khet,* the lion-head cat goddess symbolizing strength
and protection in war. Originally, she had chosen the
American Indian name, Azona, meaning shadow of the wind.
But when she did her first ritual for the group, she
realized she was ready to change. As she described the

---

*Since group members consider their chosen names to be
magical, I will not use their real names, but have made up
Egyptian-sounding names to reflect the Egyptian orientation
of the group. However, I have used the qualities associated
with the real names.

transformation:

> "I suddenly felt my name slip away, and I was no
> longer Azona, and I became aware of how much I still
> had yet to learn. Then, two weeks later when I did
> a ritual at home, I saw Khet first begin to manifest.
> I looked in the mirror, and though I have brown eyes,
> I saw two green eyes peering at me, and I didn't know
> at first what it was. But then a few weeks later at
> a Walspurgisnacht ritual with two members of the Py-
> lon, I felt the entity manifest again. I felt a
> tugging at my heels and at first thought it was my
> cat. But when I looked, my cat wasn't there. Then,
> I experienced myself growing taller, for instead of
> looking up at the pentagram, I was now looking
> directly at it, and the others in the room experi-
> enced the change. Finally, at the Pylon ritual a few
> weeks later, the entity Khet manifested in me fully,
> and several others in the group could see the entity
> was there."

Others have reported similar, but not so dramatic, experiences of feeling an entity become part of them. For
example, one Priestess who took the name of the Egyptian
queen Naptha when she was a novice Hutian, found one day
that she no longer felt herself to be this entity and was
ready to assume a new identity. In her next ritual, she
experienced herself becoming Armat the vulture and felt the
image fit, since she had previously imagined herself to be
like a bird. At first, she perceived the vulture that
selected her as a small bird. However, after about a year
of working with this image, she felt another aspect of the
vulture goddess, Luk, manifest through her, and she experienced herself as a 65-foot mother bird.

Other Hutians have been attracted to names associated
with personal interests and activities. One woman selected
Ardis the magician, since she had always liked castles and
reading about magic. Another woman felt an affinity to
frogs and often received frogs as gifts; so she chose the
name Wik symbolizing frogs. An Adept selected the name of
a snake Rath, since he had been interested in snakes and
vampires since childhood.

Other names represent warrior gods and goddesses;
hunters and huntresses; powerful animals like crocodiles,
cats, lions, and ant-eaters; physicians and healers;
pharoahs; and desirable qualities, such as strength, power,
wisdom, passion, and love. Frequently, a single name is

associated with several qualities, and the Hutian can draw
on any or all of the qualities associated with it. However,
he is not limited to these associations, since in ritual he
may experience and adopt additional qualities for that
name.

Since the Church's symbolism is heavily Egyptian, most
Hutians—about 25 members—have Egyptian names. But others
have adopted names from other religious traditions. One
Adept chose Fenian, the Celtic god of healing, since he
used this identity when he played Dungeons and Dragons before joining the Church, and he felt comfortable using the
same name. Another Adept previously had little interest in
Greek or Roman mythology, but when she was looking for a
name to choose, the image of the Greek goddess, Athena,
came to her, and after she began working with this identity,
she realized the warlike associations with Athena suited
her well. In another case, an Adept especially interested
in Norse mythology took the name Odin because he liked the
associated imagery of the hammer of the gods of the under-
world.

Hutians claim that taking these names helps the individual develop the desired qualities associated with that
entity. For example, Athena found that the feminine
aspects of the name "Athena" made her feel more feminine
and noticed that she began wearing frilly blouses and lacy
garments which she never wore before. A Priest observed he
became more fearless after taking the name of the dragon
Wif and was able to do things he previously couldn't—such
as drive on the freeway without feeling anxious.

Hutians work with these names by invoking the entity
called by that name in ritual and then taking on the attributes of that being. Hutians see this as a different
process than being possessed by an entity who takes control
as in voodoo, because in their system the powers of the
entity and individual merge together so the individual gains
greater power in exercising his will. Since he is not taken
over by these powers, he can use them as he wishes in working magic.

The process works like this. In the beginning of a
ritual, the Hutian typically stands in front of the pentagram silently for a few moments and concentrates on
invoking or becoming his magical entity. Once he assumes
this new persona, he addresses Hu through the pentagram,
saying something like: 'Hail, Hu. I stand before you as
Astarte, goddess of love and war, and as Astarte I send

forth my will."

Because the magical name is so personal, members can
select the same name as others in the group if it feels
right to them and if there is no strong reason why they
shouldn't take that name. A few Hutians have made the
same selection: two Adepts became Ardis the magician, and
two Priests selected Wer the hidden one. But most members
choose different names, and there is strong pressure not to
take certain ones. For example, higher-ups advise lower
degree members not to take names assumed by the priesthood.
Although it is likely the higher-ups don't want them to
take these names, since doing so might undermine the
Church's hierarchical structure, the usual reason they give
is that names have power and responsibilities associated
with them, and the individual must assume these responsibilities in taking that name. But if he is a low degree
member he probably won't be up to handling the power or
responsibilities of a priestly name.

By the same token, certain names are considered inappropriate for anyone to take. For instance, when I first
joined, I initially selected Khepri, the Egyptian beetle,
which is a symbol of the rising sun. But Armat, the
Priestess of my pylon, firmly advised me not to take it,
since the word "Xephering" derived from this beetle; thus,
my having this name would "defeat the whole system." Then,
when I selected Maat, which represents the principle of
justice and truth, she told me not to take this name either,
since "everyone in the Church is working in the spirit of
Maat, and at times they invoke Maat to oversee their
rituals." So this was not an appropriate name for me either.
However, when I finally settled on the name of an ordinary
goddess, Astarte, which no one else was using, that was fine.

Once the Hutian chooses a name, he not only uses it
in personal rituals but with other Hutians, for in group
activities members tend to call themselves by their Church
titles or degree (i.e. Priestess Smith, Adept Jones) or by
their magical name. They do so to remind each other they
are magical beings who have achieved a certain level of
magical growth. When Hutians engage in mundane activities
together, like shopping or going to the movies, they
generally employ regular names. But in ritual, they always
use their magical name, and in group meetings members
usually use either their magical name or title, a practice
the priesthood encourages. If a Hutian forgets and says a
given name, another Hutian will often correct him. In fact,

upper status Church members consider using magical names so
important that two Masters changed their names legally.
One woman adopted Belial, representing a female demon, as
her first name, and another woman changed her last name to
Huf to identify with the cat goddess.

Although Hutians do not always use their magical name
appropriately and sometimes alternate between using their
magical and given name, they try to employ their magical
name as much as possible in suitable contexts. For example,
when I was driving to the national conclave with four
Hutians, we had been using our given names for about 20
minutes when the Priestess announced that we should use our
magical names since we were on our way to the conclave, and
we did so for the next few minutes. However, when we suddenly got a flat tire and clunked to a stop at the side of
the road, all efforts to use magical names immediately
ended, for we were our mundane selves again. Before we
could become magical beings, we had to fix the tire.

This shift back and forth between magical, mundane
names, and titles occurs most often for those lower in
status. But as Hutians rise in the hierarchy, they are
more likely to use their magical names or title with other
Hutians to express their magical or evolved being. For
example, Masters and the Magus rarely use common names.

However, at all levels Hutians vary in whether they
prefer using their magical name or title. The variation is
usually due to personal style. Hutians who tend to be more
formal and distant from others tend to prefer that others
use their title as a sign of respect. Those who are more
informal and casual tend to prefer their magical name.
Some don't care.

Typically, when Hutians first meet or begin corresponding by letter, they indicate which they like. In some
cases a Hutian will use his title with those he doesn't
know well, particularly if they are lower in status. But
as they get to know each other or the person moves up in
rank, he will use his magical name instead—a sign of growing closeness. The permutations reflect a mixture of
personal taste, social relationships, and hierarchy. Hutians
use names, like other symbols, to express their status and
their relationship to others in the group.

6

The Role of Ritual

Hutians consider performing ritual of prime importance,
since in ritual, one invokes the magical personality,
strengthens the will, and communicates with Hu to gain
assistance growing to become higher man. In ritual, the
individual can as his magical self project his will to
"bend" or "break" the natural order to obtain what he
wants. Further, a group ritual is a form of celebration,
which provides group support for personal objectives and
beliefs.
      Hutians perform these rituals in groups or indivi-
dually to achieve various goals. Besides looking within
for insight, a Hutian can perform a "compassion" ritual to
gain mundane success, such as a better job or more confidence; do a lust ritual to obtain a desired love object;
or get back at someone through a destruction ritual, commonly called a DR. Yet, regardless of the specific purpose,
the overall goal of ritual is to grow to "xepher ir xem,"
become of the gods.
      Because Hutians value rituals so highly, they perform
them frequently—usually once or twice a month, though many
Hutians, most notably the priesthood, do so more frequently
—perhaps once or twice a week. In the ordinary ceremonial
magic ritual, Hutians believe they can "bend" the natural
order to increase the possibility of likely events occurring. However, they consider the rituals of the priesthood
to be more powerful and call them "workings," since these
go beyond bending the natural order to "break" it and
thereby cause improbable events to occur.
      Typically, Hutians perform personal rituals alone, in
keeping with the group's emphasis on self-growth, although
occasionally a few Hutians get together informally to do a

ritual.

Larger celebratory rituals occur at pylon meetings or at conclaves. In the L.A. and San Francisco area, pylon meetings occur about once a month; and after a preliminary business and study group meeting, the group ritual high-lights the evening. Usually, about 5-8 members attend these meetings: the Priest or Priests leading the pylon, the handful of lay members of the pylon, and occasionally a visiting Hutian.

At times, Hutians in distant cities visit each other or gather in a central location for a "mini-conclave" of perhaps a half-dozen members, and again ritual plays a central part in the visit. Most active members also come together to share ideas, learn the latest Church doctrine, and perform ritual at the group's annual conclave, held for the second time in June 1980. About 30 attended each year.

Because of the group's emphasis on personal develop-ment and creativity, the ritual structure is very flexible to permit spontaneity and each ritual is unique. In con-trast to the rituals of the Church of Satan, Hutians need not follow any formula or use specific magical words. Instead, within a loose ritual framework, they look within themselves and experience or express aloud personal feel-ings and insights.

Within this flexible structure, each ritual generally consists of these key elements:

- Setting the stage, usually through meditation, so participants experience an altered state of con-sciousness in order to enter another "dimension."
- Requesting Hu's presence and assistance.
- Taking on the persona of one's magical self, sym-bolized by one's magical name.
- Opening the gates to the magical realm, by visual-izing and affirming aloud that they are open.
- Using visualization, guided imagery, affirmations, and other techniques to project the will and see oneself successfully achieving one's goals.

Typically, the Hutian performs the ritual in front of an altar and pentagram and sets up a ritual area or chamber in his home for this purpose, although in a pinch he can do a ritual mentally without any paraphenalia. These home ritual centers range from the very simple to the highly elaborate, since some Hutians have permanent altars and pentagrams or specially designated ritual rooms, while some only put up a pentagram and make-shift altar for the ritual,

since they don't have a private area for them and want to
conceal their religious beliefs from non-Hutians.

In keeping with the Church's individual emphasis, each
altar is distinctive. Some Hutians use bookshelves; others
small tables; still others construct a special platform.
Some use these surfaces as they are; others cover them with
a dark, usually black, cloth. Most have assorted statues,
candles, icons, and magical equipment on the altar, drawn
from Egyptian and other traditions. For example, one of
the Priests leading the San Francisco pylon has his altar
in a special ritual room where he has a library of books on
magic. A large black pentagram on the wall high above the
altar dominates the room, and in the darkness a blue neon
light under the pentagram casts an eerie glow around it. To
the left of the altar, a statue of Anubis, the jackal-headed
god of embalming, stands on a small oak table and appears
to stare around the room, while next to him an Egyptian
king stands stolidly with his hands folded across his chest.
On the opposite side of the altar, a ceramic bust of Sekmet,
the powerful lion-hearted goddess, gazes steely ahead, as
the Preist's "watcher" who is supposed to watch and protect
the ritual area from outside interference. On the altar
itself there is a large metal bowl containing an incense
burner, and around it assorted ritual tools, including a
long knife, wand in a black felt case, silver chalice,
golden bell, and a few personal momentoes: a pine cone and
rat skull.

During a ritual, the Hutian can use these magical tools
or not, as he chooses. However, when he does use them, they
have certain standardized meanings. He uses the bell to
shatter the natural order; the incense to create a protective circle separating the magical realm from the mundane;
the wand to expand his power and will; the chalice to con-
tain the liquid representing Hu's essence; and the knife to
draw a pentagram or cut the circle off from the mundane
world. Most Hutians also have a watcher in the form of a
statue, mask, or bust of some deity which they charge to
protect the ritual area or their home.

When the newcomer joins the Church, he learns a basic
ritual structure for white ceremonial magic. These procedures are used to set the stage for the ritual, open the
gates to the magical dimension, and call on Hu for assistance. However, once he is skilled in regularly using these
techniques, Hutians consider him an accomplished magician
or "adept" and believe he no longer needs to use a formal

ritual structure. Instead they claim he can readily enter
the appropriate ritual space by directing his mind into the
altered state of consciousness these procedures are designed
to produce. Thus, as individuals advance in the Church,
their rituals become much simpler. For example, as an
accomplished magician, the Hutian can without fanfare simply
walk up to the pentagram or visualize walking up to it and
open the gates.

Because of this attitude toward ritual, the Priests
advise newcomers that the ritual structure they learn is
only a suggested one and they can change the order or eliminate steps as they wish. However, in their first months of
membership, newcomers usually follow the basic structure as
explained by members of the priesthood or described in the
White Tablet, an introductory book of ceremonial magic for
neophyte Hutians.

To prepare for this basic ritual, the Hutian first
puts on his robe, which must be black, and the pentagram
medallion. Secondly, he lights the candles and incense and
puts on some ritual music, typically something with an
other-worldly haunting sound, to reinforce the ritual mood.
Next, he walks around in a circle with the censer to separate the ritual area from the mundane world and place it in
another space-time dimension. Then, to shatter the natural
order, he rings the bell. Usually he does so nine times,
since this number was sacred to the ancient Egyptians, and
since it reaffirms the importance of the Council of Nine,
the governing board of the Church.

The next step is evoking or summoning the elemental
forces to lend their strength and power to the ritual. Like
most other groups involved in magic and Witchcraft, Hutians
believe in four elements: fire from the South, air from the
East, earth from the North, and water from the West. To
summon them, the Hutian turns successively to each direction, moving counterclockwise to reverse the natural order,
and visualizes each element having physical form to give it
more power. For example, as he turns he might say: "And
now, from the South, I evoke the searing flames of fire
which scorch the earth," or "Water, I call on your swirling
energies to purify this ritual."

Then, he opens the gates and invites Hu into the
chamber by greeting him: "Hail, Hu," and drinks from the
chalice, representing Hu's essence. If others are present,
he passes the chalice to them first, and after the cup circuits the group, he drinks everything remaining in it to

absorb the essences of all present, as well as of Hu.

Next comes the body of the ritual, which can be almost
anything the Hutian wishes to promote personal growth or
achieve a goal. For example, the Hutian might stare into a
crystal or mirror, light a red candle for a lust ritual,
burn a black candle for a destruction ritual, consecrate a
new ritual implement, or quietly talk to Hu to resolve a
problem. To conclude, he simply closes the gates and
leaves the ritual area.

After he turns off the ritual music and turns on the
lights, he is back in the mundane world. Once he is,
Hutians believe he should put the ritual behind him, meaning he should not think about it or discuss it with others.
Hutians advocate this avoidance and reticence on the grounds
that the ritual energy has been sent out to do its work in
achieving the ritual's purpose, and to think or talk about
it at length would short-circuit or limit this energy.

Most First Degree Hutians use this ritual form when
they first become members. But once familiar with procedures and able to readily enter an altered state, they
drop the formalities for a more simple structure. For instance, to communicate with Hu, a Hutian versed in ritual
may simply light a single candle on his altar, perhaps play
some background music, announce aloud or mentally that the
gates are open, and begin talking to Hu. Hutians call this
a communication ritual, and it is their most common ritual
form.

In some cases, Hutians even dispense with the pentagram, music, and ritual chamber and perform a ritual wherever they are, if they feel a need. For example, one
Priestess thought she was cheated by a man who sold her a
car which developed mechanical difficulties. She confronted
him with her complaints and had a raging argument with him,
which ended with him refusing to reimburse her for repairs.
As she drove away livid, she decided to perform a ritual,
pulled off the road, and closed the car windows. Then she
meditated briefly, mentally opened the gates, and began
screaming curses at the man at the top of her lungs, while
visualizing him having problems with his own car and projecting her will to make these problems come to pass. As
she explained it, her screaming raised her emotional power
to a peak, so she could direct it, and she didn't need the
pentagram, since she could perform the necessary operations
mentally. Furthermore, she felt her ritual objective—
damaging his car—a fit recompense for his wrong against her.

Group rituals can be similarly impromptu. For instance, on the first night of the conclave, three Adepts and a First Degree were in a motel room discussing their relationship to Hu, when one Adept, Lat, suggested they do a ritual. When the others agreed enthusiastically, he unpacked his penta- gram, which he had constructed on a piece of black cardboard, and set it upright on the small table between the two beds. He lit a small black candle, dimmed the lights, and the four lined up at the foot of the beds. After they meditated several minutes in silence, Lat softly announced: "The gates are now open...Let us hope that the coming gathering will be an experience of peace and growth." Then, he asked anyone who wished to address the pentagram. Cru stepped forward, called on the elements, and asked Hu to help the group avoid stasis. Next, Haren went up to the pentagram and asked everyone to stand closely around him and feel the bonds linking the group, while he as a warrior offered the group his protection. Finally, Lis, a First Degree, de- scribed how a door had opened for her in a recent ritual, so now she was ready to experience even more.

In contrast to the simplicity of individual or small group rituals, formal group rituals usually involve much ceremony and require prior planning to determine what will happen. Although Hutians can organize these formal rituals at any time, most typically they occur as the high point of the monthly pylon meeting. Traditonally, members of the priesthood lead them as an example to the laity. But in the San Francisco pylon, the Priestess established a new tradition of rotating the ritual leadership each meeting from member to member to help the laity learn.

To give a flavor of these rituals, I will describe a typical pylon meeting and a "working" conducted by this Priestess, and then briefly discuss the major ritual themes.

***

The pylon members gathered for the regular monthly meeting on Friday at 7:30 p.m. in Priest Baker's small San Francisco apartment. Six Hutians were there—three Priests and three lay members, including myself. As usual, we sat in his dimly lit living room, illuminated by only a thin candle and dim red bulb, so there was just enough light for us to see each other, read, and take notes. Baker kept the lights low, since Hu is a deity of darkness.

Above two low couches, a portrait of the Egyptian queen

Cleopatra stared out across the living room, and on the
opposite wall a framed scroll showed off profiles of the
gods Anubis and Thoth. Priest Baker exhibited these pictures as symbols of his membership in the Church and his
role as assistant pylon leader.

After some initial socializing where we chatted about
the latest happenings in our lives and described personal
rituals we had performed in the past month, Priestess
Irwin called the meeting to order. At her request, Adept
Arnold, the group's secretary, read the minutes of the
previous meeting, and each member of the laity read his own
impressions of that meeting. Then, preliminaries over, we
discussed the assigned reading—a selection about Aleister
Crowley from Colin Wilson's The Occult. The reading and
discussion were designed to help the laity understand the
principles of the group.

After a break for refreshments, it was time for the high
point of the meeting—the monthly pylon ritual. Silently,
we put on our robes. These were black to express the
group's darkness motif, yet uniquely designed to express
personal interests. While I had acquired an inexpensive
black choir robe from a church specialty store, others
lavished much attention on these robes. Thus they made
them by hand or had them specially made. For example,
Priestess Irwin, who called herself Armat to represent the
vulture goddess, made a robe with large floppy sleeves and
silver stripes, which suggested a large black bird. Adept
Arnold, who called himself Rath after the snake god, wore
a Dracula-style cape to underline his love of vampire
literature and films.

To complete our costumes, we put on our pentagram
medallions, so they showed clearly against our robes. Our
colors indicated our group status. Thus, Khet and I wore
white medallions signifying our First Degree status, while
Rath wore the red medallion of the Adept. The three
Priests, Armat, Rif, and Sardis, wore the black medallion
of the Priest.

Once dressed, Armat disappeared into the ritual chamber and closed the door to prepare to lead the ritual.
Meanwhile, Rif set up the tape recorder to play soft haunting background music and turned off the lights. Sardis
stepped into the open doorway of the living room opposite
the ritual chamber, her hands folded across her chest. She
meditated there for several minutes, as the rest of us sat
quietly in total darkness.

Then, Sardis lifted her arms outward and intoned in a
whispery voice: "And now I experience beside me the
presence of Rif. Let Rif come forth and stand beside me."

Quietly, Rif got up, stretched out his hands and stood
before her. They linked hands and gazed into each other's
eyes for a few moments. Then Sardis motioned for Rif to
move into the hall and stand outside the door of the ritual
chamber.

She closed her eyes, meditated briefly, and intoned
again: "And now, let Khet come and join me."

Similarly, she asked Rath and me to come forward together, held both of our hands, and gazed into our eyes.

We lined up behind the others in the hallway, and
waited silently for several minutes, until Armat opened the
door to begin the ritual.

"They are prepared," Sardis said.

"Then let them enter," Armat replied.

As we filed in, Armat gently guided us into a semi-
circle around the dark chamber, lit solely by the bluish
glow of a neon-bulb that projected out from the wall under
a large black wooden pentagram. Just beneath this was the
altar, a high table covered with a black cloth. It contained
various ritual tools, including a large bowl holding a metal
censer for burning charcoal, a wooden chalice with grape
juice, a large bell-shaped crystal with 24 facets, a knife,
a black candle, and a bell. Next to the altar were several
statues of Egyptian goddesses, including the cat-like face
of the goddess Sekmet, who faced the altar as a watcher.

Although participants don't always stand in the chamber
according to rank, our semi-circle reflected the group's
pecking order. Armat, the pylon Priestess, stood in front
of the altar. Sardis, the Executive Director of the Church,
stood directly to her right. Next came Rif, the assistant
Priest of the pylon; then Rath, an Adept; next Khet, a
First Degree; and finally me, since I was the last First
Degree to join the group.

We stood silently, heads down, as Armat turned on a
tape of ritual music. The music was haunting and other-
worldly. Then, with the tape still playing, Armat faced
the pentagram, placed her hands on the altar, looked up,
and addressed Hu.

"They have come into this chamber," she intoned. "They
are ready. Come join us with your presence in this chamber."

She stepped back from the altar a few steps, raised
her right arm in a stiff salute, and called out: "Hail, Hu."

We similarly raised our hands and chanted in unison: "Hail, Hu."

Next, Armat picked up the chalice with grape juice, faced the pentagram again, and held up the chalice.

"Let your essence become part of this liquid we. drink," she said.

Turning to the group, she held the chalice high, walked over to Sardis, and extended her right hand, while holding out the chalice in her left. Sardis clasped her extended hand, grasped the chalice, and stood quietly as Armat gazed deeply into her eyes, no longer her mundane self, but now Armat, the vulture. Then, in slow measured tones, almost in a whisper, Armat spoke:

"My sister, I see you as the crystal, which shines forth with your very essence. So now, drink of this and share of your crystal essence."

Slowly, as they continued to stare into each other's eyes, Sardis lifted the chalice to her lips and sipped from it. Meanwhile, the rest of us held out our hands palms up or crossed them across our chests to send our energy to strengthen their energy exchange. Then, throughout the ritual, we continued to send energy to support the efforts of the central ritual participants.

After her exchange with Sardis, Armat moved to each of us in turn, and still in a trance, said what inspired her. Usually her words referred to some incident or condition involving the person. For example, as she stood in front of Rif, who took the name of a crocodile god, she remarked: "I see within you the red fiery light and the crocodile teeth that bite with sharpness." Before Rath she talked about seeing the eyes of a snake. To Khet, who had recently discarded an old name for her present one, Armat commented: "I see you as a new being born from your growth." And to me, she said: "My sister, I welcome the light from your eyes and ask you to share your essence with mine." After she spoke to each of us, she bid us to drink from the chalice as Sardis had done and we did.

After Armat completed the circuit of the group, she stood in front of the altar again, held up the chalice, and intoned: "And now, as I drink, all our essences meld into one." Then she drank from the cup, symbolically joining Hu's essence and the essence of the others present with her own.

Through these preliminary procedures, Armat prepared the foundation for the rest of the ritual. Although she

didn't formally open the gates to the magical realm, she
opened them symbolically by calling Hu into the chamber and
having us drink of his essence. Then, the gates open, she
was ready to begin the main ritual, which would be a "working" rather than an ordinary ritual, since she was of the
priesthood and hence could break through the natural order.

She came over to me first, and guiding me by the hand,
led me into the center of the circle. As I stood waiting,
she lifted the large many-faceted crystal from the altar and
held it in front of my eyes. She gazed into them intensely
and asked:

"Sister, are you willing to undertake the journey? Are
you willing to look deep within yourself? Are you ready to
commit yourself to Hu?"

She looked at me closely, waiting for my answer.

"Yes I am," I finally said softly.

"Then, stare within the crystal and see the pentagram
within. And see yourself, Astarte, within the crystal.
See where you have been and what you will become."

At first, I thought she expected me to see something
and started to describe what I saw. "I see the lines of
the pentagram reflected in the crystal. I see a bluish
light like the opening of infinity."

But Armat hushed me. "No. Do not speak. Just experience. Just be."

So I stared at the crystal for a few minutes until
Armat asked me to step in front of the pentagram and express silently or out loud what I experienced. Following
her example, I put my hands on the altar and looked up at
the pentagram. Then, quietly, slowly, I described what I
had seen.

"I saw the points of the pentagram like lines on the
road and the blueness like the infinite drawing me deeper
into myself."

When I fell silent, Armat led me back to my place.
Then she went over to Khet and held the crystal before her.
Similarly, she asked her if she felt ready to undertake the
journey despite its difficulties. When Khet agreed, Armat
again held up the crystal. But she gave Khet different
instructions than she did me, for she spoke in response to
her intuitive feelings, which she believed reflected Hu's
guidance manifesting through her.

"Now, as you look within the crystal," Armat told Khet,
"see yourself emerging as the new being you are. Experience
the fragments of light in the crystal like the fragments of

yourself. Then experience those fragments coming together
within you to form a new unity. That unity has emerged in
you as Khet. You have left your former self behind and now
experience your growth as this new entity you have become."

As I had done, Khet gazed into the crystal suspended
before her eyes. Meanwhile, the rest of us directed energy
to her with our hands.

Then, firmly, Khet strode up to the altar and standing
rigidly, as if to enact her warrior goddess role, she
announced to the pentagram:

"I now come before you as Khet. I am Khet. I come
with the power of a warrior. I am healing. I have magic.
I have left my old being behind. Know that I am now Khet."
She seemed to exult in the feeling of power evoked by this
warrior image.

After Khet strode back to her place in the circle,
Armat approached Rath, asked him the usual questions about
readiness and told him to see himself as Rath the snake and
reflect on his true essence and on his growth as this being.
When Rath subsequently went up to the altar, he spoke of
seeing the two eyes of a snake peering at him in the crystal

When he returned to his place, Armat approached the
altar alone, and addressing Hu, she spoke of the growth she
perceived in all pylon members. Then, she lit the black
candle with a match and intoned:

"In the blue flame lives the black light through which
we can see into ourselves and share our essences with Hu."

Next, laying the crystal on the altar, she called on
the other Priests, Sardis and Rif, to come to her, and they
formed a circle with their arms around each others waists.
As before, the rest of us continued to send energy with our
hands.

Soon, they began to breathe heavily and sway from side
to side. In rhythm, Armat began to speak softly:

"We are three of the nine...But also among us are Wer,
Sooth, Kel, Fiero, Firth, and Ta...And now let the spirit
of Maat, of justice, come down and enter the circle...Let us
experience the being and wisdom of Hu...Let us manifest it
in our very being...Xepher Ir Xem."

As she spoke and swayed back and forth with the group,
their breathing got heavier and heavier and faster and
faster, until finally, almost like an orgasm, their energy
peaked and dissipated away. Quietly, they split apart, and
Armat led them out of the room, closing the door behind
them. Although the reason for this departure was unclear

at the time, the Priests had left to let us lay members
continue the ritual on our own to make us a more tightly
knit group, strengthen our ability to conduct ritual, and
thus better prepare us to move into the priesthood.

For several minutes after they left, we stood without
speaking, not certain of what to do. Then Khet approached
Rath and asked him if he really wished to continue to be
Rath, the snake. Perhaps he did not, she suggested, for
"Rath is known as the battler of Hu, and his movements
limit him to the ground." Although it was unusual for a
First Degree to advise an Adept, Khet felt she could do so,
because she believed she was working at the Second Degree
level, though not yet formally recognized, and she doubted
if Rath should be recognized at this level. When she was
raised in status and Rath demoted about two months later,
her perceptions were confirmed.

After hearing her query, Rath considered the matter
thoughtfully. Finally, he replied that he saw himself as
the power, strength, and cunning of the snake, but not as
the battler of Hu.

However, Khet remained unconvinced. "Perhaps you
still might be ready to take another name," she prodded.
"Maybe you might soon be ready for the skin of the snake to
come off and reveal another being."

Again, Rath thoughtfully reviewed her question, then
said that he had received no call to do so yet—in keeping
with the Church's belief that a person should only change
his name when that new name chooses him, as occurred when
Khet adopted her name after the lion goddess pounced on her
like a cat.

But Khet persisted and urged Rath to approach the
altar to ask Hu if it was time to consider a new name.
"Just to be sure," she said.

Without much enthusiasm Rath did so, and after standing silently at the altar for a few moments, he reported he
still had no call to take another name. Then, Khet walked
over to him and embraced him gently as if to comfort and
reassure him that despite her challenge, she still accepted
him as one of the group.

Soon I moved over to join them and we stood in a small
circle for several minutes clasping each other's waists
until Khet announced that she felt it time to close the
gates for herself. She visualized them shut mentally and
quitely left the room. Shortly afterwards, Rath closed the
gates in the same way and followed her out. After a few

moments I joined them.

Now that the ritual was over, the usual post-ritual
discussion or "decompression" followed. In contrast to the
seriousness of the ritual chamber, this is a time of light
discussion, and often joking, which gives Hutians a chance
to relax and discuss what happened if they have questions
or feel something unusual occurred in the ritual.

In this case, Rath had some questions, since Armat
remarked she had done a "working," rather than an ordinary
ritual.

"What was the difference?" he wanted to know.

Although Rath should have known this principle of
Church doctrine as an Adept, Armat explained: "A working
involves moving outside the natural order to exercise and
direct the will, while a ritual involves using ceremonial
magic within the confines of the natural realm. Usually,
the priesthood does workings, and the laity does rituals.
But if a Second Degree does a working, this means he is
close to being ready to move into the priesthood."

In our ritual, we had gone outside the natural order
by gaining insights to our own growth through the crystal.
In addition, the priesthood had invoked and worked with the
spirit of Maat.

***

Other group rituals use different techniques to achieve
personal growth. For instance, in one ritual Rath led us
each in turn to a mirror he had placed on a small table in
a closet. He asked us to sit down, gaze at the mirror, and
see in it our own essence. In another case, Armat moved
around the group with a goblet of water and asked each to
look at it as she intoned: "It is pure, it is clear. It is
filled with understanding. It is new being. It is truth.
It is Xepher Ir Xem. Drink of this and drink of the potential that is within you and without. Drink of the essence
of yourself, of your new beginning, and of Hu." Later,
during the same ritual, Rif brought out a large sword and
exclaimed as we clustered around it: "Look well on this
sword. It has two sides. The magician walks on this thin
line. The choice is ours. We are mighty and we are weak.
Together we are strong. Alone we are strong. Move forth,
magicians. Show us your strength. Grab hold of this sword
and with your will manifest your magical essence." He
thrust out the sword and we grabbed it, placing one fist

above the other. Then, as we held on, he spoke of how we
all needed to work on growing, though it might be hard to
do.

Still other rituals are designed to achieve specific
ends. For example, when it was my turn to lead a pylon
ritual, Armat asked me to lead one on jobs, since the pylon
members were having trouble finding, holding, or liking
their jobs. As a result, after discussing the format with
Armat, I led a ritual on this topic. To begin, I asked the
eight participants to form a circle, and I went around the
circle three times carrying a large silver bowl with a burning ember. As I made each circuit, I handed each person a
piece of paper, and asked him to see written on it what he
wanted to have happen in one month, three months, and at any
time in the future. Then, I asked him to place the paper
in the flame and visualize the desired event occurring as
the paper burned.

Ritual is also used to reaffirm the hierarchy of the
group and the member's commitment to it. For instance, at
the end of my ritual, Kel, the High Priest who had paid a
rare visit to the pylon, felt inspired by his guiding magical entity to lead his own ritual. He walked up to each of
us in turn, stared hard into our eyes, grabbed our hands,
and pressed his ring with two jutting ram horns against our
palms for several minutes. The pressure hurt and left a
distinctive red mark which lasted several hours. Symbolically, this mark and Kel's action was supposed to impress
upon us that Kel was the opener of the way.

Ritual also reaffirms hierarchy in less dramatic ways,
since in a formal group ritual, members typically enter the
ritual chamber by rank, the highest ranking members first,
and during the ritual, the leader goes to each individual
in turn, based on seniority. Likewise, when Hutians go up
to the pentagram to speak to Hu, they frequently go in order
of rank.

Any change in status is also recognized formally in
ritual, as occurred at the end of Rath's pylon ritual. As
soon as he closed the gates, Armat asked the laity to leave
the ritual. After the Priests conferred for several minutes,
Armat invited everyone inside again, and after we arranged
ourselves in a circle, she asked Lat to step to the center.
Then, as everyone moved in around him, Armat placed her
hands on his shoulders, gazed into his eyes, and announced
his rise in status by intoning:

"Welcome, my brother, for if ever anyone was, you are

ready. All of the priesthood has seen it, and so now, step
forward to put on the red medallion."

Ritual is additionally a time when Hutians take on or
confirm a new name. For instance, at the beginning of the
national conclave, several First Degrees and Adepts who had
not yet chosen a magical name discussed how they had considered certain possibilities, but hesitated to choose them,
since they did not feel comfortable with them yet. However,
that night, at the First and Second Degree ritual, each of
them stepped forward to the pentagram to announce before Hu
that they had chosen the name they had considered. In turn,
the group celebrated this great step they had taken, for
after each person announced his new magical being, several
Hutians came over and hugged them. Then, Lat, the leader
of the ritual, formally acknowledged their act by standing
before the pentagram and declaring: "Hail, Hu. Witness
this night, a new magical entity is come into being."

Another ritual function is protection, and Hutians
frequently perform rituals to protect themselves, other
Hutians, or the group as a whole. For example, in one
group ritual, Rif announced before the pentagram: "Today
this chamber has been burglarized. It's sanctity has been
disturbed. By my power and the power of Hu, may this protection prevent this from happening again. And my curse on
those who do me wrong. Shall they receive back that wrong
1,000 times." After he stepped back into the circle, each
pylon member went up to the pentagram in turn and sought to
increase the power of Rif's demand and curse by projecting
the power of his magical being to aid Rif. Lat, whose magical name was that of a bird, announced: "Let Lat, the wonder
of the skies, swoop down and pluck out the eyes of he who
enters." Rath, who saw himself as a snake, proclaimed:
"Hu, my brother, let those who have defiled this chamber
suffer in such a way that is fitting. I, Rath, the snake,
watch for him and attack him quickly without mercy. My jaws
open wide and my fangs of poison are ready to sink into them.
May they taste bitter fruits that defile, and let anyone
who dares violate this chamber suffer the same fate. And
let all who enter who are brothers and sisters be protected
by that same power. So it has been said, and so it has been
done." Others similarly shared by speaking to Hu and projecting their anger against the burglar, using imagery
related to their magical being.

The large rituals at the conclave not only serve the
more usual ritual functions of seeking protection and

sharing personal concerns with Hu, but they play a major
ceremonial role as well. They give Hutians a chance to
participate in a grand display of pageantry, hierarchy, and
power; and they reaffirm their unity as a group, for the
ceremony gives Hutians a feeling of being interconnected and
bound together, while reinforcing each Hutian's position
within the group.

At the second conclave, held at the High Priest's
mountain retreat and spiritual home of the Church, two such
rituals were conducted. The first night, the First Degrees
and Adepts held their ritual in the outer ritual area,
while the priesthood performed theirs in the inner court
higher up the mountain. In both, participants marched into
the ritual area by rank as ritual music played. Then,
after participants ceremonially closed the circle and invoked the spirits of the four quarters, each Hutian
approached the pentagram in turn to share with Hu and the
others his personal concerns and his hope that the Church
continue to grow and be protected from any harm.

For example, in the laity ritual, Haren, an East Coast
Adept, approached the pentagram, placed his sword on the
altar, and announced that all who wished might take it up
and use its power in the ritual. "But let none who are not
up to its use take it up," he warned, "for they shall be
destroyed." When the 14 other participants approached the
altar, five picked it up and described what they would do
with it. For instance, as Athena held it aloft, she
bellowed: "I hold this sword up and call on the spirit of
Maat. Let this hallowed ground of the Church be protected
from all who would do it harm, and may this sword smite and
destroy any who would harm it. May they be cast from this
hallowed ground." Later, when Lat held the sword, he cried
out: "May I be able to use this sword well to cut through
anything holding me back from my personal growth."

These great ceremonial rituals are additonally a time
of special bonding between those who feel connected because
they share similar names or characteristics. For instance,
during the laity ritual, two Hutians who had both taken the
name Ardis—one on the West Coast, one on the East Coast—
dashed from the circle to the pentagram together. As they
held hands, the West Coast Ardis announced: "We are far
apart in geographical distance. But tonight, in ritual, we
two become one." Later, when Nal, a Hutian from New England
who had adopted the name of a warrior, entered the circle,
she addressed the pentagram and came over to Athena and me

in turn, for we too had selected the names of warrior goddesses. Then, as she stood in front of each of us, she
pressed her outstretched palms against ours, gazed into our
eyes, and intoned: "So we are one, my sister. Let us join
our forces together, and may our strengths become one."

The mixture of pageantry, personal sharing, and bonding, combined with an altered state of consciousness, leads
participants to experience phenomena at rituals, which can
be powerfully moving and can produce great personal changes,
as Hutians try to explain or deal with these phenomena.
For example, when she led her first ritual, Khet broke into
tears after the Priests suddenly left the room. Although
they had left to let the laity continue the ritual themselves and develop a group closeness, Khet didn't understand
this at the time and felt abandoned. So confused, she
sobbed: "Our priesthood has left us. There is so much I
do not understand." Then, to add to her confusion, she
felt her old name slip away, and over the next two weeks,
she experienced a deep personal struggle over who she was
until her new name grabbed her like a cat in a personal
ritual.

In another case, Lat looked into the mirror and saw
his own image disappear. As he later explained, he interpreted this experience to mean he was now face to face with
his own magical entity, and having this encounter helped
reinforce his belief he was on the right spiritual path.

Hutians consider this confrontation with the magical
entity especially significant, since they see it as a confirmation of ritual effectiveness, because it indicates the
ritual is occurring on a higher dimension which transcends
time and space. Armat described the experience this way:
"The first time it happened, it was eerie, uncanny.
When Kel walked around and I looked into his hood, there
was no one there, and I knew I was looking at the manifestation of Hu."

In other cases, Hutians have reported seeing images of
the magical entities assumed by other members. They have
seen Khet as a cat, Rif with a crocodile head, and Armat as
a huge vulture. Some have seen other unnamed presences.

The reason for these phenomena, as Armat explained, is
that, "When the priesthood does a ritual, incredible things
happen, the energy is so great. Once, for instance, we
evoked the old ones, and when I looked against the wall,
they were there. I could see them as gray misty presences,
and when I spoke to Ardis, she saw them, too."

Finally, since Hutians see themselves as members of an elect, the ritual becomes a testing ground, where each individual's appropriateness for this elect is measured. Hutians claim this testing occurs because Maat reveals the true essence of where the individual is "at." If he performs well in ritual and has "good energy," Hutians consider him a worthy member who is well suited to grow and evolve within the Church. But if he does not perform well, he must subsequently measure up, or he will lose his status among the elect.

In sum, a concern with ritual performance pervades the Church, and each Hutian is expected to participate in personal or group rituals regularly—at least once a month—to remain in good standing. Conversely, those who don't perform enough personal rituals or who detract from the energy of a group ritual have problems in maintaining their status or staying in the Church.

Ritual is so important because Hutians not only use it to contact Hu, exercise their will, and experience personal growth, but also ritual brings Church members together in a close intimate relationship, where they feel emotionally and psychically linked. Moreover, the phenomena produced in ritual help to validate the Hutian's beliefs about Hu and his own magical powers. Although some lay Hutians initially attribute these phenomena to physical or chemical changes (for instance, they claim the pentagram seems to move because they have been staring at it for a long time), later they learn to sense a presence or energy they believe comes from someone else. Then, this experience leads them to believe that Hu's power has become manifest.

The outsider may dismiss these claims to see phenomena as pure hallucination. But Hutians consider this experience a natural part of growth. Thus, as the newcomer repeatedly has his own experiences in ritual and hears other Hutians repeatedly assert that this phenomena is real and is due to magical power, his experience is validated, and he comes to believe.

7

Group Structure and Hierarchy

The group's concern with elect status, personal growth, and
power is reflected in its rigid hierarchical structure,
where progress towards becoming higher man is represented
by degree status. Despite the group's small size, there are
six degree levels within it, and personal relationships are
affected by the level achieved.

At the top Sixth Degree Level is the secular head or
Pharoah, called the Ipsissimus, who primarily handles
administrative matters. The position is now occupied by
Ipsissimus Andrews, who founded the Church and was its
original High Priest. When he passed the mantle of priesthood to Kel in 1979, he moved into the newly created
Ipsissimus role.

The Magus or High Priest, considered a Fifth Degree,
is the authority on points of doctrine. In this position,
Kel establishes guidelines for appropriate behavior and
keeps members informed of policy through the Church newsletter and occasional meetings he attends.

His priestly leadership is further enhanced by the
mountain retreat he lives in with Ba, one of the Priests,
about two hours north of San Francisco. This retreat,
called HuXem, is not only his home, but the Church considers
it the spiritual home of the group and therefore held its
second annual conclave there.

The site consists of 20 acres of largely undeveloped
steeply sloping land, a three-room wooden house, and two
cleared and leveled ritual areas. It is located at the end
of a narrow twisting mountain road. Next to it are 20 more
acres of land which the Church recently sold to two L.A.
Priests.

To get there, one must park several hundred yards away

and continue up a steep, twisty dirt road on foot. At the
entrance, visitors encounter a skull fitted on a tree trunk
just above a sign that says: "HuXem. No trespassing."
Then, about 20 yards up the dirt road one comes to a small
meeting area about 10 yards in diameter, where several
benches form a circle. Another 20 yards up there is a somewhat larger leveled area with a small altar surmounted by
a jackal figure, and a few yards beyond that several more
benches.

After climbing another 20 yards, one arrives at the
house—a brown wooden structure consisting of an outer living room area containing a wide bench and four chairs, a
tiny kitchen, and a small inner bedroom. Reminders of the
site's magical nature are everywhere. In the living room
a red stained glass window depicts Hu climbing through a
pentagram; in the bedroom a small draped altar displays
statues of Egyptian gods and ritual paraphenalia. Even in
the outhouse directly outside the house there are magical
reminders, since a sheet of paper hangs facing the commode
with the typewritten message: "You are now sitting on the
throne of Hatchem...Honor him, as you honor yourself. And
recognize that you are evolving even now."

From the house, a narrow path leads upward, and the
high priest views this path in magical terms, too, since he
describes it as the initiatory path the magician follows as
he evolves from laity to priesthood. About 100 yards up,
this path leads to another cleared area, called the inner
court, used for ritual and other gatherings by Priests and
members of higher rank.

Dominating the area is a large silver pentagram which
hangs freely about 10 feet above the ground on a rail between two tall white posts. Although Hutians usually place
their pentagrams inside a silver circle, this pentagram has
no boundary, because according to the Priest, "On this
mountain, we are already outside the natural order."

The altar—a long table draped in black containing the
usual ritual implements and two Egyptian statues—is under
the pentagram on a raised dirt platform. To its left is a
throne with two jackal figures, representing the High
Priest's magical entity, and to its right is another small
altar inscribed with mystical symbols. These symbols express the Church's belief system. A bird with one wing
represents higher man. An image of Hu climbing through the
pentagram underlines the importance of using the pentagram
to communicate with Hu. And five colored columns or pylons,

representing the first five degrees in the Church, are colored
to symbolize that one degree emerges from the preceding one.
Thus, the first pylon is white for the First Degree and
rests on a green base symbolizing growth. The Second is
red and rests on a white base; the Third black on a red
base; the Fourth blue on a black base; and the Fifth purple
on a blue base. On the altar itself there stands a statue
of a large falcon, representing Horus to symbolize the magical Aeon begun by Aleister Crowley, and behind him a double
crown, representing the two aspects of Horus-Hu, before he
became Hu.

During ritual, the High Priest stands in the center of
the platform before the altar, while the Masters of the
Church stand to either side. The Priests stand in the
slightly recessed area below the platform. When the laity
are invited to attend these priestly rituals, their place
is in a more deeply recessed area further from the altar.

Thus, the physical layout of the ritual setting reinforces the hierarchical system, and this structure is further
reinforced as one winds up the mountain. For example, Kel
plans to build a museum and library with Church artifacts
and books behind the altar and make this area available to
all Hutians. But beyond this point, sections of the mountain will be reserved for the priesthood alone, and the
highest areas for the highest ranking Hutians. As Kel explained at the conclave, he plans to build a pyramid on the
next level for the priesthood, and has already created a
small clearing where Priests can spend the night alone for
a personal initiation. However, further up the mountain
at the rock where he first uttered the word "Xem," he
expects to build a small building where only Masters and up
can go. The rationale behind this restricted use of space
is that at each level of development, Hutians know and have
evolved more; so they are entitled to go higher on the
mountain path representing their magical growth.

Below the High Priest are the Masters of the Church.
Hutians frequently call them Magisters or Magistras, since
they feel the Latin form sounds more magisterial and formal.
Currently, there are seven Masters, all previously in the
Church of Satan. One was promoted to this position at the
1980 conclave and one only a few months before.

Since the High Priest makes these promotions to Master
on intuitive or magical grounds, the criteria for advancement
are unclear. Thus, Hutians typically explain this advancement with vague or cryptic comments such as: "You know when

you have achieved that level," or "The High Priest just
knows," or "Everyone knows." But generally, those who become Masters are the most involved in developing Church
doctrines and writing about them.

Like the High Priest, Masters tend to be remote from
the laity. Hutians, in turn, agree this should be be case,
because "the Masters have evolved so much more and therefore form an elect within the elect." Several Masters
commented on this remoteness at the conclave and explained
that it occurs because the Masters are so much more involved in magical things than the laity and have less time
to deal with the mundane. Also, some Masters feel uncom-
fortable with the First and Second Degrees because they
don't know what to say to them.

By contrast, the Priests and Priestesses—the Third
Degrees—are considered a bridge between the laity and the
more evolved Masters and Magus. Sometimes Hutians call
them the teaching degree, since they lead the pylons. Of the
11 Priests, 6 were formerly Satanists.

According to Church doctrine, a Hutian becomes a priest
when he gains the gift of Hu—the sense of "knowing" Hu is
real and can manifest through him. Then, he knows he is a
Priest and sees himself as a full-fledged black magician
who can break through the natural order to transcend time
and space.

Again, it is hard to specify precisely what this knowing entails, since Priests explain their advancement
cryptically to the laity, much as Masters do: "You'll just
know when you're there." However, by inference, Priests
seem to characterize knowing as the inner feeling that Hu
does exist and believe that a Priest should see his central
being expressed by being a magician and Priest of Hu. He
should also feel the magical world takes priority over the
mundane. As one Priestess explained this outlook: "If I
participate in any worldly activities, such as going to
work, seeing friends, or going to the movies, I do so as a
Priestess of Hu." Thus, even when he participates in mundane activities, the Priest sees himself as part of an elect
group and not just as a regular "human."

There are some parallels in this belief in getting the
gift of Hu and the Christian idea of getting the "call of
God" to the ministry. However, a key difference is that
Hutians view Hu as a higher being to be honored as a friend
and teacher, rather than a God to be worshipped.

Hutians believe that once one has this gift, no one can

take it away because Hu has given it and has conferred his
priesthood directly on the individual. When the Magus
recognizes the Priest, he simply confirms what is already
known.

Thus, Hutians claim the Priest can never lose his
priesthood, and no one can take it away. Yet, in practice,
this Church doctrine is sometimes breached since the Magus
has "kicked" a few Priests out of the Church for personal
problems or because their ideas about Hu deviated too far
from accepted doctrine. In one case, a Priest became an
alcoholic, and in another two Priests moved to California
and then asserted that Hu was not an entity who resided in
the stars but a force existing in all Hutians.

The most significant division in the Church is between
the priesthood and the laity, and to emphasize this, all
members of the priesthood belong to the Order of Hu, which
has its own newsletter to discuss the finer points of Church
doctrine and meets occasionally, such as at the national
conclave. This division is further highlighted, since only
the priesthood can serve on the Church's governing body,
the Council of Nine. This body is patterned after the
Council of Nine in Nazi Germany, since Hutians admire the
organization, discipline, and power image of the Nazis,
though not how they used this power. The Council is composed of three Masters and six Priests.

Council members vote on all Church policy matters, including the recommendations of the High Priest, who is not
a voting member of the Council. They are also responsible
for selecting and confirming the High Priest in his office.
Thus, they act as a check on his powers, though in practice
they normally approve and carry out his wishes.

The highest ranking lay members are the Adepts or
Second Degrees, who are considered accomplished white magicians who can bend or nudge the natural order with their
magic. Ironically, Adepts do not need to believe in Hu,
although they must at least entertain the possibility he
exists. But, generally, most believe and aspire to the
intense encounter with Hu that will advance them into the
priesthood.

To become an Adept, a Hutian must be recognized by at
least one of the two Priests to whom he is assigned as an
accomplished ceremonial magician. However, if two or more
Priests feel negatively about him, they can prevent his
advancement. Again, there are no clear criteria for deter-
mining exactly when a Hutian has become sufficiently

accomplished at magic to be an Adept. Instead, the Priests
claim to "know," for they believe a Priest can talk to any
Hutian and know immediately his degree status.

Becoming an Adept is a significant achievement, for it
is the first permanent status in the group. According to
Church policy, newcomers must achieve this status within
the first two years of membership or be dropped from the
rolls. But once an Adept, the Hutian can remain at this
status indefinitely, as long as he communicates with his
Priest representatives and shows them he is continuing to
evolve. However, if he doesn't communicate or if they don't
think he is evolving, either representative may demote him
to First Degree status until he is back on the path.

Becoming an Adept also marks a significant change in
how other Hutians regard him. As long as he is a First
Degree, he is in the Church on a trial basis, and much group
knowledge is closed to him. But once he advances to Adept,
this is an indication of group acceptance—that higher-ups
consider him worthy to go on.

This acceptance is signified in a number of ways.
First, he can now purchase a large binder, called the Red
Tablet, which contains detailed information about Church
structure, policies, and beliefs. Also, he can join Ground
Floor, a Church research organization open to Adepts and
above, which is designed to investigate strategies for
survival so members can live through the collapse of society
they believe is coming. Some Ground Floor members have been
combing the literature to develop a library of survival
strategies, and one member is working on a book dealing with
the basics of survival, such as making a fire with sticks
and stones and building a leaf shelter.

Currently, there are 13 Adepts, most of whom were not
in the Church of Satan. Rather, most learned about the
Church through friends or relatives already in it. A few
also joined after hearing a talk by a Master at a local
gathering, although the Church does little active recruit-
ment.

Finally, on the bottom of the pecking order are a
handful of First Degrees, called Hutians. All learned about
the group through friends and relatives, except for Rath, a
former Satanist who became an Adept but was demoted. Newcomers begin at this level and go through a trial period to
show they are seriously dedicated to their own magical growth
through the Hutian system of magic. Like Adepts, they are
not expected to believe in Hu, but are expected to work with

Hu in ritual as if he does exist.

Although a First Degree can remain in the Church up to
two years without being promoted to Adept, if at any time
a member of the priesthood feels he is not suitable material,
he can recommend to the Council that the neophyte be asked
to leave the Church, and if the Council agrees, this occurs.
Conversely, one of the two Priests overseeing his magical
development can recommend he advance to an Adept. Then, his
advancement will be automatically accepted since the Magus
does not need to approve it as he does when an Adept moves
up to Priest.

To systematize the recognition process and link together Priests and laity, Kel developed the "Pyramid Project"
in mid 1980, whereby he assigned two Priest to each Master
and four or five Adepts or First Degrees to each Priest, so
that each lower degree member ended up with two higher
status representatives who would play a kind of "big brother"
or master-apprentice role. Kel's philosophy in designing
the project was that lower status members could show the
upper degrees that they were evolving appropriately, while
the upper status members could share their higher knowledge
with them and recognize and recommend those operating at a
higher level for higher status. Also, the project would
link together members all over the country to create a
tighter national network, as members corresponded, called,
or visited with each other. Further, Kel and other higher-
ups felt this process would reveal the "dead wood" who
weren't doing anything, so they could eliminate them from
the group.

This tight military-like structure reflects the group's
elitist growth-orientation, for the more magically developed
the Hutian is thought to be, the higher his status in the
elect. At the same time, Hutians believe their entire group
is becoming more magically powerful as more and more Hutians
rise in the structure. Also, they believe that members of
each degree are becoming more evolved as well, so that newcomers are at the level of magical development formerly
expected of Adepts, and Adepts are now at the level once
expected of Priests. In turn, Hutians attribute this individual and group upgrading to the Church's creation and
change orientation, which is making the whole structure
evolve, as well as the individuals within it.

Thus, they believe their degree structure must remain
flexible to reflect this, through the creation of even higher
degrees representing higher stages of magical evolution.

As Hutians explain, when the group first organized in 1975,
there were only five degrees. But when Andrews passed the
mantle of Magus to Kel, he moved up to the new Sixth Degree
position, Ipsissimus. And now Kel is intimating that a
seventh degree may be manifesting.

Although Hutians view this degree creation process as
a response to their continuing magical and spiritual evolution, and claim it keeps motivation high, since there is
always something more to strive for, the process of advancement and degree upgrading can also be regarded as a kind of
ego enhancement, representing a response by members to
their status deprivation outside the group and their need
to compensate through status recognition within the group.
This interpretation seems especially inviting, since the
objective criteria for advancement are so nebulous that they
allow those deciding who will advance wide leeway for subjective judgment. Moreover, Hutians can use this judgment
of magical growth to excuse personal failure outside the
group and to convert a failed outside status into high
group status.

This process is demonstrated in the movement of Hutians
up the hierarchy, for as they rise, many Hutians claim they
have more trouble operating in the mundane world but explain
this by saying they are becoming more magical beings. On
the other hand, the individual's failure to operate successfully in the mundane world may lead him to invest more of
his energy in the Church and to consider his status within
it more important. Thus, by achieving within the Church,
members can compensate for their failure to fit in and
achieve within the mainstream. As Hutians often comment in
meetings and in conversation, they already felt weird and
alien from mainstream society when they entered the Church,
and they are aware that moving up the degree ladder tends
to produce even more feelings of alienation.

However, since Hutians see themselves as an elect, they
can turn this sense of alienation around. Thus, instead of
feeling downgraded by their difference, they can see their
uniqueness as a sign they are better than mere "humans" outside the group. Further, using the same logic, they can
claim that the increasing alienation higher-ups experience
as they move up in the Church is one more sign they are
evolving into a higher and better being. In other words,
the higher the person's degree, the more highly evolved,
and the more he is likely to be alienated from mainstream
society. So degrees play a crucial role not only in locating

the Hutian in the group, but in explaining or justifying his
lack of fit outside it.

To an extent, the important role degrees play in the
Church derives from the group's origin out of the Church of
Satan, in response to LaVey's sale of degrees. LaVey considered their sale perfectly acceptable and not hypocriti-
cal, since he felt degrees could be used in negative ways
to manipulate and control others by using degrees to reward
or punish. So making them less important by selling them
was a means to reduce manipulation and control. However,
to the dissidents who joined the Church, these degrees were
a sign of advancement and status representing years of work
and study in the Satanic Church. Then, when they left because the degree system was undermined, they invested
degrees with prime value in the new Church.

In turn, the degree system plays a major role in
structuring relationships and interaction patterns within
the group. For example, as Hutians move up the ranks to
Master status, they tend to become more reserved and formal
with lower status members and have little social contact
with them. As Masters, they may socialize with members of
the priesthood; but generally, not with the I's and II's.

Similarly, Priests may socialize with some lay members
if they are already personal friends or have a dating or
marriage relationship. But otherwise, Priests are more
likely to socialize with each other.

By the same token, the higher-ups encourage the I's and
II's to get to know each other, since they feel the lay members are more likely to understand one another or know
"where each other is at," because all newcomers go through a
similar learning experience. For instance, I's and II's are
typically fascinated by the phenomena observed in the pentagram; but to the priesthood seeing them is "old hat."

The use of titles, medallions, and magical accoutrements
further reinforces the status positions. Although Hutians
use their regular names in everyday interaction, in group
meetings and rituals they use their magical names or titles
and try to avoid their mundane names. Also, at all group
events they prominently display their color medallions indicating status. Some Hutians also wear small pentagrams
of the appropriate color as necklaces or on rings in daily
life to show pride in their membership. The higher Hutians
rank the more likely they are to wear such jewelry outside
of the group.

Likewise, Hutians use magical gear as a sign of status,

for as they advance they tend to acquire more and more
statues and magical tools, such as swords, knives, and power
objects, which further attest to their magical knowledge and
prowess.

The robes used in ritual show status, too, for the
Hutian can only add a trim in the color of his own degree
or less. Thus, a First Degree can only trim his robe with
white or silver, while a Second Degree can add red or orange.
The Priest can wear all of these colors plus black, while
the Master can add blue and the Magus purple. When he
applies this trim, the Hutian must keep the main body of
his robe black, since Hutians are a people of darkness.
But the trim provides a dramatic and attractive statement
of status and pride, for as the Hutian advances in rank, the
splendor of his robe typically increases.

Other signs of degree recognition occur during the
ritual itself, when lower status members symbolically honor
higher-ups by facing them, raising their arm in homage, and
addressing them with the phrase: "Hail..." followed by
their magical name or title. For example, at the conclave,
the Magus and Masters led the Priests and laity to the inner
court and stepped onto the central platform under the pentagram, while the Priests and laity watched. Then, facing the
pentagram, the High Priest intoned loudly: "Look, Hu, here
are your royal ones." In response, the Priests and laity
raised their hands to salute the Magus and Masters and
cried out: "Hail, royal ones." At times the higher status
member may hail the lower status person back; but usually
he does so in a manner that reasserts his higher status.

An instance of this occurred at the conclave when the
laity were about to begin their ritual on the first night.
They were grouping together to make a procession, when Kel
approached. "Do what you will do well," he said, holding
out his hand in salute. At once, all members of the laity
turned to him, similarly raised their arms in salute, and
chanted several times: "Hail, Kel...Hail, Kel." Kel smiled
broadly and saluted the group in acknowledgement. "Hail,
Hutians and Adepts," he said, stating their rank as if to
reaffirm their lay status.

The ritual procession usually reflects rank, too, since
members typically enter the ritual area in single file by
rank and seniority. Thus, when the whole Church participated
in a ritual procession on the last night of the conclave,
the High Priest came first, followed by the Masters lined
up in order of seniority. Then came the Priests, similarly

ordered, and finally the Adepts and First Degrees.

Advancement in status is likewise made much of. As each member moves up in rank, he acquires an initiatory certificate indicating his degree, which he is supposed to display prominently on his walls. This certificate, called the "Stele of Xeper" or becoming, is modeled after the ancient Egyptian funeral stele or standing stone, which was embossed with images of gods and messages in hieroglyphs.

The Church's version depicts the beetle god Xepera or Khepri pointing to the pentagram at the top of the stele, and beside him, the Egyptian hieroglyphs for apes, mankind, and divine persons are arranged in ascending order to symbolize the evolution of the elect. On the other side of the stele, Hu, with his usual beak-nosed head on a human body, sits on a throne holding a scepter to signify he is guardian of the Church. He holds the ankh of life as a symbol that believers in him will achieve immortality. Also, the stele includes four lines of hieroglyphs stating that Hu resides in the heavens in the astronomical north pole and that the named member has "come into being" as the designated degree. The recorded date of this noted event is counted from the first year of the Church of Satan. When Adepts and higher ups receive their stele, it includes two additional lines stating they have gained mastery of what it was set forth for them to do for Hu on earth and that they are now in the company of the elect.

When the Hutian first joins the Church, he gradually learns about this structure and his place in it. After he first reads about it in a flyer or hears about it from a Hutian, he merely needs to indicate he wants to learn and is willing to commit himself to become a Hutian. However, he is permitted no trial period, for he must decide on the basis of this limited information whether he wants to be a member or not. The group's rationale for this approach is that the prospective Hutian is either one of the elect—or potentially so—or not. He is either inside the group or out. There is no middle ground.

In some cases, geographically isolated Hutians learn about the group through one other Hutian and depend on this person for their early learning. For example, one Canadian First Degree found out through her boyfriend, a Priest, and learned most of what she knew from him. An Adept from Nebraska first heard a Master speak and gained her initial training from him.

However, most newcomers are in the San Francisco or

Los Angeles area and learn about group beliefs in a more
organized way, such as from the pylon's monthly study group.

Typically, new Hutians go through a period of questioning in which they ask themselves if they are on the right
path, and many wonder if they are truly of the elect. The
result is often weeks and months of soul-searching and
questioning to decide. For example, the Canadian First
Degree vacillated for several months about whether to stay
in the group, because she was dating a priest and wanted to
be sure she was really making the decision for herself
rather than because of the relationship. But finally, after
much reading and study, she decided she was of the elect,
unlike her ordinary friends and acquaintances who wouldn't
understand the Church's philosophy.

This long questioning process occurs because the Hutian
way involves accepting a totally new way of thinking and
viewing the world, which Hutians call "the left hand path."
It means casting aside old ways of understanding and per-
ceiving to think magically, and see oneself as a causal
agent who has the power to effect external events. It involves looking for links between otherwise apparently random
or chance occurrences. Thus, becoming a Hutian is not an
easy decision, and often Hutians go through a period of
several months when they feel their foundations stripped
away, as Khet experienced for about six weeks after she performed the ritual during which she realized how much she
didn't know and how much she had to learn.

The process is made more difficult for newcomers, since
the Hutian is supposed to take the initiative in order to
prove to himself and others that he is of the elect. He
should not, according to the Magus, be "spoon fed;" therefore others should not give him too much help. As a result,
higher-ups generally leave him on his own and avoid giving
him explicit directions about what to do to grow, although
sometimes his Priest representative will give suggestions
or instructions. For example, when the pyramid project was
started, most Priests wrote an introductory letter to their
lay assignees, describing how much they had gained personally from being in the Church. Then when some of these
neophytes didn't respond after a few months, the Priests
followed up with brief, angry letters demanding to know why
they hadn't answered and if they were still in the Church.
In another case, Armat, my Priest representative, called me
after my first ritual to set up a meeting so she could further explain the approach of Hutian magic, since the images

of light I used in my ritual demonstrated I didn't understand some basic Hutian principles. Nevertheless, apart
from specific situations where the Priest feels intervention
necessary, the First Degree must normally initiate action to
prove he is seriously interested and hence of the elect.

Generally, this neophyte stage lasts at least six
months and more commonly a year, though the First Degree has
two years to prove himself an accomplished white magician,
so he can advance to Adepthood or be dropped from the group.
Under special circumstances, such as an illness or unusually
heavy job demands, the Magus might exempt the neophyte from
this two year requirement, but normally the two year limit
prevails.

As the First Degree progresses—or doesn't—he gets
feedback through critiques of his ritual, reactions to his
remarks in study group, or informal comments. Thus, before
he actually advances, he may feel he is about to move on.
For example, when Khet was a few months away from becoming
an Adept, she began to talk about how she was working high
in the first and near the second.

Then, when the First Degree's Priest rep considers him
ready, the neophyte exchanges his white pentagram for a red
one in a ritual, symbolizing he has advanced to Adept. Often
he expects this advancement, as occurred with Khet. But at
times, the new Adept is surprised at his changed status and
goes through another period of questioning about whether he
is worthy.

This occurred when Lat was recognized in the pylon
ritual. At first he was ecstatic that the group had acknowledged him. But that night at home, he awoke at four in the
morning, and contemplating his pentagram, he asked the question again and again: "Am I really worthy?" He wasn't sure
if he was, and his crisis of faith lasted for several hours,
until he felt Hu's presence beside him. If Hu was there,
he concluded, he must be worthy, and he recommitted himself
to the group.

Because of the group emphasis on evolution, advancement,
and self-observation, Hutians continually observe themselves
for signs of readiness to move on wherever they are on the
degree ladder. Thus, Adepts talk about how they are working
higher and higher in the red as they become more confident
of their ability to perform magic, while Priests look for
signs they are approaching the Fourth Degree.

Frequently, these indicators of change are subtle personal changes, which are only readily apparent to the Hutian
himself. Hence, it is important to share personal feelings
and experiences with higher-ups, so such changes can be
recognized. For instance, one L.A. Hutian felt he had become more focused and better able to concentrate when he
moved from First Degree to Adepthood. But others didn't
notice this change until he shared.

Hutians also suggest changing a magical name to produce
change, and they believe a name change can be a harbinger
of change, in that after it occurs a degree change may
follow. For example, shortly before she became a Priestess,
Armat gave up the name of an Egyptian queen to become Armat,
the vulture. Then, when she felt she was working at the
edge of becoming a Master, she began to call herself Luk,
a larger and more powerful form of the vulture goddess.

Just as Hutians look within for signs of progress, so
higher-ups observe those below them. Then, when they see
lower status members evolve or fail to do so, they share
this information with other higher-ups so the official with
jurisdiction can recognize a lower member to the next level
or take other action, as appropriate.

Because of all this sharing, there are few secrets in
the Church. In turn, Hutians feel justified in passing on
information about other members even if someone tells them
in confidence, if they believe it will benefit the Church.
For instance, when Rath was an Adept, he shared his doubts
about some Church policies with three other lay members,
Lat, Khet, and myself after a pylon meeting. He complained
that the Church's ideas about evolution and growth seemed
vague, and the priesthood didn't even know what they meant.
He said that he wanted to be open and truthful about his
feelings and was sharing them in confidence. However, immediately after the meeting, Lat and Khet called Armat to
report his comments, since they felt his doubts could become
a threat to the Church and they believed they should make
this information known, in keeping with the Church principle
of working with the Spirit of Maat or truth.

The exchange of letters between lower and higher status
members is part of this sharing process, too, and like other
information, the contents of these letters is spread to
others in the Church. Priests frequently circulate the
letters they receive from their pyramid assignees to other
Priests, or they advise their assignee to send a copy of his
letter to his other pyramid rep. Masters circulate letters

from the Priests assigned to them among themselves. And
lower degrees often share their letters from higher status
members, too, to obtain new ideas. The purpose of this sharing is to provide all members with further insights on the
growth process, and show the higher ups how well each lower
degree is growing.

In sum, concern with the growth process pervades the
Church, since all are striving to evolve. In turn, the
degree system, symbols, socialization patterns, and pyramid
communication system reaffirm the group hierarchy, which
reflects this process of growth in structural form. As
members appear to Hutians to become more evolved, they move
up the hierarchy, and the symbols of status and honor they
acquire as they rise provides a growing assurance that they
are of the elect. Although this process of advancement
contributes to the Hutian's alienation from outsiders, it
simultaneously compensates for this alienation, since members feel increasingly of the elect as they move up in the
Church.

Unfortunately, this sense of being increasingly elite
creates some problems in the Church, since some higher
degrees look down on lower degrees. One Priestess found when
she first joined the Church that several Priests and Masters
wouldn't speak to her or treated her abruptly. But once she
became a Priestess that changed. As one Priest who previously
scorned her explained: "Since you're a Priestess, I can talk
to you now."

Many higher-ups are concerned about this potential for
divisiveness in the Church. Thus, the Magus and other
leaders frequently urge other higher-ups to remember they
were lay members once and should respect present lay members
who "are still of the elect." But the admonition doesn't
always work, and many higher status members are often distant
and critical of lower degrees, because they consider themselves more magically developed, and hence the "elect of the
elect." Since the group places so much stress on evolution
and hierarchy, such an attitude seems almost inevitable, even
though many higher-ups wish to change it.

8

The Role of Magic, Ritual, and
Elect Status in Everyday Life

Being in the Church affects the Hutian's experiences of
everyday life, since believing in magic, ritual, and elect
status changes the way he thinks and acts in the world.
These different perceptions and experiences then confirm the
Hutian's beliefs. Whereas First Degrees are only learning
this perspective, Adepts and higher-ups have adopted it to
a greater or lesser degree.
   This unique perspective has these major effects. First,
since Hutians consider control and discipline. crucial to
magical growth, they modify their lives to promote these
qualities. Thus, they generally do not drink, because they
feel alcohol detracts from personal control, and a few former
heavy drinkers or alcoholics gave up drinking when they
joined the Church. The concern with control also leads
Hutians to become increasingly remote, rigid, and emotion-
less as they remain in the Church. Thus, even those who
feel genuinely warm toward one another tend to show their
affection in a controlled, reserved way.
   Secondly, the Hutians' emphasis on gaining power, personal development, and self-interest tends to produce a
self-centered, abrasive, inconsiderate personality, which
is characteristic of many Hutians. They want what they want
when they want it and try to keep others out of their way.
For example, at the conclave one Midwestern Adept told me
proudly that whenever she had a question, she called other
Hutians to discuss it, even at three in the morning. "I know
I harass them," she said, "but if it's important, they should
get up."
   Because of their magical beliefs, Hutians look for examples of coincidences, signs of personal power, and proofs of

performing effective rituals everywhere. Often they claim
an event has occurred because they performed a specific
ritual or that something favorable happened because they are
an elect powerful person.

For example, when several Hutians met for a mini-
conclave at the home of a New England Hutian, they observed,
as one wrote in The Papyrus, that the kitchen was dark when
they entered although the light switch was in the on position. Then as they stood beneath the light, it suddenly came
on. Soon after when a Priest stood in front of a hanging
wall rug, it suddenly fell. To the Hutians these events
were signs their presence had a magical effect on the world
around them and caused these out-of-the-ordinary events.

A few Hutians even feel their personal power extends to
controlling the weather. Thus, they consider themselves
"weather witches," and look for examples that their willing
has produced the desired results. For example, on the trip
to the conclave, Athena, a Nebraska Adept, remarked that she
could make good weather since she didn't like rain. As proof,
she claimed that several times when it was raining, she made
the sun shine in her immediate area. In fact, she claimed
since she became a Hutian two years ago, the average yearly
rainfall in her community went down.

Hutians also believe they have the ability to communicate with others in non-ordinary ways, such as through telepathy, and see this as another indication of personal power.
For instance, a Priest from Georgia told me that he had been
corresponding with a Master from California and that they
responded to each other's needs and wishes without having to
express these in words. As he explained: "Whenever I feel
down, I get a letter from her to cheer me up. And when she
has the blahs, she gets a letter from me. It's as if we
both know what we each need without anyone saying anything."

Some feel a special bond with others who share the same
name or have a name with similar qualities, and view this
bond as another source of power. For example, at the conclave, I was sitting on a bench with two Adepts, Athena and
Nal, who had chosen names which had warrior associations
like mine. Suddenly, Nal remarked that it was significant
that the three of us with this warrior identity were located
in almost a straight line from one end of the country to the
other, she on the East Coast, Athena in the Midwest, and me
on the West Coast. It was as if, she suggested, the country
was divided up into three large territories for us to protect.
"So you'll have to be our protectress on the West Coast," she

told me, "while we take care of the other areas."

Hutians see ritual success as another sign of personal power, particularly if they can point to evidence that the ritual has "broken" the natural order by causing a rare or improbable event. Higher-ups frequently talk about such cases with each other and the laity to show off their magical abilities. For example, in one widely discussed case, a Priestess did a destruction ritual against a photographer who had threatened the man she lived with, and in her ritual she visualized the photographer having an auto accident. A few hours later, he was in a car crash which totalled his car, and when she learned about this incident a few weeks later, she was certain her ritual caused it.

In another case, she put some wood on her porch and performed a ritual in which she placed the wood under the protection of the Egyptian statue of Cleopatra which served as her watcher. The wood remained there for almost a year, and shortly before the 1980 conclave, she offered it to Kel in lieu of a $25 registration fee. He said he would arrange to pick it up but didn't say when. A few days later when she returned home, she noticed the wood was gone and thinking it stolen called the police. As it happened, Ba, the Priest who lived with Kel, had picked it up in his truck. Ironically, about an hour later, as he was driving on the freeway, another car rear-ended his truck, totally demolishing the wood. According to the Priestess, the accident happened because her watcher's protective power over the wood continued even when she was away. As a result, as soon as she thought the wood was stolen, her watcher's power caused the person taking the wood to suffer the consequences. And so Ba had his accident. However, as the Priestess explained, Ba wasn't hurt because of his own personal power. Any other driver would have been decapitated by the wood going through the cab of the truck. But Ba's magical powers protected him.

Hutians are also constantly on the lookout for signs telling them they should do something or warning them not to do it. For instance, Ardis, an Adept from Massachusetts, got an insight in a ritual that she should move, but decided not to act immediately because of current commitments. Then, about two weeks later, she was in a car accident which severely dented the side of her car, although she was not hurt. Like Ba she took her survival as proof that her magical powers gave her special protection. But Ardis interpreted the accident as a warning she should move. In her view, the accident occurred because she hadn't acted upon the

insight she gained in the previous ritual. As a result, in
a few days she moved to another city where two other Hutians
lived and within one day found a job. This success, in turn,
convinced her that her original insight was correct.

Since then, she and the two other Massachusetts Hutians
received several signs suggesting that they should move to
California, and in the conclave ritual, she got a further confirmation they should do so. As Ardis described it, she saw
the image of a city and heard the words "one of the three and
two of the two." Since there was one Priest or III in their
group, and two Adepts or II's, she felt the words referred to
them, and the city represented San Francisco. Thus, she
concluded, this was another sign they should move to San
Francisco.

While a non-believer would argue that there is no justification for making such connections between signs, meanings,
and events, and that the believer simply makes these links
to support a desired reality, Hutians dismiss such arguments
as non-magical thinking. In their view, they can make such
connections, since one can know intuitively that a certain
effect is due to a certain cause, such as a ritual, and that
a certain occurrence is a sign. Hutians believe they have
acquired this knowing through their development as magical
beings, and hence can accurately link cause and effect.
Moreover, they believe magical training gives them the ability to know they know. By contrast, they claim those who
constantly ask for proofs of effects are magically naive,
since the magician should take it for granted that coincidences and signs are real and not question their validity.

In short, Hutians believe in magical thought and practice, and they relate to the world and interpret events in
magical terms. They can even explain apparently non-
confirming events in this context, so the system is pre-
served. For example, since they believe that every cause
has an effect and that the time between a ritual and its
effect is open-ended, they claim that performing a ritual
will eventually produce an effect. This effect may not
happen immediately or as soon as they would like, but it
will occur. As they see it, once the energy of the ritual
is sent out, it will work when it is ready.

When possible, Hutians make note of desired results
which occur after a ritual, and they refer to them as proofs
of effectiveness. Thus, if a desired event occurs soon after
the ritual, Hutians point to it as a confirmation the ritual
has worked. But even if the Hutian has no way to confirm his

ritual, he still assumes it will work. For instance, when
Armat cursed the garage mechanic who she thought cheated her,
and when Rif wished harm against the person who burglarized
his house, neither had any way to tell if the offender was
hurt. But both felt sure the offender would eventually "be
taken care of" because as Armat put it: "The energy has been
sent."

Even when events occur that might appear to disconfirm
belief in personal power, Hutians continue to believe, since
they interpret or reinterpret the events to preserve their
beliefs. For example, when I drove to the conclave with
Armat, Khet, Lat, and Athena, numerous problems plagued our
group from the outset. First Lat was late, and we weren't
able to leave until about an hour later than planned. Then,
after we had driven for about 15 minutes, as Athena and I
discussed how we purchased our robes, Armat suddenly remem-
bered she forgot hers and turned back to get it. About a
half-hour later, when we were on the freeway, one of the
tires went flat, and we had to pull off the road. Armat
took out the spare, and we put it on. But as soon as Lat
removed the jack, she discovered this tire was flat, too.
As she hiked off to call the AAA, the rest of us waited by
the side of the road.

However, having these problems did not lead anyone to
question their possession of magical powers, since Hutians
can dismiss such day-to-day problems on the basis that magical power is best reserved for personal magical development,
not trivial mundane matters. Yet, they can resolve the
difficulty through magical means, if they wish. Accordingly,
about ten minutes after Armat trudged down the road to find
a phone, Athena reassured us there was no need to worry, because she was working magically to handle the matter. "No
sweat, no sweat," she said. "I've already put out the message. We'll be on our way in 30 minutes." When the AAA
truck arrived shortly thereafter, Athena interpreted this as
a sign her magical willing had been effective in getting the
AAA to respond to Armat's call. However, neither she nor the
others saw having the flat as an invalidation of personal
power.

Likewise, when serious incidents occur, such as near
fatalities, Hutians reinterpret them to suggest they weren't
more serious, because the Hutians involved had personal protection. For instance, the Priest and two Adepts from
Massachusetts arrived at the conclave about six hours late,
since their plane had had a near accident when it lost an

engine, and they had to change planes twice. Then, when they
checked at the bus depot for their luggage, it hadn't arrived.
The depot agent assured them several times it would arrive
later that night and subsequently said it would come in the
morning; but by the following evening, they still had no
luggage. However, again, the Hutians interpreted the incident to support their magical belief system. Rather than
wondering if the accident called their own power into question, they concluded they had not been in a fatal accident
because they were protected.

Similarly, when Ba's car was pushed off the mountain
road by a speeding car three weeks after the accident with
the wood, he focused on his survival, rather than the accident, and saw this incident as still another reaffirmation of
his magical being. He claimed this was so, and Kel agreed,
since the car flipped over three times and came to rest
against a large rock which prevented it from hurtling several
miles down the mountain. Also, Ba only suffered a few bruises.
Thus, the outcome of the accident was less serious than it
might have been, presumably because of Ba's personal power.
As Kel observed: "If it was someone else, he probably would
have been killed."

In short, even when Hutians experience major problems
or a series of difficulties, they tend not to question their
ability to exercise magical power, but look on the positive
side, so they continue to believe in their magic.

Hutians also maintain belief by claiming the problems
they experience are part of their magical growth. This
occurs in two ways. First, the individual regards these
problems as a learning experience that furthers his magical
development. And secondly, he encounters more problems as
he evolves magically, since he is less able to deal with the
mundane world. In either case, whether the Hutian successfully achieves his goals or not, he can still see himself as
a powerful magical being.

This happened when one Priestess experienced a series of
personal crises for several months which involved changing
jobs, looking for a new apartment, and not having much success in developing a good relationship with a male. But she
never doubted her powers as a Priestess because of these
problems. Rather she regarded them as indicators she was
growing, evolving, and moving closer to becoming a Fourth
Degree. As she explained when an Adept assigned to her asked
why she hadn't answered her 20-page letter: "I'm balancing
on the edge of a major transition. So it's becoming harder

to relate to the mundane."

Thus, instead of making the individual question his
magical abilities, difficulties become a confirmation of
magical growth. Ironically, many Hutians are attracted to
becoming magicians because they feel a lack of power in
everyday life. Once they become Hutians, they may confront
the same problems and perhaps other difficulties, but they
think about them differently in that they look at them
positively or consider them a sign of magical evolution; as
a result they feel powerful and magical in spite of these
problems.

A similar transformation occurs in the way Hutians
regard and relate to outsiders which helps them feel powerful, too. As noted, many Hutians considered themselves
weird or were rejected by others and were disturbed by this
self-image and rejection before joining the Church, such as
the Priestess who observed that others seemed to move away
when she walked into a room. But after becoming Hutians,
they see this rejection as one more sign of their magical
development and elect membership. Whereas outsiders are
"mere humans," they are "evolving man." If humans treat them
badly, they do so because they are inadequate themselves and
only worthy of scorn. One L.A. Priestess expressed this
scorn that developed as she felt herself transformed, when
she wrote in a letter: "You begin to realize that you are
superior to the humans around you. It shows and they sense
this and react accordingly. I have had no bad experiences
with humans, but I tend not to pay attention to people who
do not matter."

Another Hutian who worked in an occult shop frequently
described her customers as fools, because she charged: "All
of them seem to want instant miracles. They think all they
have to do is burn a candle, wear a charm, or say a spell,
and they don't understand that achieving these goals requires
hard work."

Thus, Hutians often try to avoid "mere humans;" and when
they do have to relate to them they tend to use various
strategies so these "humans" will bother them as little as
possible. For example, when Khet walked to and from work,
she put out energy so others would avoid her, and she looked
directly ahead so she wouldn't see them. At the conclave,
Athena and Nal indicated they each had an internal robot,
and when they had to work with humans, they sent it out to
interact for them, in effect putting themselves on automatic
pilot. Then, they could respond by rote, so the annoying

humans would have as little impact on them as possible.

In more personal situations, Hutians evolve other strategies to keep outsiders at arms length or in their place. For
instance, Athena lived with a "human" she had been married to
for 20 years, 18 of these before she became a Hutian. Prior
to joining the Church, she found him "pleasant enough." But
being a member increasingly alienated her from him, as it did
from other humans, so now she considered living with him "a
major annoyance," and barely spoke to him or did anything
with him. Instead, she generally went her own way, and
eventually she planned to leave him and move to California
to join the core of the Church.

Other Hutians seek to relate to humans in ways that
emphasize their elect status—using humans to serve their
own ends. Nor, a Hutian from L.A. who prided himself for his
intelligence as a member of the high I.Q. Mensa Society, described this strategy in the Hutian newsletter. Hutians, he
observed, have a "natural tendency" to dismiss people outside
the Church as "mundane" and unimportant to the Hutian. But
Hutians should not dismiss them so readily, because each
Hutian has only limited time and resources to devote to the
important work of higher evolution, due to mankind's coming
annihilation. Thus, Hutians should not only do all they can
to avoid the disaster, but they should use every available
resource,"including that of our less fortunate cousins, the
humans. There is simply no point to a superior Being dupli-
cating efforts that lesser individuals are capable of and
are achieving."

Besides disparaging outsiders, minimizing contact with
them, and thinking up ways to use them, Hutians enjoy antago-
nizing or "baiting" them and relating these incidents. These
actions represent one more method the Hutians use to put down
outsiders, make themselves feel more self-important and powerful, and strike back against their experience of rejection.
At a pylon meeting, Rath described one such incident. A
Jehovah's Witness appeared at his door and urged him to get
religion and a Bible. "But I already have a Bible," Rath
told him and gleefully went to get it. When he returned, he
thrust a copy of the Satanic Bible at the Jehovah's Witness,
whose face blanched as he retreated in shock. "It was won-
derful," Rath smiled.

In another case, two Adepts at the 1979 conclave at a
Midwestern Holiday Inn visited all of the motel rooms they
shared and drew pentagrams in the Bibles. Although several
higher-ups later chided them for their immaturity, the

incident is another dramatic example of how Hutians enjoy
startling others with their beliefs.

The Hutian's desire to proclaim differences and shock
others is tempered, however, by an awareness of the need for
secrecy. Hutians recognize they must generally be discreet
about who they are and what they believe, since their beliefs
may seem weird and threatening to others and may lead to
negative repurcussions they are not powerful enough to prevent. For example, some higher-ups have lost their jobs due
to their beliefs, as occurred when Firth, a Hutian from
Southern California, was fired from his bank job when his
boss learned about his religion. Thus, believing most people
won't understand or fearing negative consequences, most
Hutians are circumspect and do not tell others, even friends,
about their Church membership. Some even claim outsiders
will react as they do because they are only humans. As Wik
from Canada observed: "Why should I tell anyone. They
wouldn't understand. They're not of the elect."

In some cases, this concern for secrecy leads to paranoia. For instance, before the conclave, the higher-ups
constantly warned everyone to be circumspect and not mention
the Church, since the People's Temple had gotten a great
deal of publicity in the area, and the locals might be fearful
of another unusual religious group arising in their community
and act accordingly.

Then, when we first gathered at the motel, they warned
us several more times not to call the group a church. "If
anyone asks," Armat said, "say you represent the American
Egyptological Order or an Egyptian lodge."

Besides experiencing rejection as individuals and rejecting others, Hutians at times experience outsiders
rejecting or avoiding them as a group. But again they
reinterpret this avoidance as another sign that they are
superior, elect, and powerful, and that "humans" fear their
power. Thus, when people move away, Hutians recount this to
each other with a perverse pride. For example, at the conclave Athena proudly boasted that when the Hutians gathered
in the halls of the hotel or walked to the elevator at the
previous conclave, people frequently opened their doors, saw
them, and retreated back into their rooms. Likewise, when
Wik and her boyfriend were visiting three Hutians in New
England, and they went to a nearby restaurant for breakfast,
she reported in the Papyrus: "Our eating section slowly
started to empty. It appeared that no one wanted to sit near
us." The implication was that once again the "humans" sought

to avoid the Hutians out of fear of their superior power.

Given this negative and scornful attitude toward humanity, it is not surprising that Hutians hold other religions
in low regard. Although their literature states that they
consider other religions irrelevant and do not wish to
attack them, in practice Hutians disparage other religions.
Primarily they argue that other religions are dogmatic and
controlling, whereas their religion encourages individual
creativity and freedom. However, they have their own form
of dogma and control.

Hutians are particularly hostile to Christianity, since
they reject its ideas about sin and suffering, feel it encourages human weakness, and makes man subservient to a
strong outside god. Also, they reject the contemplative
Eastern traditions and their ideas of karma and oneness,
since they claim that the black magician transcends and
therefore is not bound by the laws of Karma. They believe
that humanity is not one, because they are an elect. As for
the humanitarian concerns of other religions, Hutians reject
these, too, since they are not interested in solving the
problems of humankind generally; they consider humans unworthy of concern and want to survive the coming annihilation
themselves.

Similarly, Hutians are not receptive to other forms of
magic. These are, they assert, wrong, filled with mindless
superstition, and outdated because they employ old unneeded
formulas, which depend on the magician performing procedures
properly or invoking gods outside himself to do the magic.
Instead, the magician must depend on his own will for magical
success. Hutians are also especially opposed to white magic.
They think white magicians weak and unable to break the magical order, because they are too "white light."

Although holding these negative attitudes to other
humans, religions, and magical systems helps the Hutian feel
a sense of personal worth and power by putting down others
and elevating himself, this critical negative outlook can
create difficulties in how Hutians relate to each other.
Sometimes it leads to personal crises as well. The major
reason for this difficulty is that believing he is of the
elect tends to make the Hutian highly self-judgmental and
critical of other Hutians, if he detects signs that he or
others are not performing up to elect standards.

When all goes smoothly, this sense of election draws
Hutians closer together by creating a bond which separates
them from outsiders. Wik noted she felt this way at the

conclave. "When I arrived," she said, "meeting other Hutians was like coming home." Several others remarked they felt this strong bond, too, because they found others like themselves in the Church. Hutians also experience a sense of closeness when they perform rituals together or share ideas.

Yet, there is an underlying criticalness that occasionally surfaces over certain key concerns. Is the Hutian working hard enough to evolve? Does he have the requisite personal qualities to evolve along the Hutian path? Is he as powerful magically as he appears to be? These issues are critical for the Hutian, because they raise the question of whether the Hutian truly has the potential to remain among elect, and if so, is he exercising this potential appropriately? Is he truly a superior being? And is he doing enough to express his superior nature?

Given these concerns, Hutians frequently discuss how well others are performing, and their letter exchange becomes a window on each Hutian's growth. Although this constant communication about growth can help the Hutian grow by stressing its importance and providing useful techniques, this exchange can also alert others when a Hutian is not growing correctly or enough.

When this happens, Hutians tend not to be very supportive. They take this position, because they believe magical growth is one's personal responsibility, and if one is not growing properly, one should quickly get back on track or drop off. In the early stages of inappropriate growth, another Hutian might point this out to the offender. But after several months, if the errant Hutian doesn't shape up, Hutians believe he is no longer worth helping, for he has, by his difficulty, shown himself to be another "mere human" and not of the elect.

Hutians express their criticalness towards others in several ways. Sometimes they disparage another Hutian's personal qualities; sometimes they attack his level of magical development. One Hutian often described certain other Hutians as "very weird." A Priestess stopped attending meetings of the San Francisco pylon because she didn't like several members. A few Hutians repeatedly remarked that another Hutian couldn't explain group ideas very well. And often Hutians told me or each other about other Hutians they didn't like.

In some cases, Hutians question whether others should be recognized to a particular level or whether they are sufficiently magical. Before Rath was demoted, Khet discussed

with others whether he should be at that level. Later, when
Rath was put on probation, he questioned why another Adept
who did even less than he and didn't come to meetings should
be an Adept. In another case, Armat told me that she doubted
the magical abilities of someone she had been living with who
was involved in the group. In ritual, she felt, he "put out
negative energy." When he left the group, she felt his
departure confirmed her initial impression.

At times, members of one group question the magical
ability of another. For example, a Priestess of the San
Francisco pylon occasionally praised the San Francisco group
for working at the highest magical level, but criticized the
L.A. group for not having as good an understanding about
magic and for not being as well organized. As she explained:
"When I asked them what they were doing, the Priest told me
'We sort of meet one time a month, and we sort of do a ritual,
and sort of talk about the reading.' But here we have regular
study groups. And they don't really understand the concept
of 'Xem.' They only perceive it, but don't understand it as
we do. Here we're light years ahead of them magically."

In turn, this criticalness can lead to changes in the
status of members when higher-ups think they are not performing properly. For example, when Lol, an Adept in Los Angeles,
wrote a letter to Huf, her Priestess pyramid rep, Huf felt
her letter was a First Degree letter, because it didn't show
sufficient understanding about magic. As a result, Huf wrote
to Lik, the Priest heading the L.A. pylon, and told him to
demote Lol, which he did. At this, Lol wrote back protesting
that a demotion for a single letter was unfair, though she
acknowledged it was a First Degree letter. When Huf finally
relented, Lik restored her to Adept status four months later.

In another case, Rif, now a Priest, was demoted from
Adept to First Degree, because he had stopped doing rituals,
and his Priest rep felt he had become complacent. Rif agreed
he had, and explained this happened because: "I knew I could
do it, and I felt I didn't have to prove that anymore, so I
stopped doing anything. I was demoted to show me I had to
keep working." In this instance the punishment worked and
soon Rif was regularly performing rituals again. In a few
months his rep restored his status.

This criticalness has also led to extensive efforts to
get non-performing members out of the Church. These efforts
began in late 1979 when the Church leadership launched a
major house-cleaning to get rid of any Hutians who were not
actively practicing the Hutian way. The leadership decided

to "get rid of the deadwood," because as one Priestess put
it: "They're not doing anything. They're just out here, but
no one has heard from them in months or years." To begin
this process, Kel instructed the Priests to write to the
First and Second Degrees assigned to them to find out what
they were doing. Then, if they didn't respond after two
letters or if their letters showed they didn't understand
the ideas of the Church, the Priests should drop them from
the group because they had shown they were not of the elect.

In some cases, this criticalness intensifies other
pressures the Hutian experiences in developing magically, and
some Hutians have trouble maintaining their balance, resulting in intellectual, emotional, or spiritual conflicts. The
priesthood talks about this problem frequently, and points
out that Hutians must learn to achieve a balance between the
magical and the mundane worlds they live in by integrating
their mundane and magical selves into one.

But these efforts don't always work, and as a result
the Hutian may experience "the wigging out syndrome," a
phrase that refers to members who come to disagree with
Church ideals and policies or become unbalanced by losing
touch with reality due to their magical development. One
Hutian was accused of having this syndrome soon after the
Church broke away from the Church of Satan, because he continued to hold onto Satanic beliefs about the value of
indulgence and personal gratification, rather than accepting
the Church's new emphasis on personal growth. Thus, as other
Church members changed more and more, he became increasingly
isolated by his old concepts until he eventually dropped out.
When he did, other Hutians claimed he had "wigged out."
They made similar charges when a Priest became an alcoholic
and left the group. And when the two Priests who moved to
California began to think of Hu as part of all things, Kel
claimed they had "wigged out" and "kicked them out" of the
Church.

In a few cases, the exploration of new magical ways of
thinking has led Hutians to experience difficulty in separating reality from fantasy or to engage in bizarre behavior
patterns. Although some of these Hutians may have been un-
stable personalities prior to getting involved in the Church,
the development of an alternate magical persona and the focus
on personal change and growth helped to trigger the emotional
crisis or odd behavior. In one such incident, Trak, a former
Adept in the San Francisco pylon, went to a movie with
several Church members, and when the car stopped at a light,

he suddenly jumped out of the car and ran off. Another time
he wandered away from a group party. When he didn't return
after a few hours, the others became worried and several
went outside to look for him. They found him about an hour
later walking up and down the street crying. A few weeks
later, Trak had an argument with one of the Priestesses and
tried to attack her with a fork. For Kel, this incident was
the last straw, and he wrote Trak a letter telling him he
was demoting him to a First Degree and then expelling him
from the group.

This problem of wigging out is well recognized by
Hutians, and one Master, Firth, wrote a detailed article
about it for the Papyrus. The key source of the problem, he
claimed, was the creation of two personalities in the new
initiate—the magical and the mundane—in the process of
developing magically. Unfortunately, he wrote, the new
initiate may have trouble expressing each personality in the
appropriate sphere. He may mistakenly create a new self by
fusing his old self and adopted magical personality instead
of keeping them separate. He may let his subconscious become so powerful that his inner drives overwhelm him. Or he
may become so enraptured by his unusual experiences and
fantasies that he gets lost or falls off the path and cannot
return to the objective universe.

Although Hutians acknowledge that such problems arise
due to their magical training program, they offer little
support to the Hutian having these problems. Initially, they
may try to talk to him. But they do little more, since they
believe it is up to the individual to take charge of his own
growth. If he can't, they conclude he is not of the elect and
therefore doesn't belong in the Church.

Firth expressed this make-it-on-your-own-or-else philosophy in a Papyrus article when he wrote: "We...cannot
treat it; all we can do is remove the victim from our midsts
...The cause of the wigging out syndrome resides solely in
the individual initiate." Though he acknowledged the syndrome might be generated by the "aristocratic structure of the
organization" and "the stresses of magical discipline," he
argued that it was up to the individual to face and deal with
any difficulties himself. If he couldn't, too bad, for "once
the syndrome manifests, we cannot do anything about it."

In other words, as long as the Hutian conforms and shows
signs he is of the elect, other Hutians will support him in
his position in the Church. But should he stray from the
path, other Hutians will turn against him, for they no longer

consider him of the elect.

In summary, being a Hutian means assuming a new persona
with certain characteristics, but doing so entails certain
risks. Since Hutians see themselves as magical elite beings,
they seek to develop personal power and confirm that they
have it by looking for ritual effects, disparaging outsiders
as less than they are, and criticizing other Hutians who
appear not to measure up. In turn, these attitudes can
create intense stresses for the Hutian, which may lead to
self-criticism, doubt, and unusual behavior. However, when
this happens, other Hutians do not give much support, since
they expect the Hutian to develop on his own. Then, if he
cannot, they feel he is not a fit Hutian and doesn't belong
in the group. Although they acknowledge that the group's
beliefs about magical growth and its hierarchical structure
can create certain heavy stresses, they feel the individual
should overcome these pressures. If he can't—too bad—he
is not worthy of the group.

9

Dealing with Deviance

The issue of social control is of major concern for a group
with a rigid hierarchical system, highly specified belief
system, and conception of elect status, since the group has
a highly formalized structure and self-image to maintain.
This is why Hutians consider the distinction of who is inside and outside the group extremely important and require
members to behave and think in certain ways to remain inside
the group. Even though Hutians claim the Church is free of
dogma and encourages personal freedom unlike other religions,
in practice, the Hutians substitute another kind of dogma
and control based on their own beliefs, and the leaders soon
eliminate from the group individuals who do not think or act
appropriately.

Hutians look on this elimination process as a means of
getting rid of "deadwood"—those who are not elect. However, from another perspective, eliminating such members is
a means of protecting the group's unity from those who might
challenge central premises or have disruptive personality
conflicts with other members.

I have previously described several occasions when
Hutians have dropped out or been dropped because of incor-
rect beliefs, insufficient interest, bizarre behavior, or
psychological problems. Here I want to focus on the techniques the Hutians use to maintain control and then highlight
two dramatic incidents involving a demotion and an expulsion
to illustrate in depth how the social control process oper-
ates when Church leaders feel threatened by deviant behavior
or beliefs.

Like other religious groups, Hutians use the control of
belief and practice as one means of social control. Maintaining these within certain limits contributes to group

cohesion by providing members with a similar world view so
they interpret events and relate to each other in a similar
way. To remain in good standing members must appear to
believe what is acceptable. While newcomers have more freedom of belief because they are learning, established and
high status members, as they rise in rank, are subject to
more control, since they have more influence in the group.

In the Church, belief is controlled by the requirement
that all Hutians must eventually come to accept certain key
beliefs and practices previously discussed: a belief in Hu,
the practice of ritual, the use of a magical name and pentagram, an acceptance of the Church hierarchy, a commitment to
evolve to higher man, and a belief it is possible to break
the natural order. Even though Church leaders urge members
to question all premises of belief, including the existence
of Hu, by the time they are Adepts members must accept these
critical premises or be eliminated from the Church. As one
Priestess put it: "These beliefs are the bottom line."

For Hutians, the study group is an important technique
for maintaining control, since in it newcomers learn what
they should believe and others hear accepted beliefs restated.
Although members may question higher-ups about principles and
present their own ideas, they still must come to agree with
basic Church principles, or higher-ups will criticize them
for their lack of understanding. Then, if they continue to
resist, they will be demoted or expelled from the Church.

A dramatic example of using criticism to control dissent
occurred at a San Francisco pylon study meeting, when the
group discussed The Psychology of Man's Possible Evolution,
in which P. J. Ouspensky argues that man evolves by making a
conscious choice to do so. During the discussion, Sooth, the
Master leading it, agreed that anyone had the ability to
evolve and could be magical regardless of setting. However,
Rath, then an Adept, argued that social background affects
one's development. "After all," he said, "poor people are
struggling to survive."

However, his explanation angered Sooth. She stood up
and stomped into the kitchen, bringing the discussion to a
halt. Then, returning after a minute, she looked at him with
piercing eyes, and snapped: "Yatata...Yatata...I don't see
any point in going on like this...Read the material again.
Then, you will understand." Later, this interchange was considered along with other factors leading to Rath's demotion
to a First Degree.

Critiques of rituals performed by First Degrees and

Adepts are another form of control, for they help the lower
degrees bring their practices into conformity with group
ideals. An example of this occurred after I did my first
ritual, when Armat and Rif told me that the way I set it up
and my opening meditation were wrong. As Rif explained:
"You used too many candles (I had used five), and these made
the ritual chamber much too light. After all, Hu is a
creature of darkness, so the chamber should be dark." Similarly, he pointed out that I erred in leading a white light
meditation when I instructed everyone to visualize themselves
in a white protective bubble. Not only was the white imagery
wrong, but the idea of a protective bubble was, too. "You
want to open up all barriers between you and Hu, not close
them off," Rif said.

A few weeks later, Armat came over to my house to give
me further instruction in how to properly conduct a ritual
and what to avoid. Besides the points Rif raised, she noted
several others. "You don't want to be so cosmic and draw on
the powers of the natural order. You want to stand outside
it. And you want to be more forceful. You don't want to
ask for assistance from the elemental spirits. You want to
demand that assistance. And remember, the power is coming
from within you. It's your will. They are only helping you.
But you're doing it."

After these critiques of beliefs or ritual practice,
the criticized member is expected to change his behavior.
Otherwise he will eventually be demoted, as occurred to
several Adepts who were not actively practicing ritual, or
dropped, as occurred to the two priests who came to believe Hu
was within all members.

Beyond having the right beliefs, the Hutian must also
show sufficient interest, or be eliminated. The priesthood
has adopted this policy because they feel there is no reason
to waste time with someone who doesn't take the initiative
for his own growth. In the Papyrus, Kel underlined this
attitude in a letter to the members: "No III is going to
waste valuable time and effort trying to prod the complacent
or apathetic. Those who receive guidance from the Priesthood will be those who are actively working toward Magical
evolution...The end of any phase of initiation is merely the
beginning of another...Thus inactivity is intolerable in the
Church. Every Initiate must actively engage in Xeper."

Huf, a Master from New Jersey, seconded this at the beginning of the conclave, when she proclaimed: "Everyone in the
Church must be actively Xephering. If you're not, you don't

belong here and should get out."

When Kel initiated the pyramid project, part of the
purpose was to police this process by having lower status
members keep higher-ups informed about their Xephering progress. When about two dozen Hutians failed to respond,
despite warning letters, they were dropped from the Church.
Most were former Satanists who got involved when the Church
first split from LaVey.

Although the recent tightening of controls has reduced
the Church's size approximately one-third—from about 60 to
40 members—the priesthood considers it a healthy clearing,
which will make the Church stronger and more cohesive through
eliminating non-contributing members, who are a drain on the
Church. At one pylon meeting, Armat strongly agreed with
this approach. She held up a letter from an Adept she wanted
to drop to illustrate. "He's just out there waiting for the
Church to come up with the answers. He isn't doing anything
about Xephering or Xem. We don't need members like that."

To make sure this housecleaning continues, Kel recently
established the policy that lay membership renewals are no
longer automatic but must be endorsed by a Priest. Thus, if
a Priest thinks a lay member assigned to him has not been
evolving or growing appropriately, or if he isn't sure because the member hasn't communicated with him, the Priest
can refuse to endorse him or recommend he be dropped. As I
will describe at length, this happened to Rath when his
membership came up for renewal. Demoted from Adept to First
Degree, he refused to accept the decision of the priesthood
as fair, kept protesting, and stopped doing rituals. Thus,
when his time for membership renewal came up, he was suspended for six months.

The Church's concern that members show a high level of
interest and commitment is, in turn, due to its stress on
quality, not quantity, as an organization of the elect. If
members don't show enough interest, they are not evolving,
and therefore don't belong among the elect. For the same
reason, higher-ups seek to control individual behavior so it
conforms to the Church's image of what is proper and presents
the group in a good light.

Church leaders seek control in many ways. They tend to
distance themselves from lay members. They demand that
underlings treat them in a respectful, formal way, such as
calling them by their formal title. And they often issue
military-like directives, which others must follow or else.

For instance, before the conclave, Armat informed the pylon
that Kel had issued certain instructions to be followed at
the conclave. "If you don't follow them," she warned, "you
don't have to come." As an example, she told us that anyone
who didn't make the morning caravan to HuXem "might as well
go home, because he won't be able to come up."

When individuals don't conform properly at Church events,
when their behavior threatens the group's network of relationships, or when their unusual actions outside the Church
prove embarrassing and call into question their elite status,
they are demoted or asked to leave. For example, at the
group's first conclave, Church leaders dropped a woman who
did a great deal of bedhopping, since they felt her behavior
was too enthusiastic, although the group espouses sexual
freedom. In another case, a Master was attracted to Salo,
a female Adept he met at the first conclave, but she liked
another Church leader and fantasized he would leave his wife
for her. When he didn't respond to her letters and calls,
Salo began calling other members to ask assistance, while
rejecting the overtures of the Master who was still in pursuit. Since her activities disturbed many in the Church,
Kel asked her to leave, too. Likewise, Kel dropped the young
man, described earlier, who began to behave bizarrely by
suddenly walking away from others and becoming violent.

Finally, Church leaders may drop a Hutian who experiences a psychological crisis, since once this crisis
develops, they feel they can do nothing, because magical
growth is an individual accomplishment. Thus, when a Hutian
fails to grow properly or becomes unbalanced and "wigs out,"
they claim this is his own failing and shows he is not of
the elect. So they drop him, as when they dropped the Hutian
who became an alcoholic and two others who lost touch with
reality as they got more involved in practicing magic.

Hutians consider these demotions and explusions necessary to preserve the group's elite character and protect its
members. Yet, since the Church is small, each time someone
is demoted or expelled, the incident creates reverberations
through the group, as members readjust to the loss of a member or to changes in status. As Nal from Massachusetts
described it: "The Church is like a spider web. Anytime
anything affects someone, the effect radiates outward and
affects everyone."

Besides causing this reassessment as members adjust,
penalizing or expelling others draws current members closer
together, shows them the limits of acceptable behavior, and

impresses upon them the importance of conforming, or they
will be out too. To grow magically and maintain group support and love, they must recognize and work within the limits.

Finally, Hutians consider control important, since it
increases respect for discipline and loyalty, and they believe
these qualities will be needed in the coming difficult days
when most of humankind perishes to enable the group to endure.
Since they believe only the elect will survive, they feel
that the Church must be sure its members are only of the
elect or it will become weak. The winnowing-out process is
thus designed to strengthen the group.

Two dramatic examples of the demotion and expulsion
process occurred during my study.

The demotion involved Rath, an Adept when I joined, who
was demoted to First Degree. Initially, he had joined the
Church of Satan because he hoped to develop his will to obtain more material pleasures and manipulate other people to
do what he wanted. But he only got a membership card, statement of principles, and a newsletter. Then, when he ran
into several Church of Hu members at a New Age Awareness
Fair, he joined thinking it would offer what he had wanted
but hadn't gotten from the Satanists.

In his first year, in a pylon led by Ba, he was very
active and contributed extensively to the discussion and to
the Papyrus. But he never took a magical name, and the
priesthood felt he only understood the Church's ideas on a
philosophical level and did not have a magical or metaphysical understanding based on intuitive knowing. As long as
he was a First Degree, they could accept this level of
understanding, but as an Adept, they expected him to in-
ternalize and apply Hutian concepts.

However, he didn't appear to do this though he had been
in the group for a year and seemed eager to learn. Thus,
after the first conclave, they decided to promote him to an
Adept, thinking the new position might help him advance. But
still, Rath continued to discuss magical principles abstractly
and did not make what Hutians call the "metaphysical flip"—
turning abstract ideas into intuitively understood concepts.

Then, a series of events occurred which led directly to
his demotion. Ba decided he didn't want to continue to lead
the Ba Pylon, since it was a long trip to San Francisco from
the mountain where he lived with Kel; so the pylon dissolved.
However, Armat agreed to start a new pylon with Rif, and in
September of 1979 they held the first meeting. Besides Rath,
there were two members, Khet and Lat, who became Adepts in

six to nine months.

    Unfortunately Rath had a personality conflict with the
new leader. He found Armat domineering and extremely critical, and he complained that she generally told him what he
did wrong or what not to do, rather than praising his efforts
as had Ba. "You give me negative reinforcement, instead of
positive encouragement," he told her at one meeting, citing
numerous examples. For instance, when he disagreed with
points of Church doctrine, she told him to be quiet. Armat
argued that she was justified in doing so, since she was
trying to help him understand Church beliefs and assume the
responsibilities appropriate for an Adept. However, Rath
continued to claim he had a right to his own opinions and
that her requirements were oppressive.

    For a few months Armat and the other Priests tolerated
his divergence in belief because of his long involvement in
the Church. But in time this resistance contributed one
more reason that the priesthood decided to demote and then
drop him from the Church.

    The next problem arose over Rath's choice of a magical
name. Before Armat formed the Horus Pylon, Rath had been
using his real name, though Ba and other Priests in the Ba
Pylon had suggested he choose a magical one. But now, Armat
gave him an ultimatum, as she did to Lat and Khet. "Choose
a magical name by the next meeting."

    Since he liked vampires he chose Rath, the snake. But
this choice, too, contributed to his difficulties because
Armat felt his choice didn't show much understanding of the
group's conceptual system or "the energies it was working
with," since in Egyptian mythology, Rath is a low unevolved
creature that crawls on the ground and battles with Hu.

    Then, in January, another serious problem occurred. Lat
was supposed to conduct the ritual at the next pylon meeting,
but about a week before he called to say he would be out of
town, and Armat asked Rath to lead it since he was scheduled
to lead the ritual the following month. At first Rath resisted, since he had never led a ritual before, though he had
been a Hutian for about a year and a half, because Ba and
other Priests had led them. Thus, he felt insecure leading
a ritual at such short notice. But Armat persisted until he
agreed. However, when he arrived at the meeting, he was
unprepared for he did not bring his magical implements and
had not planned the ritual. Rif was furious and wanted to
kick him out of the group immediately, but Armat calmed him
down, and Rif told Rath how to conduct the ritual. Then Rath

led it, and the ritual proceeded smoothly—he asked everyone
to contemplate his own image in a mirror and share in front
of the pentagram.

However, as a result of the incident, Armat warned Rath
that he was on probation for three months, and if he didn't
pull himself together she would demote him. Her hope was the
threat would make him "straighten up" as occurred with others
who had been demoted, such as Rif.

Unfortunately, the warning only made Rath angry, and he
found it even more difficult to do rituals at home, since
his resentment towards Armat and Rif made it hard to concentrate. Also, he complained they were picking on him because
they "were jealous" of his many interests outside the Church
such as school, work, and jogging. But Armat argued his
interests had nothing to do with it. He could do magic and
his other activities, too, as long as he participated in
these activities as a Hutian, and thus used them to advance
his personal growth. In reply Rath argued that his activities did contribute to personal development, and he couldn't
see what Armat meant. Thus, he continued to feel she and
the other priests were jealous, and this contrary view contributed to his growing alienation from the Church.

Meanwhile, tensions continued to mount. At the next
study group meeting, Rath argued with Sooth over the principle that anyone regardless of social status could evolve.
She felt they could, while he said the poor were held back
by social restraints. Then, at the February pylon meeting,
Armat asked him to take over as secretary since Ardis, the
Adept who was secretary, could no longer attend meetings.

However, this new responsibility only added to the tension, because Rath resisted writing some of the articles
Armat asked him to write. For instance, at the April meeting, she asked him to combine everyone's opinions about the
March meeting into an article for the Papyrus, and Rath said
he wasn't sure how to do this. He felt the others might be
angry at him if he selected the wrong opinions to emphasize.
Also, he complained it was a dull article to write although
Armat wanted it in the newsletter to show Church members in
other areas what the San Francisco group was doing. Ultimately, Rath wrote it, but his initial refusal left bad
feelings.

A few weeks later, Armat began to question his magical
ability. As a Second Degree, Rath was supposed to be an
"Adept" ceremonial magician. But Armat felt he was not doing
enough rituals at home, didn't talk about magical topics in

the beginning of group meetings, and most importantly,
didn't manifest his magical entity in ritual. Whereas she
claimed to see the magical personas of the other Adepts and
Priests, she couldn't see his. Also, she felt he was still
asking questions about subjects he should know about as an
Adept, such as the differences between a ritual and a working.

As a result, she conferred with the rest of the San
Francisco priesthood and with Kel, and they decided to demote
him to First Degree. Since Rif was Rath's local pyramid rep,
he informed Rath of this decision at the May meeting. To do
so, he invited Rath into the ritual chamber, handed him a
letter explaining the reasons for the decision, and for about
half an hour discussed why the decision had been made and
what Rath should do. Then, to symbolize the demotion, he
asked Rath to remove his red pentagram. When they left the
chamber and rejoined the group for the regular pylon meeting,
Rif requested that no one ask any questions about what
happened. But everyone knew because Rath's pentagram was
missing, he looked very upset, and talk about his conflicts
with the priesthood had been widely aired.

Then, at the June study meeting, Rath tried to bring
up the matter for reconsideration before the whole group on
the grounds that his demotion was due to personality reasons
and that he had been an active loyal participant for almost
two years. But Armat cut off discussion. "I don't want to
start a debate." So Rath became quiet and simmered.

After the meeting, he discussed the issue with Lat,
Khet, and myself over coffee. Unfortunately, Rath's arguments only convinced Lat and Khet that the decision had been
the right one, since he disputed points of Church doctrine
and questioned the fairness and judgment of the priesthood.
For example, he said he didn't see the point to all the abstract talk about Xephering, since the idea of growth was so
nebulous. Besides he was interested in enjoying himself
through indulgence and using his will to manipulate others—
the basic ideas that had drawn him to Satanism. He argued
that he didn't see much point in doing inner work, since if
he wanted inner peace, he would have joined another sort of
organization. Further, he claimed that the priesthood wasn't
sure what Xem was all about; so why should he be required to
know this.

Lat and Khet tried to defuse his arguments. Inner
growth, they explained, was necessary to gain the material
control he wanted. Also, he needed an overriding goal or
identity to unite his individual personality fragments. But

Rath was adamant in opposing his own ideas to established
Church principles and affirming his right to disagree. "The
idea of Xem and inner man evolving are just abstract, metaphysical opinions, and anyone can have an opinion," he
claimed. "And what's the point of growth if it's hard and
unenjoyable." Lat tried to explain that in the long run the
difficult process of growth would be worthwhile since one
would gain a great deal, but Rath couldn't see its value.
Finally, he attacked the group itself. "The group is dogmatic in many ways," he charged. "If I wanted to be accepted,
I could go around mouthing certain words about experiencing
Hu, growing, and Xephering, as others do. But I don't see
the point. It would be phony."

Not surprisingly, Lat and Khet were extremely upset by
these revelations, and even though Rath had spoken in confidence, both Khet and Lat called Armat later that night to
tell her what happened. Later Khet said it was appropriate
for them to do so since the group was working under the
spirit of Maat or truth, and Rath should know that the truth
came first over all else since the concept had been discussed
at the meeting. Thus, both Lat and Khet put their loyalty
to the group above their loyalty to individuals within it.

Once alerted, Armat became very concerned and had long
conversations with Lat and me to get our opinions. She felt
that Rath's questions about basic Church principles were
creating confusion for everyone and that the matter now
needed to be discussed openly. In her opinion, seconded by
Lat and Khet, Rath didn't seem to understand what the Church
was about, although he had been in it for two years. Although she didn't expect him to understand Xem, since the
priesthood was still working out its meaning, she felt Rath
needed a solid understanding of Xephering to proceed to Xem,
but the recent events indicated he didn't have this. He
seemed to be stuck at the level of the Church of Satan,
oriented to will and indulgence, and didn't realize the
Hutians had gone beyond this. Also, she was concerned that
he didn't seem to be working with Hu in ritual, wasn't performing enough rituals, and thought coming to meetings was
enough.

As a result, she decided to hold a meeting to discuss
the matter with Lat, Khet, Rath, and me to show Rath that
he was not demoted for personality reasons, as he believed,
but because he was not working on a high enough magical
level. She felt he had potential to develop magically if he
could understand and thus thought it worthwhile to try to

get through to him. Although Rif should normally attend as
Rath's pyramid rep, she decided not to include him, since she
felt Rif didn't express himself very clearly in words and
would only "muddy the waters."

About a week later, we met at my house. Armat asked me
to get my pentagram because she wanted to hold the meeting
in a ritual setting where she could open the gates so we
could deal with the problem under the guidance of Hu and the
spirit of Maat. Under these circumstances, she felt, only
truth would be spoken and Rath would recognize he had been
demoted for magical reasons, not personality ones.

After I got my pentagram, Armat set it up on a small
bookcase in the living room and asked us to sit around it
silently. Then, standing in front of the pentagram, she said
quietly: "Hu, be present with us here tonight. And I invoke the spirit of Maat to be here with us, too."

Then, sitting down again, she told Rath she realized he
was upset with his demotion and didn't understand why it had
happened. But now the matter needed to be discussed, because
his demotion had caused much confusion in the group.

In response, Rath raised most of the issues he had before. He claimed that the demotion was unfair and personal
and that some members resented his outside interests. He
said the priesthood had been very supportive and encouraging
when he was in Ba's pylon. But this changed when Armat took
over the pylon, and this lack of support made it hard for
him to progress. However, he did not mention his doubts
about Xephering or Xem. Instead, he said he hoped to become
a Priest eventually and was upset by the demotion because it
suggested that: "Any time somebody doesn't like something,
they can take the priesthood away."

Again, Armat argued he didn't understand the reason he
was demoted. The demotion occurred solely for magical
reasons, because he wasn't in touch with the magical part
of himself. For example, in ritual, she explained, she
became Luk, the 65-foot vulture, and at other times Armat,
a smaller bird. Khet pointed out that she could look in a
mirror and see eyes in it that were not her own. Lat observed that when he moved his arms in ritual he felt he was
moving the arms of a bird.

"But do you really become Rath in ritual?" Armat wanted
to know. As a First Degree it was acceptable for him to
explore and act as if he was the magical personality he
assumed. But as a Second Degree he must do more—he must
experience a complete magical transformation in ritual and

become his magical entity.

To illustrate, Armat held out her hand to Rath and asked him to stand in front of the pentagram. "Now call forth the spirit of Rath," she told him, "and speak in front of the pentagram."

Without much enthusiasm, Rath did as she said. Quietly, he faced the pentagram, meditated briefly, and spoke to it: "I call on you, Rath, to manifest yourself."

"Now observe the pentagram," Armat told him. "Remember, we are acting in the spirit of Maat, so truth will come forth."

For several minutes, Rath stood silently in front of the pentagram. Armat walked over and stood behind him, holding her hands outward to send him energy. Then she asked him to sit down.

"What did you experience when you looked at the pentagram?" she asked.

Rath explained he had seen the pentagram begin to move to the right in a circular motion and had never seen this happen before.

"This is the kind of thing you're supposed to see," Armat said. "The points moving...eyes in the circle."

Then, she asked if he had been his regular self in the ritual or his magical self. When Rath said he wasn't sure what she meant, Armat talked about seeing the magical entities manifest in ritual. "For example, in one ritual, I saw Kel's beak in his cowl. It was really eerie."

No, Rath acknowledged, he had never seen such things.

"That's just the point," she concluded. "You're not operating magically. I've never seen Rath manifest in ritual, though I've seen the magical entity of the others."

And on that note the meeting ended. Armat told Rath to think about what was said and let it "jell."

Her hope was that Rath would recognize why he had been demoted, accept the fairness of this action, and recommit himself to practicing the Hutian way. However, in subsequent discussions with Kel, Armat, Khet, and Lat, Rath maintained his original views and continued to complain that the demotion was personally motivated. In turn, Armat felt he continued to think this way because: "He's still thinking on a mundane level, and not magically."

But she took no further action, and the situation dragged on for another five months. Rath decided not to attend the conclave because of work commitments, and after the conclave Rif asked him to write a letter describing his

views about Church doctrine. Rif planned to use it in deciding whether to renew Rath's membership, which was coming
up for renewal in August. Rath agreed to do it, but stalled
for several weeks in writing it. In the meantime, the Horus
pylon broke up since Armat decided she didn't want to run it
anymore, and Ba, who planned to form the new pylon, invited
Rath to dinner. Again, Rath complained about his demotion,
and Ba reassured him that perhaps in a few months he would
be restored to status; but first he must write the letter
Rif wanted.

Reluctantly, Rath wrote it. Perhaps Rath could have
restored himself to the priesthood's good graces with a
conciliatory letter at this point. But, instead, Rath held
firm and stated what he believed. Though some of his beliefs
were at variance with Church doctrine, Rif might have been
able to accept this. But Rath continued to claim the priesthood was being unfair. This accusation, spelled out now in
writing, was a direct affront to the authority of the priesthood.

For about a month Rif pondered the matter and finally
asked Rath to come over one evening for another discussion.
Unfortunately, this meeting never took place and was the
source of further misunderstanding. Rath claimed he arrived
at the time Rif asked and rang the bell, but Rif didn't
answer it. Conversely, Rif claimed the bell never rang and
was angry Rath didn't show up. A few weeks later, when Rath
discussed the matter with Ba, who had previously been supportive, he told Ba he thought Rif was lying, and Ba became
extremely angry that Rath would dare to make such an accusation, for a lower degree had no right to impugn the integrity
of a Priest. Besides, as Ba claimed, a Priest wouldn't do
such a thing, since "He is ordained by Hu."

Matters dragged on for another month. Then, in early
November, shortly after the second meeting of Ba's new pylon,
Rif sent Rath a letter suspending him from the Church for
six months. The gist of the letter was that Rath had been
given plenty of time—about 2-1/2 years—to learn Hutian
principles. Though he recognized what they were, he had
failed to "incorporate them into his being," and was not
Xephering. He had been demoted in May to relieve him of
the responsibilities of an Adept until he could "get himself
together." But he failed to respond, and any discussion
ended up in a debate. Also, Rif charged, Rath didn't show
the priesthood enough respect and didn't recognize their
wisdom. "The truth is something one either comprehends or

does not," Rif wrote.

Thus, Rif recommended that Rath focus on his interests outside the Church, "For perhaps then he will come to understand the difference between Hutian magic and other paths." In six months if Rath got over his anger and recognized the real reason for his demotion, he could approach the Church again.

So Rath was out. He had continued to challenge both Church doctrine and leadership, and after a time, these challenges became too threatening to the Church. So finally, the priesthood dropped him though with the possibility he might get back in if he showed he was willing to accept Church authority. However, his return is not likely. As Rath told me, he had enough. Not only did he still hold the views outlined in his letter, but he rejected the Church's claims to eliteness, its use of jargon like "Xephering" and "growing," which he felt became meaningless through overuse; its position that the priesthood could do no wrong; and its belief that unusual perceptual phenomena, such as movements in the pentagram, were due to spiritual rather than psychological causes. As he put it: "I feel like the child who sees the Emperor has no clothes."

Rath's long period of conflict with the Church not only affected him but stirred up other pylon members, since the issues raised by his demotion led them to consider more intensely the meaning of being a Hutian. For example, at the conclave, Kel observed that the I, II, and III degree stages were equivalent to the three aeons of magic: will announced by Crowley, indulgence announced by LaVey, and Xephering announced by the Ipsissimus. But Lat had trouble reconciling these ideas with Rath's demotion. "I'm confused again," he told me and Armat. "I thought Rath was demoted because he didn't show enough magical development. But now it sounds like a II only has to be Xephering to remain a II."

"Both are true," Armat assured him. "Rath wasn't Xephering and so he didn't show enough magical development. You have to Xepher to develop magically."

But Lat was still confused and continued to discuss the issue to clarify the expectations for a I and II. The issue troubled him, since it made him wonder about his own acceptance as a II and what being a II meant. Before Rath's demotion, he thought he knew, but now he was uncertain about the Church's criteria for status.

In short, the circumstances surrounding Rath's demotion and subsequent departure caused much concern. The priesthood

had originally promoted him to Adept because he showed
interest, and they hoped his ideas would fall into line with
Church beliefs if they promoted him. But his views did not
change, and his questions continued to challenge basic
Church principles such as the belief in Hu, the value of
ritual, the use of magical names, and the value of Xephering
to higher man. Since he questioned these premises, he
couldn't remain an Adept. Yet, if he had been with the
group for so long and still questioned—why? How could he
still not understand? Moreover, his questions raised the
issue of what are the criteria for judging magical growth and
evaluating the Hutian; and they challenged the authority of
the priesthood since the criteria are so vaguely defined.

Thus, his continued presence as an Adept represented a
threat to group principles and practices, and after he was
demoted, his continued doubts and criticisms of the priesthood represented a further challenge. So, ultimately, Rath
was suspended. Although the priesthood claimed to act
against him on magical grounds, both the demotion and sus-
pension can be seen as actions taken to protect the Church
and its belief system from an individual with alien ideas.

When alien ideas become too threatening, the group will
take more drastic action and immediately throw the person
out. This happened when the two Priests formed a new conception of Hu as a force in everyone, not a deity in the
stars. And it occurred even more dramatically at the conclave, when the priesthood decided I did not have the right
motives in joining the group because I did not appear to be
primarily interested in Xephering. However, instead of
calmly discussing the matter with me, the group acted as if
I was an alien sinister presence and responded with a melo-
dramatic scenario, worthy of a television spy thriller. The
circumstances of the expulsion were this:

After about four months in the group, I told Armat, then
the Priestess of Horus Pylon, that I might be interested in
doing a study of the Church and wanted to be sure she and
other members were comfortable with this. I suggested we
might discuss the matter at the next pylon meeting, told her
I would not write anything without permission, and said I
would show her what I wrote for her comments. She commented
that it might be nice to have something done on the group,
but suggested putting off any discussion until after the conclave when she would discuss it with Kel. Meanwhile, I
continued to tape meetings and rituals with the approval of
the pylon members.

Then, at the conclave, I asked if I could take photographs and tape two of the general meetings and Kel agreed. When I asked to tape a I and II discussion, no one objected either. Also, everyone appeared open and friendly when I asked about their backgrounds, reasons for joining, understanding of Hu, experiences in growing, and similar questions. I found many higher-ups remote and cool as Armat had forewarned me; so I talked mainly to I's and II's.

However, as I later learned, many Hutians gradually began to feel I wasn't Xephering properly, and thus began to see my taping and questions in a sinister light. For example, when I had a long conversation with Lat and two L.A. Adepts, Haren and Lol, I observed two guns in the room which belonged to Haren and another Hutian, who were in police or military-related occupations. When Haren mentioned that he and another Adept would be going around the grounds to shoot snakes the next day, I said I would be interested in learning to shoot snakes, too. But later, I learned my comment unnerved some higher-ups, since they wanted members to learn to use guns to survive the coming annihilation and felt his interest could be easily misunderstood.

Others felt I did not talk enough about my own personal growth or magical being, and when I participated in the ritual, they claimed I was not in the appropriate magical space. For example, one Adept later told me that I did not appear to move my arms spontaneously, but seemed to be patterning my movements after what others were doing. He also said I wasn't forceful enough when I went up to the pentagram to share, so that I did not seem to be really assuming my magical identity or projecting my will. In addition, Huf, the Master from New Jersey, was unnerved when I came out before the ritual wearing not only my robe but a furry white hat that Ba suggested I wear because I said I was cold. "You can't wear that," Huf glared at me. "It'll distract others because it's so bright." I took it off, and Ba found a more suitable black cap a Witch friend had given to him. But the damage had been done.

My apparent lack of Xephering led a few I's and II's to question whether I was appropriate Hutian material, and they expressed their concerns to some Priests and Masters. As a result, the group now saw my taping, notetaking, and photography in a different light. If they regarded me as a true Hutian, they would have approved it. But since they now questioned whether I should be in the Church at all, they viewed these activities as spying.

Yet, as these backstage discussions were occurring, no one said anything to me. It was as if my alien presence convinced them I had sinister intentions, and so they had to secretly mobilize against me to confirm what they believed and confront me with their discovery. Meanwhile, since a few higher-ups told me they had heard all about me from Armat or hoped to talk to me about my writing, I blithely assumed everyone knew and approved of what I was doing.

That night after the ritual as people were milling around and chatting informally, the plot to unmask and expel me began to unfold. I was sitting on a log talking with two Adepts, Athena and Nal, when Armat came over to inform me that Khet and I would drive back in another car. Originally, Khet and I had driven from the motel to the mountain with Armat, Lat and Athena. But now, Armat asked us to join the Priest and Adepts from Massachusetts, so she could drive back with Wif, the Priest from Georgia on the ruling council.

Then, about an hour later, as I was writing up my field notes, Athena, who shared the room with Khet and me, appeared. Khet was curled up under the covers trying to sleep, but Athena plunked down on her bed and commented: "I really envy you keeping a diary like that. I wish I had the perseverance to do it." Then, innocently she added: "Say, do you think I could read your diary? I'd like to recall where I've been when I was a First Degree."

Politely I declined by telling her it was private and that I would be glad to write her a letter about my feelings. She seemed to accept that and our conversation continued for another ten minutes. Then, she got up, said she would be back in a few hours, but didn't return.

About nine in the morning, I awoke to a pounding on my door and heard Athena calling out that she wanted to come in with someone to get some coffee. Since we were sharing the hospitality room, I quickly dressed, assuming they wanted to have the coffee here. But when Athena came in with Wif, she announced that they were going out and invited me to join them. Not suspecting anything, I said "Sure," delighted to have the chance to talk to them. Then, as we started out, Athena suddenly hesitated, and as if remembering something, remarked: "Oh, I nearly forgot. There's something I have to do in the room. I'll join you in a few minutes."

So I left alone with Wif, totally unsuspecting that anything was afoot, although I later learned that Athena and Firth used this opportunity to read my field notes. However,

Wif gave no indication anything was unusual. Instead, at
the restaurant he chatted enthusiastically about his activities in Georgia, his experiences in ritual, his relationship to Hu, and his reasons for getting involved in the
Church. He even paid for my breakfast.

When we returned, Athena was in front of the motel
waving. "Where have you been?" she asked. "I couldn't find
you." Then, Wif excused himself to take a box of cigarettes
to Firth, and I returned to the room to make some notes on
my conversation with Wif.

Afterwards, I went outside and talked to Wik and Nis
from Canada. The conversation was casual and friendly, so
still I suspected nothing. Then, Lik, the Priest of the L.A.
pylon and editor of the Papyrus, appeared smiling broadly.
"You're just the person I was looking for," he said. "We're
working on the newsletter now, and I wonder if we could have
your tapes." Since Lik had previously asked me to send him
the tapes so he could write up a story on the I and II meeting, I thought there was nothing suspicious about his request
and even considered that giving him the tapes would show I
could be trusted.

After I got them from my room and gave them to him, he
left, and I began talking to Ardis. Then, Athena appeared
again and excitedly told me some people wanted to talk to
me. I followed her to the second floor of the motel, and
she led me into a room where five members of the Council
were gathered—the Priests Armat and Wif and the Masters
Firth, Huf, and Lare. The latter was the chairman of the
Council.

At first, as I walked in, I was delighted to finally
have the chance to talk to some higher-ups, but in moments
the elaborate plotting that had taken place behind my back
became painfully obvious.

As I sat down on the bed beside Huf, Lare looked at me
icily. "What are your motives?" she hissed.

At once I became aware of the current of hostility in
the room, and this sudden realization, so unexpected, left
me almost speechless.

"To grow," I answered lamely. "Are you concerned about
the tapes?"

"Well, what about them?" she snapped.

"It's so I can remember things," I said.

"And the questions? Why have you been asking everyone
about their backgrounds? What does that have to do with
growth?"

I tried to explain. "But I always ask people about
themselves when I meet them. What's wrong with that?"

However, Lare disregarded my explanation. "We don't
believe you," she said.

Then Firth butted in. "We have several people in
intelligence in the group...We've read your diary..."

At this point, the elaborate plotting going on behind
my back became clear, and I couldn't think of anything to
say. It was apparent now they considered me some kind of
undercover enemy or sensationalist journalist out to harm
or expose the Church, and they had gathered their evidence
to prove this. Now they were trying the case, though it was
obvious the decision had already been made. Later, Armat
explained that they had fears about me or anyone else drawing attention to them because of the negative climate towards
cults among "humans." So they were afraid that any outside
attention might lead to the destruction of the Church before
they could prepare for the coming annihilation. However, in
the tense setting of a quickly convened trial, there was no
way to explain my intentions or try to reconcile them with
my expressed belief in learning magic. Once Firth said he
read my diary, I realized there was nothing more to say.

"So now, get out," Lare snapped. "Take off your pentagram and get out."

As I removed it from my chain, I explained that I had
driven up with several other people and had no way back.

"That's your problem," she said. "Just be gone by the
time we get back." Then threateningly she added: "You
should be glad that we aren't going to do anything else."

"There are buses," Huf remarked.

So I was out of the Church. After the meeting broke up,
I asked Firth if I could speak to him, since he had previously asked me about my writing. We found a quiet place
outside an upstairs motel room, and as we sat on the walkway
I told him that I thought everyone understood what I was
doing since Armat had spoken to them. I said I was interested in growing, too, but wasn't able to explain this at
the meeting.

"I understand what happens in the group process," he
replied. "But you don't have that Hutian spark. And now you
better go."

In short, the Church members had decided I wasn't of
the elect since I wasn't Xephering properly. Then, once they
defined me as not one of them, my questions and observations
of the group became a threat. Had I been a naive prospective

Hutian who had potential, but didn't develop it, they could
have proceeded more slowly and gently as they did with Rath.
But I wanted to write about them, and if I wasn't one of
them, they would have no control over what I might say.
Also, their fears about the coming annihilation and possibility of group destruction led them to act decisively and
at once. Not only did they feel I didn't believe, but as
an outsider, I could potentially destroy them, too. So, the
Council quickly cast me out.

The news of the decision spread rapidly, and the rest
of the group soon closed ranks against me. For instance, no
one would drive me to the bus depot, although Khet and Armat
quietly expressed disappointment over what had happened. As
I left, Armat commented: "It's too bad. An article would
have been nice." And Khet softly said: "I'd like to still
call you," though she never did.

Then, as the members of the Church gathered to go up
to the mountain for the second day, I walked to the bus
depot with my bags alone.

10

Assessing the Hutians

In summary, the Hutians are members of a tightly knit magical
society which stresses personal growth leading to magical
development, so the individual can use his will to get what
he wants and ultimately achieve perfect freedom. To attain
this end, Hutians practice ritual in which they communicate
with Hu, an ancient Egyptian sky god, whom they consider the
prince of darkness and a creature of night. They believe in
taking on the persona of a magical being and communicating
with this entity using the pentagram, so they can gain Hu's
assistance in becoming an effective black magician and
evolved higher man. They recognize each Hutian's level of
growth through a degree system ranging from the First Degree
or novice Hutian (I) to the High Priest (V) and the Ipsissimus or administrative head (VI). The group derives much of
its philosophy and structure from the ideas of the magician
Aleister Crowley and the Gurdjieff teacher, P. J. Ouspensky,
and from Egyptian religion and mythology.

Members are generally alienated from society and religion, and the Church offers them an alternate belief system
and structure where they can feel superior as a member of an
elite. They also gain a sense of direction and purpose from
the belief they are evolving to higher man and a feeling of
protection from the belief they can avoid the coming annihilation of mankind as members of the elect. Hutians
recognize the growing process will be difficult, but feel
it is worth the effort since at the end they will become
higher man who has perfect freedom, control, and immortality.

Unfortunately, the process is beset by numerous problems.
First, the group's beliefs about elite status, its concern
with who is in and out, its ideas about a coming destruction
of society, and its rigid hierarchical structure can be very

stressful for members, since they become very concerned about
whether they are performing well enough for the group and
whether they will survive the annihilation. Also, the focus
on power can lead to a paranoid attitude, since there is
always the danger that the Hutian may use power improperly
with bad results or that someone may try to direct power
against him. These beliefs and the hierarchical group
structure, in turn, tend to make Hutians even more alienated
from society than when they first joined the group.

A second problem is that the group's ideas about growth
and higher man are extremely vague and subject to constant
change. The higher-ups justify this vagueness and variation
on the grounds that the organization is dedicated to creation
and change, not preservation and rest, and that the priesthood is still working out the meaning of the terms Xepher and
Xem. Also, they tell anyone who doesn't understand or raises
questions about the growth process that he will understand
when he is ready, but now he isn't developed enough. Thus,
they easily escape answering challenging questions. No
doubt they would claim this analysis shows my own lack of
understanding.

However, this deliberate obscurity and mystification
leads to some difficulties. First, since the criteria for
growing and evolving are not completely clear, one is never
certain he is properly growing and evolving, though he may
feel he is intuitively. This type of knowing may work well
when the priesthood and member agree the member is growing
well. But, when they don't agree, the conflict can result
in the demotion or dismissal of the lower status member if
he tries to press his claim of knowledge through intuition.

Thirdly, developing a magical personality can have
hazards, since this development tends to produce a split
personality as the Hutian puts more effort into creating a
magical self distinct from his external functioning personality. Though the Hutian ultimately seeks to create a fully
developed integrated personality, in which he unites all of
his aspects to a core magical personality, in practice,
Hutians tend to have increasing difficulty in operating in
the mundane world as they go through the growth process.

Hutians talk about this problem frequently and stress
that the developed magician must have balance to effectively
coordinate his mundane and magical personalities. But maintaining this balance can be very difficult, and it leads many
to experience what Hutians call "the wigging out syndrome" or
loss of psychological balance which is reflected in members

losing touch with reality, becoming alcoholics or developing
ideas of omnipotence. Unfortunately for the victim, when
this syndrome developes, other Hutians offer little or no
support, since they believe they are members of an elite and
someone who is should be able to maintain his balance. If
he can't, the priesthood typically casts him out on the
grounds he is now no good to himself or to the membership as
a whole.

In short, the Church's belief system and structure
creates some of the stresses that can lead to psychological
problems. Then, if the member succumbs, other Hutians consider it his own fault and reject him. He is not strong
enough to make it, and his continued presence threatens the
organization.

The idea of being part of an elect also has some un-
toward effects. Although this belief does help members feel
better about themselves because they feel themselves special
and superior, it also contributes to their difficulty in
relating to others outside the organization, since it sets
them apart, as does developing a magical personality and having unique beliefs about reality. However, the conception of
being of the elect increases this alienation and justifies
it, since Hutians can regard outsiders as "mere humans," who
are not worth bothering about.

Ironically, the underlying dynamic of this casting-out
process is a reversal of rejection by others. Hutians
generally consider themselves a little "weird" when they
join, and many observe that people tend to avoid them. But
by seeing themselves as members of an elect, they can feel
people are avoiding them because of their magical power, not
their personal lacks, and they can reject these "humans" who
reject them by defining them as inferior folk of little worth.

Church beliefs and activities, in turn, help solidify
the group against the world outside and create a strong sense
of being either inside or out of it. The hierarchical
structure further reinforces this process, since as the Hutian
moves up the hierarchy, he is increasingly alienated from the
outside world and spends more and more time in group activities.

Hutians favor this growing isolation and alienation because it makes them depend more on themselves and on one
another, and thus better prepare to survive the coming annihilation. At the same time, this inward turning increases
the pressure to clear out "the deadwood" by dropping anyone
who does not accept the group's beliefs or lifestyle, or does

not show sufficient interest or dedication. In the last
year, this clearing-out process cut the group down from about
60 to 40 members.

For Hutians who stay in favor, the group can become a
refuge against the perceived mediocrity of humankind and the
threat of worldwide destruction. Yet, there is always the
possibility the Hutian may do something to displease higher-
ups and so find himself outside. As described, the disengage-
ment process can be very sudden at times, and once the group
decides, there is little redress.

In part, the Hutians' concern with eliminating those who
don't measure up derives from the group's vision of the
Church as a society of the elect. But this concern also
springs from a deep paranoia, arising out of alienation from
mainstream society, that outsiders may learn about or infil-
trate the group in order to destroy it. Then, the Church's
efforts to survive the annihilation will be of no avail, and
in their view, the Aeon of Hu will be no more.

Thus, due to its philosophy, structure, and relationship
with the outside world, the Church has become a group turning
in upon itself in response to a growing paranoia. Within the
group, members can, while in good standing, experience an
intense love and close bond of fellowship from some other
members. But they must conform. Though they are free to
explore and question ideas as they evolve and are encouraged
to do so, they must confine their exploration and questioning within acceptable limits as defined by the higher-ups,
and they must accept some basic premises about the existence
of Hu, the value of developing a magical personality, the use
of the will, and the evolution to higher man. Also, they
must accept the hierarchy and their place within it.

However, this conformity has its price, for it further
alienates the Hutian from the larger society, and the magical
growth process produces certain stresses that may lead to
severe psychological problems, as discussed. Should these
problems develop, the Hutian cannot look to the group for
help. Instead, the group will cast him out.

Ironically, individuals join the group to seek power.
Yet, to the extent that the Church assumes control over their
beliefs and activities, they give up much of their power to
the group.

Currently, the group isn't dangerous, despite its extremely negative attitudes to outsiders, since members are
still content to work on becoming highly developed magical
beings outside of the public eye. Also, the activities and
beliefs of the group can siphon off the aggressive and

hostile feelings of members and cool them off as they express their hostility in a safe way.

However, a group like this does have the potential of becoming dangerous. Its members are alienated from society; the group's beliefs and structure encourage this alienation; members seek group and individual power through a tightly knit almost military hierarchy; and the group is increasingly turning inward to protect itself from the threat of impending doom. Given the right conditions, such as increased outside pressure from society, a group of this sort could easily turn away from innocent inward growth and direct its alienation and rage outward to society. It hasn't yet; but with a change in philosophy or direction spoken by its High Priest, it could readily do so. Then, members who take their direction from him and consider his words spiritually sanctioned by Hu would be likely to follow along.

Probably this will not happen. More likely, the group will continue to close in on itself and less committed members drop out, until it is reduced to a handful of members or falls apart of its own high demands. Another reason this outcome is likely is that the group is making little effort to recruit newcomers, except through friends of members, so it is unlikely to grow, particularly since members tend to be relatively isolated from close outside personal contacts, and their membership contributes to their isolation.

Thus, the prospects for the Church are not encouraging. To members the growth process may contribute to personal development. But it is a process that has high costs—in the personal tragedy for some who can't make it; in the potential danger that the Church may direct its alienation from society outward; and in the potential destruction of the group itself, because its high standards have led many to drop out on their own or through group efforts to clean house. Thus, group structure and processes have their own effects, and these are not always what the group intends. In the Church, selected individuals go through a process they consider to be a personal evolution. But to what end? And at what cost?

PART III:

THE ROLE OF POWER AND GROUP PROCESS

11

The Use of Power Among
Other Magical Groups

Any discussion of a group oriented around using magical
power raises the questions: To what extent is it like other
power-oriented groups, particularly those focused around
using magic for personal power? To what degree do its
processes parallel those in other groups?

These questions are significant, since if the processes
are similar, the dynamics observed in the one group have
broader application and illustrate general concepts about
the desire for personal power and methods of expressing it.

Accordingly, I briefly studied a second group involved
in magic. This was a white Witchcraft group, which I will
call The Church of Empowerment, or the C of E for short. I
chose this group since it was like the black magic group in
many respects. Like the Hutians, C of E members were primarily from the middle or lower middle class and largely in
the same age group—in their 30's and 40's. In addition,
the group, though centered in Northern California, had
national connections through its links with solitary Witches
and other Witchcraft groups throughout the country. Finally,
the C of E High Priestess, like the Hutian High Priest, was
involved in writing up group ideology and spreading it
through lessons to newcomers, the Church newsletter, and
other publications.

I joined this group for four months—from August to
November 1980, when it broke up due to some dramatic power
politics to be described. I initially discovered the C of E
a few months after I left the Hutians when I saw an ad for
Witchcraft lessons in a Bay Area activities guide. A few
days after calling, I met the High Priestess, whom I'll call
Athena, in her suburban home in a middle income community

about 30 miles from San Francisco. Since her husband supported the family, she did not have to work and devoted full
time to the Craft. Also present were her husband, Jeff, who
worked as a trucker and was the group's High Priest, and the
two males members of her coven—Alexis, in his early 20's,
who worked in sales in a record store, and Frank, in his mid-
30's, who did promotional work for a public service organization. Later, I learned Athena had one other initiated member
in the coven—Andrea, a woman in her 30's who worked as a
word processor. Additionally, she had a dozen students who
were taking her Witchcraft course by mail or in person and
were in various stages of becoming Witches.

      After a brief conversation, Athena signed me up as a
student, and I began to take her course consisting of seven
lessons. After reading each lesson, answering a quiz on it,
and sometimes doing an assigned project, I met with her to
discuss the Craft. In addition, I participated with the
group in two seasonal rituals, attended by a dozen other
members of the Witchcraft community, went to a weekend
Witchcraft conference with about 40 Witches in Texas, and
spent a few social evenings with group members.

      In this chapter I will briefly compare these Witches'
use of power with the Hutians.

                          Major Beliefs

      In many respects the Witches and Hutians share similar
beliefs. Most centrally, the Witches, like the Hutians,
believe that they can gain access to special powers, that
these powers lie within the self, and that they can use these
powers to change the course of events in the natural order.
However, whereas the Hutians believe they can get outside
the natural order to control events, the Witches feel they
can speed up the clock to make things happen faster or make
them increasingly likely to happen. The reason for this
difference is that the Witches see themselves as part of the
natural order who can change it by understanding and influencing natural forces, whereas the Hutians see themselves as
above and beyond this order. Furthermore, while the Witches
perceive themselves as part of an essential oneness, the
Hutians consider the world to be made up of individual entities and view themselves standing outside and apart.

      The Witches are also like the Hutians in that they

consider the energy used in magic to be neutral and believe
in using it to do both positive and negative magic. Like
Hutians, they believe the energy only becomes positive or
negative through intent. As Athena once explained it:

>"You have to be willing to zap someone when the
>time comes. If you return negative energy, and the
>person gets a jolt, it will show them not to do it.
>You also have to be able to protect yourself if some-
>one wants to hurt you or society generally. So you
>have to be able to do both white and black magic.
>This also helps to maintain a balance. If someone
>does something to you and you don't fight back, it
>makes you resentful, inefficient, and will interfere
>with other things you do. So you must be able to
>fight back."

Like Hutians, the Witches feel that a great deal of
training is necessary to acquire power, and that both study
and ritual are necessary. But where the Hutians claim only
certain individuals can master this study to become part of
a superior elect, the Witches feel anyone has the potential
to learn if he is serious and committed.

These differing conceptions in turn reflect the groups'
different orientations to the mainstream world. Whereas the
Hutians reject mainstream society and further set themselves
apart by their elitist ideals, the Witches are primarily
interested in using power to become a more effective person
and better get what they want in the mainstream world—such
as a better job, more money, better health, and more love.
So they work on self-development to that end, not to become
a superior, better-than-others being. In their view, Witchcraft is merely one path to acquire better power techniques,
and they don't see themselves as a superior, higher order of
being. Instead, they want the outside world to ultimately
accept their way as valid expression of religion, and to obtain this acceptance, they seek to present themselves with a
stable, respectable, middle class image. They don't reject
the mainstream world; nor do they see it hurtling towards
some apocalypse. Instead, they want to enjoy the good things
it offers and develop their power to get them.

The Witches are additionally similar to the Hutians in
believing that a person can develop this inner power by working with outside beings who represent the forces and powers
in nature. However, where the Hutians call on the powers of
darkness which are outside of nature as well as other deities,
C of E members, like other Witches, believe that the basic

force of nature is both outside and within the self and is divided into two polarities—male and female—represented by the male god and female goddess. Further, they believe that they must work with the manifestations of this force in the form of specific male and female deities in order to relate to and use this higher force.

They claim this central Craft belief goes back to paleolithic times. In their original manifestation, they believe the male deity was the god of the hunt and the female deity the goddess of the earth and fertility. Then, as society developed, each culture created a panoply of deities representing various qualities and associations for the male and female polarities. For example, male gods were frequently associated with the sun; female deities with the moon.

Now the Witches believe they can work with any of the hundreds of ancient pre-Christian deities who represent these polar forces and have gained great strength through centuries of belief. Each Witchcraft group is free to create its own tradition and use whichever male and female deities it chooses in ritual. Accordingly, the Church of Empowerment has chosen to work with Celtic gods and goddesses, since Athena is Irish and feels the strongest identification with these deities, particularly with Cernunnos, the god of the animals, life, death, and wealth, and with Cerridwen, the mother deity who represents the moon, inspiration, and knowledge. However, when the C of E participates in rituals with groups of other traditions, members honor the other gods as well.

In sum, despite some differences, the Witches share certain key beliefs with the Hutians—the belief that they can develop and use special powers to influence events, that training is necessary to develop this power, that this power comes from the self, that this power is neutral and can be used for both positive and negative ends, and that one can call on outside spiritual beings for assistance in accessing this power.

The Role of Ritual

The C of E Witches and Hutians also share a number of commonalities in their use of ritual. First, like Hutians, the Witches consider performing ritual crucial for gaining access to the power within, and they call on various deities to assist them. The differences are in the specific practices

and symbols used in the ritual and in intent. Whereas
Hutians emphasize using ritual to look within for self-
transformation, the Witches are primarily concerned with
directing the ritual to some outside objective, such as
health, wealth, or love. Also, whereas Hutians see self-
development as the channel to all else and tend to employ
less elaborate rituals as the individual becomes more adept
in going into an altered state, the Witches are more
interested in manipulating the outside world directly and
tend to perform more elaborate rituals as they become more
advanced in the Craft since they value techniques.

For example, to make the ritual more dramatic and
intensify its power, a C of E member may use an elaborate
scheme of magical correspondences, involving combining certain colors, symbols, objects, and words, or performing the
ritual at a certain time to correspond with the planetary
hours most suitable for the ritual's purpose. In some
cases, he may even harvest the herbs he will use in a working according to astrological principles to increase the
power of the herbs.

Because of this concern with techniques, the Witches
have much less spontaneity in their rituals. Instead, they
tend to rely on specific chants, spells, amulets, talismans,
and other ritual devices learned from books, friends, or
another Witch. But their rituals involve more pageantry.

These characteristics are reflected in the personal
rituals Athena describes at length in her course literature
designed to introduce the newcomer to the Craft. In the
first ritual of dedication to the path, she instructs the
neophyte to begin by lighting a candle and incense. Then he
reads a passage dedicating himself to the gods and the old
religion and asks for the blessing of the Great Earth Mother
and the Father of the Mystic Realm, so he can be taught the
ways of the Ancient Ones.

In the next lesson, the neophyte learns about the tools
of the Craft which he must acquire to perform a proper
ritual: the athame, symbolizing the positive, active male
god force; the wand, representing life and divine wisdom;
the chalice, representing the receptive, passive female goddess force; the cord, used to draw the magical circle and
bind; the thurible for burning incense; the altar candles,
symbolizing the god, goddess, and purpose of the ritual; and
the two small bowls used to hold salt and water. Once he
obtains these tools, he performs three rituals—one to purify
himself, another to cleanse the ritual area, and a third to

consecrate the tools. He uses a formal ceremony in each case.

For the self-purification ritual, he must prepare a bath and throw three teaspoons of salt into the bath water, while he chants:

Creature of Water, cast out from thyself all the impurities and uncleanliness of this world.

Creature of Earth, allow only those powers of the pure creative force to enter so as to cleanse my soul and spirit.

Then, he must get into the bath and visualize all of the impurities of his physical and spiritual body drained away.

When he purifies the area or the room, he must dip his athame into the two small bowls containing salt and water and recite a similar chant while doing so. Then, he must take the salt and water mixture and sprinkle it around the room.

Consecrating the tools involves another series of ritual acts. To begin, he places all of his tools, along with the salt and water bowls, candles, and thurible, on a small table used as an altar. Then, he sprinkles consecration incense into the thurible, and as the smoke rises, he passes each tool through each element while chanting these lines:

Oh Tool of Thy Sacred Art,
All My Power I Now Impart
By Elements of Earth, Air, Fire, and Sea,
I Now Bless and Consecrate Thee.

Later, when the aspiring Witch performs rituals and healings, he follows similarly detailed ritual guidelines. For instance, to do most workings, he begins by casting a magical circle through this procedure. First he consecrates the water and salt by inserting his athame briefly into each bowl and reciting a chant about casting out impurities. Next, he circuits the area holding his knife before him while chanting another few lines, indicating that he is forming a boundary of protection, so all power raised in the circle will be contained within it.

Then, he goes around the circle and invokes the mighty ones by facing each of the four cardinal points, pointing his athame to the sky and offering the appropriate element to each one while chanting this invocation:

Ye Lords of the Watchtowers of the (North, East, South, West), I do summon, stir, and call you up, to witness my rites and to guard this Circle. So mote it be.

Now with the circle created and the deities invoked, he can perform the desired working—to heal, gain love, obtain wealth, or whatever—or he can celebrate the season or the phase of the moon. To do so, he employs a variety of ritual techniques, including calling on the powers of certain deities, burning candles, or doing more chanting to raise power and direct it to his objective.

Finally, at the conclusion of the working, the Witch closes the circle. He dismisses the mighty ones, thanks the lords of the watchtowers for their presence, and draws up the circle, by walking around it in a counter-clockwise direction as he points his athame at its rim.

The specific techniques for performing a working in a ritual are similarly highly structured. For example, to gain love, Athena advises her students to place seven tea-spoons of sweet basil in a clear jar at midnight of the New Moon. Next, the Witch should place the jar in a window where it will catch the rays of the moon, and place a tall pink candle to the right of the jar and a tall gold candle to the left of it. Then, each night as the moon begins to shine on the jar, he should light the gold and pink candle in turn and direct loving thoughts into the jar, while he recites the following chant:

> By the power of Earth
> and Fire,
> Bring to me the one
> I desire.
> The moon grows full, so
> does ___(name)___
> love for me. As I will
> So mote it be.

After letting the candles burn for an hour, the Witch should snuff them out.

As Athena advises, he should follow this procedure each night until the night of the full moon when he should invite his desired one for dinner. He should place plenty of sweet basil in the food, and before the loved one arrives, he should burn the gold candle. Then he should burn the pink one during dinner. Presumably, the object of all these attentions will be enchanted by the spell.

Other techniques are used to regain the affections of a loved one, gain money, get a good job, and heal. These in-volve chants, burning candles, and using talismans or herbs. For instance, Athena told me she puts Irish moss under her doorstep to bring in business and uses Lily of the Valley in rituals to increase her business success; she advised me to do the same.

Once the neophyte learns these basic guidelines he is
free to design his own ritual, since Witches, like Hutians,
believe the meaning behind the words has the real power;
they consider the symbols only a focus for improving concentration and thereby helping the individual draw on his
inner power. Yet, even so, they continue to use the ritual
trappings and perform even more elaborate workings as they
become more advanced in the Craft. They do not gradually
drop the ritual forms as do the Hutians, who believe there
is less need for external techniques as one can more easily
enter the ritual state.
     Nevertheless, despite these major differences in ritual
form and content, the Witches and Hutians use ritual for the
same purpose—to raise and direct the powers within to
achieve a desired goal.

Reasons for Joining

     Socially and in their motivation for becoming members,
the Hutians and Witches are much the same. As noted, the
C of E Witches were in middle and lower class occupations;
they included a truck driver, social worker, word processor,
and salesman. Other Witches I met at the national conference comprised a mixture of engineers, teachers, secretaries,
a computer programmer, a security guard, and others with
middle range occupations.
     Like the Hutians, most came from Christian backgrounds,
most notably Catholic, but got disenchanted with Christianity.
However, the Witches didn't appear to have the same degree
of hostility to conventional religions as the Hutians; instead, they typically found something missing and wanted
something with more personal involvement and emotional intensity. For example, Athena had been a Catholic but felt
that the Catholic ritual was dead, whereas the Craft was a
way to return to the roots of religion. Another Witch at the
national conference, Ty, had been a Baptist, but was turned
off by its message of fear, suffering, sin and guilt.
     Frequently, as among the Hutians, individuals were
attracted to the Craft because they were experiencing some
difficulty in life leading them to feel a lack of power.
They were dissatisfied and wanted something that would enable them to take control of their lives again.
     For example, Anne, a C of E student, decided to learn
more about the Craft since she had made some very bad

decisions which led her to contemplate suicide and felt she was at a turning point in her life. But rather than taking the ultimate step, she decided to find some system which would give her power and began reading occult books. Then, when she read a book on ancient Witchcraft, which described magical techniques she could use to achieve her goals, she chose to get involved in the Craft and asked about it in metaphysical shops. In one of them she met a woman who directed her to Athena.

Another Witch at the conference, Irene, had a similar experience. She was a married Catholic and went through "hell," as she termed it, when her husband sought a divorce. She felt she had failed and began to ask questions about the meaning of life which the church couldn't answer. Also, maintaining her ties with the church made her feel so alone, because when she talked to her priest, he told her she could still take communion and come to church as long as she didn't remarry. Then, while she was feeling very confused and lonely, she met a woman who was interested in the psychic world and began taking psychic lessons from her. This helped, but still she felt something was missing. Finally, after she experienced still another family tragedy when a close relative died, she felt she needed to have power over people and, therefore, decided to become a Witch.

Other Witches joined because they experienced some major danger and saw the Craft as a way they could protect themselves. For example, Paul, another Witch at the conference, had once been a member of a fundamentalist Christian group but dropped away and became an agnostic. Then, one day in the late 1960's when he was fighting in Vietnam, he was huddled down in a trench trying to avoid a mortar barrage and suddenly experienced the feeling of being protected. He wondered where this feeling of power came from, and after he returned from Vietnam, he tried to find out by studying astrology and yoga and then worked with some ideas about the male and female polarities and intuition. He studied on his own for about 12 years when he met one of the leaders of modern Witchcraft. He realized as they talked that he had been involved in Witchcraft on his own all this time without calling it this, and so he formally became a Witch.

In other cases, Witches had dabbled in the occult for years, generally on their own, and decided to join to be with others with similar interests. Then during this search, they learned about the C of E or another Craft group through an ad, newspaper article, or metaphysical store salesperson.

    Soon after they became involved, the Witches, like the
Hutians, usually had some sort of confirmation experience
which led them to feel that this new religion would work for
them and give them the power they sought. Often this experience occurred after they did some ritual technique; then
something happened which they took as a sign of confirmation.
Some experienced this confirmation as a sudden insight;
others had a series of confirming experiences.

    For example, Dave, a Witch from Texas, said his belief
was confirmed when he found he could move the light of a
candle with his mind. Paul, a Virginia Witch, was very
skeptical at first, but was convinced when a woman had an
apparently "miraculous" recovery from a serious coronary.
As Bill described it, the woman was near death in the hospi-
tal when his group sent energy to her. But the next day,
the woman woke up feeling better and the doctors said they
could find no trace of the coronary.

    Andrea, a student of Athena's, became more involved
when she found that one of the spells she read about in one
of the books for the course seemed to work when she tried
it out. She made tea from rosemary and thyme, and as she
drank it, chanted a spell to relieve her loneliness and
attract a man. Although the spell was supposed to take six
weeks to work, after two days of tea drinking the super-
visor in her office asked her to get something for him, and
when she returned he commented on how attractive she was.
Andrea took this compliment as an indication the spell was
working. As she commented: "If that happened after only
two days, just think what else might happen."

    Other Witches experience this confirmation of belief
more gradually. For instance, Andy, a North Carolina Witch,
noticed after doing rituals for several months that his per-
cent of successes increased, and he found the associations
and coincidences in his life so marked that he became convinced his rituals were effective.

    For still other Witches, the confirmation experience
involved the feeling that they had been transformed into a
new being. Alexis, of the C of E, told me he had this
gradual sense of being transformed as he read and studied
about the Craft under Athena's direction and worked with his
new magical name. After two months when he was initiated
into the group, he felt like a totally changed being.

    Athena reported this experience of transformation, too.
She had studied about the Craft on her own for about three
years, when she finally found a Witch in the Southwest who

would initiate her. She flew there one weekend and when
she returned from her trip, she felt different and even her
neighbors asked what had changed.

Such stories about making contact and experiencing
confirmation were similar to the Hutians' accounts of why
they got involved. However, whereas the Hutians were particularly attracted by the idea of seeing themselves as
being better and not just different than others, the Witches
were more interested in doing things better than others
through acquiring special techniques. Unlike the Hutians
who often saw themselves as weird or different and sought to
transform that conception into seeing themselves as part of
an elite, the Witches did not experience this same intense
alienation from others. They felt a similar lack of power.
But instead of seeing the group as a way to get power to be
better than others, they sought power to do better than
others.

This orientation is, in turn, linked to underlying
philosophical ideas about the nature of humanity. Whereas
Hutians do not believe in a oneness and stress their indi-
viduality and specialness, the Witches see themselves and
others as part of a common unity. They may want more power,
but they are still part of this larger whole. The Hutian
wants to step outside.

Group Structure

Like the Hutians, the Witches also measure magical
growth through a degree structure. However, whereas Hutians
have six degree levels, the Witches have five. These are
the neophyte student; the initiate Witch who wears the red
cord to symbolize his new birth into the Craft; the second
degree Witch who wears white to symbolize he has advanced
to the realm of the Goddess; the full-fledged Witch who
wears purple, the color of the crown or highest chakra, to
show he knows the inner meanings and has been initiated into
the mysteries; and finally the queen Witch, who has taught
other Witches who have hived off to form their own covens.

These differences in the degree systems are related to
differences in group structure, which are based on different
ideas about the source of power. Whereas the Hutians see
one primary deity, Hu, as a major source of power and have
a single pyramid-shaped structure which parallels the members' growing expertise in working with Hu, the Witches see

the underlying power of the universe manifested as a duality, represented symbolically through numerous spiritual beings and deities. In turn, their ideas are reflected in a multi-unit structure, in which different groups or covens work with different spiritual beings and gods, and are linked to other covens in a kind of Witchcraft federation.

Within the coven, the high priestess is the head, since she draws on the powers of life and fertility, represented by the goddess; but she works closely with a high priest so there is a balance between the two polar energies of nature. Then, under her, the coven members, who are first and second degree Witches, are much like a family which works together as a ritual unit. Finally, lowest in the degree structure are the neophyte students just beginning to learn the Craft.

One problem with this kind of structure is the difficulty of creating a philosophy unity, which was the theme of the Southwest conference. Each Witchcraft group has its own ideology and traditions, reflected in different symbols, rituals, deities, and even certain equipment. So there is a tendency to fragmentation, particularly since Witches have a spirit of independence and anarchy and like doing things their own way—in contrast to the Hutians who accept their place within a rigid hierarchical structure. Yet, in spite of their differences, Witches share a common belief in one power manifested through the goddess and god which draws them together.

The Role of Magic and Ritual
in Everyday Life

Despite specific differences in group organization, ritual, and symbols, the Witches and Hutians use magical practice for much the same purpose in daily life: to get what they want and to get back at those they feel have wronged them. Like Hutians, Witches use both personal rituals and group rituals, and they also interpret events magically—claiming one event is caused by another through intention or will, or pointing to events as signs that something else may occur.

Like Hutians, the Witches view the force they use as neither good nor evil. Rather, they see it much like electricity, nuclear energy, or any other power. It can be used for good or bad ends, but it is inherently neither one. Furthermore, though they see themselves as white Witches,

they believe a Witch must be able to use power for good or
ill, for as Athena frequently observed: "If you can't hex;
you can't heal," meaning if you restrict your use of power,
you are limited in what you can do.

Like Hutians, the Witches were reticent to talk in detail about a ritual until it worked, since they felt talking
about it would diffuse its power. But once it seemed effective, they willingly shared ritual techniques to get new
ideas or see how other Witches performed rituals.

They similarly used rituals frequently in everyday life
to achieve desired goals. However, where the Hutians typically used brief rituals with concentration, visualization,
and sometimes the pentagram to project their will, the
Witches generally used more elaborate rituals with a variety
of magical paraphenalia to increase their focus on the goal.

The act of doing a ritual and looking for signs of
effectiveness occurred repeatedly. For example, at our first
meeting, Athena talked about doing a working to sell a truck
so she could get money to buy a desk. Afterwards, she was
so confident her ritual would work that she bought the desk
before selling the truck and urged her husband not to worry.
She had done a ritual, so the truck would sell. The next
day, when a man phoned, offered $1900 for the truck sight-
unseen, and subsequently bought it, she took this as a sign
of her ritual's power.

In another case, Athena went to a Southwestern city to
get initiated and arrived while the high priest and priestess
were feuding about who should initiate her and other matters.
For awhile it looked like neither would initiate her. He
said it was up to the high priestess to perform the initiation, but the high priestess said she didn't want to. Athena
returned to her motel room extremely discouraged. Then, she
did a working that the high priestess would initiate her and
would call within 45 minutes to say so. When the high
priestess did call within 30 minutes to say the ceremony was
on, Athena felt her ritual had been successful.

Athena also performed rituals to make her classes go
successfully. In one of these, she took a stack of papers
she had prepared for the class and charged them in a circle.
When several prospective students called about the class in
the next few days, she deemed the ritual a success.

In some cases, she did rituals to make things happen
more quickly, as occurred when she wanted to get a book
another Witch was sending to her. Normally the book would
take about three weeks to arrive via fourth class mail, but

Athena did a ritual to make it come faster, and the book
arrived the very next day—one day after it was sent—a sure
sign, she claimed, that the ritual worked.

Other Witches I met at the conference described similar
ritual success stories. For example, Paul from Virginia
described numerous experiences, including several successes
in controlling the weather. In one of the most memorable,
which happened when he was in the military, he had his men
set up their tents at night and in the early morning he was
about to have them take the tents down when it started to
rain. Though the weather forecast said it would continue,
Paul was determined that it shouldn't rain now, since it
would be impossible to take down a soggy tent and his men
would have to wait around until the tents dried out. Thus,
he concentrated intently and "put out the thought" that he
wanted clear weather. Then, within minutes, he reported,
the clouds parted and the sun came out for a half an hour,
before it rained again—just long enough to take down the
tents.

In addition, Paul found he could use his intuition to
answer questions or gain information otherwise unavailable
to him. For example, to make a decision or find an answer
he would think: "I'm seeking this information in the name
of the goddess," relax each part of his body, and concentrate
on his question with his third eye, located in the center of
his forehead, until he got back an answer. In one dramatic
incident, he used this technique to locate someone in Atlanta.
A friend told him that a certain businessman occasionally
turned up at a certain address though he wasn't often there,
and Paul set out to find him. However, once on the freeway,
he discovered he had lost the address and directions, so he
decided to try letting his intuition guide him to his desti-
nation. He concentrated on the question: "Where should I
go?" When he got the feeling he should get off, he turned
off the freeway and then, in response to his feelings, he
made two more turns, which led him to the correct street.
Incredibly, he said, as he arrived at the right house, the
man he wanted to see drove up in a station wagon, and this
experience convinced him of the power of magic.

Marie, a Witch from Texas, used other techniques to
make things happen. Sometimes, she told me, she wrote what
she wanted on a xeroxed picture and burned it in a ritual, so
the heat of the fire would lend its strength to her desire
to make the event happen. At times she wrote the name of a
loved one on a piece of paper, put it in a doll, and burned

it in ritual to inspire the loved one to feel the heat of
passion. And when she invited a man she liked for dinner,
she used candles, incense, and music to set the mood, and
added certain herbs to his food. "When you do all that,"
she said, "you have a more positive attitude and cannot
fail. He hasn't got a chance."

Many Witches seek to increase their power by wearing
charms they have charged with a desired objective, or they
wear them for protection. For instance, at one class meeting, Athena showed me the High John the Conquerer Root she
wore for both purposes. "It's good luck," she said, "and
if your lover touches it, he's bound to you for life."

Some Witches light candles as they think about what they
want and chant to charge the candles with their feelings.
And some use divination to get insight on what is likely to.
happen; then they use this information to determine what kind
of ritual to perform. If they favor the possible event, they
do a ritual to make it happen more quickly; if they hope it
doesn't occur, they do a ritual to alter the flow of events.

Witches also use everyday rituals for healing. For
example, Paul once was walking along a beach when he came
upon a man who had nearly drowned. The man was as cold as
ice and not breathing, and several people had already tried
mouth to mouth resuscitation without success. Then, as he
stood amongst the crowd of onlookers, Paul felt a sudden
urge to go over and put his hand on the man's forehead, and
when he did, he felt a strong surge of energy flow through
his hand. In seconds, he felt the man's forehead turn from
cold to warm; then the man opened his eyes and sat up.

Witches use these rituals for protection, too. Artemis
from Illinois described at the conference how she visualizes
a white light around her head and whole body. "Then," she
told the audience, "no one can hurt me."

Others use protection devices to ward off perceived
dangers, and look for signs that the ritual protected them.
Athena and her husband, Jeff, once felt another group of
Witches were trying to "zap" them with negative energy, because a number of things had gone wrong in the house—a fuse
blew several times, some appliances suddenly didn't work,
and Jeff cut himself badly as he worked in the garage.
Thus, they decided to "zap" the others in return. They put
a black candle in the living room to collect the negative
energy and did a ritual to send the bad energy back. The
result, Athena claimed, was the house was protected so things
stopped going wrong, and later the people sending the energy

came down sick. Moreover, as further proof the ritual was effective, Athena observed that shortly after the ritual the electricity went out for ten minutes all over the neighborhood for several blocks except in their own house—a sure sign they had been working with a high level of power.

In another case, Artemis feared that a man in a relationship that was going sour was going to harm the woman and directed her will to block the man from doing harm. When the couple decided to end their relationship a few days later, Artemis felt she had effectively blocked the danger.

Like Hutians, Witches also do rituals to hurt others who have hurt them, and they justify these on the basis of getting retribution for a wrong. For example, Sam, a Witch from Texas, retaliated when someone hurt him by making a mirror image in his mind to send the harm back.

In some cases, Witches feel their power is strong enough to operate against someone who has wronged them, even if they don't do a ritual to retaliate. An example of this occurred when Athena was angered by an article which described her in unflattering terms by linking her with another Witch she didn't like. She performed no ritual, but when the writer lost his job soon after the article appeared, she regarded this as one more indication of her power. "People who cross me have problems," she said.

Like Hutians, Witches sometimes do group rituals to raise more power to attain their goal. For instance, Athena and six other Witches did a ritual in Sacramento when the Attorney General was trying to promote a bill authorizing him to launch an investigation of religious groups. They didn't want the bill to pass and set up an altar in a parking lot near the capitol to do a ritual to prevent it from happening. After they cast the circle, they burned some black candles, and each participant wrote down statements against the bill on a piece of parchment which they burned in a thurible. A few days after the ritual, the bill was turned down; hence, they claimed their ritual had been effective.

In short, like Hutians, Witches believe they can mobilize power through ritual to increase their chances of healing, harming, protecting, and getting something; and they take favorable events that happen shortly after the rituals as signs of ritual effectiveness. Implicitly or explicitly, they deny these events could be due to other causes; or if they think other factors might be involved, they still claim the ritual helped.

Conversely, when rituals don't work immediately or

appear not to work at all, Witches, like Hutians, find
reasons to explain what went wrong, so they can continue to
believe the ritual process is still effective. For example,
when Athena did several workings to sell her house and didn't
get an offer for months, she explained the apparent failure
by saying she really wanted to hold onto the house; so the
ritual was not at fault. Then, when she got an offer but
the deal didn't go through, she explained that the time
wasn't quite right, since she had too much to do in preparing for the Witchcraft conference. But afterwards, she was
certain the house would sell.

In another instance, Athena said she didn't get what
she really wanted in a ritual because she hadn't performed
it precisely. Instead, she got what she actually asked for.
Specifically, she had hoped to get $1000 from her ex-husband,
who was coming to visit her in a few days, and in her ritual,
she wrote down her desire to obtain money from him on a
piece of paper, which she burned. But she didn't specify how
much. Thus, when he came to visit her, took $100 out of his
wallet and gave it to her without her even asking for money,
she claimed this showed the ritual was effective. "But, it
should have been $1000," she said. "The only reason it
wasn't is because I didn't do the ritual right."

Like Hutians, the Witches also enjoy showing off their
power and are pleased when others acknowledge it. This was
especially noticeable at the Witchcraft conference, which
got extensive publicity because several local Christian
groups were upset that the Witches were holding a national
meeting there and had attempted to block the conference. The
Christians put pressure on the hotel, city government, and
county sheriff, and failing to get the conference cancelled,
announced a public protest. Alerted to the conflict, the
press flocked to the conference in droves from local, national,
and even international media (two reporters wrote for magazines in France and Sweden). So there were about as many
members of the media as there were Witches—about 40 of each.

The Witches, in turn, were delighted by the attention,
and those that were public gave numerous interviews describing their powers. Many claimed the fears of the Christians
and the media interest were further proof of their power.
And many interpreted major events at the conference as signs
of personal power, too. For example, on the first day, a
caller threatened that a bomb would go off at 12 noon the
next day if there were any Witches in the motel. Thus, at
about 10 in the morning, the motel management secretly

hustled the Witches into a caravan of cars which sped away
to another motel down the road. In the afternoon when they
returned after an extensive search revealed no bomb, numerous
Witches exulted that this event was another sign of their
power. "You see," one said, "the Witches weren't harmed."

Many Witches also interpreted the protest of 300 Christians outside the motel in terms of their personal power.
For instance, Artemis had a motel room overlooking the site
where the protest took place, and on the night before the
protest, she did a ritual to make it ineffective. She put
guardian animal figures on her balcony for further protection. Then, when the protest occurred below her window rather
than on the nearby field where originally scheduled, she
viewed this change as an example of her power. As she explained it, the protest had been moved near her window,
since the Witches would be better protected because of her
ritual protecting the area. Moreover, she thought it
significant that the protest lasted only 45 minutes, instead
of the originally announced three hours—another sign that
her working had reduced the strength of the Christians.

Causing skeptics to acknowledge Witches have power makes
Witches feel more powerful, too. An example of this occurred
when several Witches gathered in a motel room and began chatting with a visibly tipsy newsman who dropped by to visit.
During the conversation, he remarked skeptically that "there
aren't any real Witches in the room." He was a Baptist, he
said, and he didn't think Witches had any power.

Alex, one of the Witches, rose to his bait. "Oh, no,
you don't," he said. "As long as you don't believe we have
power, you will find starting tomorrow morning that when you
wake up your big toe will be numb. And, beginning tonight
you won't be able to have an erection for a month.

At this point, the newsman suddenly became concerned.
What if these people really did have power? What if they
could do what they threatened? He didn't want to acknowledge their power, yet feared that just possibly their threat
might be true.

Thus, for the next half hour, he and the Witches debated
the issue. "Please don't do this," he begged continually.
"Then say you believe," the Witches said again and again.
The discussion finally ended in a stalemate, with the newsman refusing to say he believed, and the Witches refusing to
cancel the spell.

In the morning, when he returned to the convention,
after being unable to have sex with his wife the previous

night and feeling his toe a little numb, he capitulated.
"Yes. Yes," he told Alex at breakfast. "I believe. I
believe those were Witches in the room." So Alex agreed to
remove the "spell," though later he commented to several
Witches that his "power" had simply been the power of psychology to make the newsman believe. But regardless of why
the "spell" worked, the Witches gloried in this recognition
of their power.

In summary, the magical practices of the Witches differ
in content from those of the Hutians. Also, whereas the
Hutians emphasize using the will, the Witches concentrate
more on techniques. But they apply magical thinking to everyday life in a similar way. Like Hutians, they interpret
events in light of their belief in magical cause and effect,
and they believe they can influence what happens through will
or ritual. Also, like Hutians, they look for experiences
which confirm their power and like it when others acknowledge their power.

The Problems of Power

Unfortunately, the focus on power can cause Witches,
like Hutians, to experience paranoia, become overly critical,
and develop an overconcern with the self to the detriment
of the group.

This paranoia may arise due to beliefs about magical
cause and effect, leading a Witch who has some bad experiences
to conclude that the events did not happen by chance, but
because someone with malevolent feelings wanted to harm him
and caused the events to occur.

This happened when Athena and Jeff had a falling out
with another group and soon after experienced a number of
breakdowns around the house. Some of Jeff's tools broke; his
truck wouldn't start; the phones went out for a few hours.
"But we know where it's from," Athena told me, and explained
that the other group was sending negative energy their way.
Then, to promote themselves and get their own revenge,
Athena and Jeff performed a ritual to send this negativity
back.

Other Witches claimed they had gotten sick or felt
drained of energy at times because another Witch tried to
get back at them with magic.

The Witches I met also tended to be very critical of
others, and were particularly incensed when others misused

power in the name of the Craft. For example, Athena frequently observed that Witches in other groups did not
practice the Craft appropriately, and her coven members
agreed. One group was too informal, she complained. Members performed rituals for trivial or inappropriate purposes;
then they called what they were doing Witchcraft, but they
were really making a mockery of it. As an example, she
pointed to a Witchcraft group with a mocking name, the
Crackpot Coven, which did a ritual in which they covered a
menstruating woman with mud and gave her a shower. She
also opposed their practice of having each person stand in
the center of the circle while they raised a cone of power
for her, since "a ritual should only have one purpose." Also,
Athena vehemently disparaged one ritual in which the larger
group split into two to do a healing and a celebration.
"You have to be of one mind to do a ritual," she charged.
"And when you have the group divided into two and do two
rituals simultaneously, you can't be of one mind."

Similarly, she and her coven members roundly criticized
Witches who smoked dope or participated in group sex on
ritual occasions. "They just want to use Witchcraft as an
excuse to justify orgies," she complained. "And they give
Witches a bad name." She even criticized some of her students for being too wimpy or eccentric.

Likewise, at the conference, I heard about a dozen
Witches criticize other groups for their ideas and practices,
even though,in theory, Witches believe in having many traditions and freely expressing ideas. In one case, these
Witches strongly criticized some Witches not at the conference who were on a T.V. talk show a few nights before and
had talked about the advantages of having multiple relationships and using abortion as a form of contraception. These
Witches had aired their views too freely, they griped, and
thereby presented a wrong libertine image of the Craft.

The theme of the conference, "Philosophical Unity,"
was chosen to deal with this issue of criticalness, and
several Witches gave speeches urging others to stop the back-
biting. However, even though the Witches are aware of it,
the problem remains, since it derives to a large extent from
the group's emphasis on power. This orientation is likely to
lead to criticalness, for when a person finds a certain
route to power effective, he may believe that other routes
are less so. This type of thinking occurs in turn because
it is hard to sustain a vision that all routes to power may
be equally good, or that some routes are desirable for

some but not others, since the agreement of others helps to validate one's own view. Divergent thinking provides no such support.

Finally, the overconcern with self arising from the emphasis on personal power can lead to difficulties which undermine the group. This was illustrated dramatically by a series of events that led to the end of the C of E.

The Witchcraft convention set these events in motion. Athena had been asked to speak at it and was looking forward to giving her talk with a mixture of eager anticipation and concern. She had never spoken to a large group before and was worried whether she could do it well. At the same time, she was attracted by the aura of power associated with the conference and the possibility she could become part of it. A few years before she had trouble finding another Witch to initiate her, and now she had a chance to work with the "biggies" of the Craft on an equal level. To her, this opportunity was an exciting and self-affirming prospect.

When she arrived at the conference site, her feeling of power grew even more, for almost immediately members of the news media accosted her for interviews on her reactions to the local fundamentalists who were protesting the Witches' gathering. Soon Andy, the Witch from North Carolina who was handling the press contact and worked with some of the most important nationally known Witches, took her in hand and shuttled her from one meeting with the press to another.

The result of all this hoopla was that Athena was turned into something of a star and gloried in the publicity. At the same time, she was attracted to Andy and as the conference went on, they spent more and more time together.

Meanwhile, Isis, who had been practicing Egyptian Witchcraft on her own for years, got drawn into the group's orbit since a C of E member, Frank, began pursuing her. She was not romantically interested in him, but began to spend most of her time with him and the other C of E initiate, Alexis, since she knew almost no one else at the conference. Then, through Frank and Alexis, she got acquainted with Athena and Jeff.

For Athena this development was ideal since it provided her a way to get more freedom to associate with the other big name Witches and with Andy. "Why don't you keep my husband amused," she told Isis, "so he won't get bored."

As a result, Isis began to flirt with Jeff, while Athena spent most of her time with Andy and the nationally known Witches. Meanwhile, Frank continued to court Isis.

After the conference, events proceeded rapidly to the
group's denouement. Athena returned to California with her
husband, Frank, and Alexis; and, at Frank's invitation,
Isis came along. But then, instead of moving in with Frank,
Isis stayed with Athena and Jeff and began to study with
Athena to become part of the coven while continuing her relationship with Jeff. However, they were discreet about it,
and when Athena was around Isis deferred to her and acted as
if there was no special feeling between her and Jeff.

Three days after they returned, Athena traveled to
Northern California for a few days to do some local publicity for a Halloween ritual. On Halloween night, Jeff,
Frank, Alexis, Isis, Artemis, and several of Athena's students drove north to join her. Then, as high priestess and
priest, she and Jeff welcomed in the new year according to
Craft tradition, while the media filmed away.

Afterwards, as the group drove home, everything seemed
outwardly normal. Athena sat in the front of the van with
Jeff, holding his hand affectionately while Isis sat in the
back with Frank, Alexis, Artemis and me.

However, two days later, Athena unexpectedly left to
become the high priestess of Andy's coven. She didn't even
tell Jeff her plans for leaving. He returned from work to
find her note. Though she had earlier talked about going
East for three weeks for a visit, this sudden and irrevoc-
able departure was totally unexpected. She simply left.

Her move in turn led to a number of changes in quick
succession. First, the coven came to an abrupt end, since
without the high priestess there could be no coven. Secondly,
Jeff filed for divorce while Athena sought to get various
pieces of furniture, equipment, and school materials, as well
as cash from the house sale as part of the settlement. Meanwhile, Jeff and Isis openly acknowledged their love for each
other and decided to get married once the divorce was final.
Frank disappeared from the group. Alexis decided to join
Athena back East and become part of her new coven. And
Armetis felt totally devastated because just before Athena
left she gave her $500 as a gift for the coven. But now the
coven was no more and Athena had taken her money.

Then, when Jeff and Isis went through the house to
organize their own affairs and locate some materials for
Athena, they found several small dolls with pins in them
which Athena had left behind to attack them. They performed
a cleansing ritual to diffuse these objects of their power
and threw them out. However, a few days later, when Isis

felt her energy very low and Jeff had some more problems
with his truck, they attributed this to another of Athena's
spells. Yet Isis was certain she would ultimately prevail.
"Athena may have me down now," she told me, "but once I get
over this, my power will be stronger than ever, and the
power she has sent will return to hurt her."

An analysis of these events illustrates the role of
personal power in influencing what happened. In essence,
this chain of events occurred because at the conference
Athena suddenly became aware of the new channels of power
open to her due to her contact with the big name Witches and
the media. She also realized this taste of power could continue if she moved her school to the East Coast and continued
to work closely with these powerful Witches. Thirdly, there
was her attraction to Andy. It was a powerful combination—
a chance for increased personal power, wealth, fame, recognition, acceptance by the most notable Witches—and love.

By contrast, in California she felt she was out of the
mainstream. The coven she created and her less powerful
husband might hold her back if she stayed. Thus, seizing
the opportunity, she left, abandoning her husband, the coven,
and her students. She grabbed the chance to increase her
personal power—though this led to the end of the group. Her
self-interest, her own needs for power, came first, even
though leaving meant breaking a number of firmly pledged
bonds. First, in the coven initiation ceremony she had
bound herself and other coven members together. Secondly,
she and Jeff had recently reaffirmed their own wedding vows
in a Witchcraft wedding ceremony called a handfasting. And
thirdly, they had planned to move to the country with Alexis
and Frank in a few short weeks, once they sold the house.
But when she left, she broke these bonds. The desire for
love and power proved stronger; self-interest prevailed over
that of the group.

Summing Up

In summary, similar dynamics occur among Witches and
Hutians since both groups are oriented around attaining and
using personal power. Members are attracted to both groups
for similar reasons; share a like interest in recognizing
levels of personal power through a system of degrees; and
seek to interpret experiences and influence events through
magical ideas and practices. In both groups members seek

positive benefits for themselves through magic, though they
may use magical strategies to get back at those who have hurt
them.

In turn, this orientation to magic and power has similar
repercussions in both groups. It can lead members to be
extremely suspicious and critical of others, and it can lead
them to elevate their own interests to the detriment of the
group.

Although specifics differ in symbols, ritual content,
and the relationship of members to the mainstream, the underlying processes are similar, suggesting that the study of a
group like the Hutians has a broader application to other
groups which likewise seek personal power through magic.

12

The Importance of Personal Power

In the preceding chapters I have shown how the search for
power is a key reason members join the Hutians and other
magical groups, and I have described how the theme of power
is reflected in the activities and beliefs of these groups
and in the relationships of members. Members are attracted
to these groups by the chance to increase their power through
learning and using magic; and the group structure, activities, and relationships make the individual feel powerful as
he practices techniques he believes will help him get what
he wants. While skeptics may question whether these techniques work, the individual using them—whether they work or
not—feels powerful because he has, he believes, special
knowledge and abilities.

This interest in power in turn raises other issues.
What is the nature of this power which members seek? Why
do they seek power? Why is it so important to them? What
are the underlying psychological dynamics involved in using
power? And what are the effects of seeking and using power
on the individual?

In describing the Hutians, I have briefly discussed some
of the processes, such as feeling more powerful by rejecting
others who might reject oneself. But now, I want to consider more systematically, and in greater depth, the dynamics
involved in the search for power in four key areas:
  · the types of power sought
  · the reasons for wanting power
  · how power is used
  · the relationship between power and personality

I will deal with each of these issues in turn in this
and the following chapter.

The Nature of Personal Power

In discussing the Hutians, I talked about their concern
with power in generic terms. However, power takes a number
of different forms—expressing aggression, seeking control,
wanting to dominate, and feeling hostility and hatred. In
its most anti-social form, the search for power can become
a desire to destroy others who appear to be weaker than
oneself or are outsiders. On the other hand, power can be
nurturing and supportive. Thus, power springs from a number
of different sources.

Since 1950, some psychologists have sought to distinguish these types of power and have been particularly
concerned with the nature of the power motive and the way
the need for power differs from individual to individual.
To learn how this motive is expressed, these psychologists
have defined it as a thought about having impact in one of
three ways: taking a strong action such as being aggressive,
controlling, or persuading others; taking an action which
makes others respond emotionally, such as crying; or expressing a concern for one's reputation or its effect on others.
Then they have shown subjects pictures with power themes
and asked them to tell brief imaginative stories to find out
what they are thinking or experiencing when the power motive
is present.[1]

These studies have shown that individuals high and low
in power motivation behave quite differently. For example,
young American males with high power needs are more apt to
watch competitive team sports, read about sex and aggression,
drink more liquor, accumulate prestige possessions, and belong to organizations or hold office in them than those low
in power needs.[2]

After reviewing the research on power motivation, David
McClelland has suggested four ways of classifying power,
based on whether the source of power comes from outside or
inside the self and whether the power is directed towards
the self or towards someone or something else. While power
can be conceptualized in other ways, this model provides a
useful clear-cut way of categorizing power. After describing
these four stages, I will point out how the Hutians and other
magical groups can be viewed in terms of this classification.

According to McClelland, in the first and most primitive
stage of power development, the individual experiences the
source of power coming from outside the self and uses it to
strengthen the self. To gain this power, he looks to friends,

associates, leaders, and others thought to have power, even
to a deity. Or he may seek power from an impersonal outside
source, such as books.[3] For the Hutians and others in magical groups, this kind of power is particularly relevant, since
they gain power from the deities they work with, from reading
magical literature, and from the support of group members.

In Stage II, according to McClelland, one gains power
from expanding or strengthening the self through acquiring
self-enhancing possessions or making efforts to develop or
transform one's personality. For example, a person who takes
up body-building, yoga, or assertiveness training would fall
in this category. The rationale behind this use of power is
that one can find sources of strength within the self, and
draw on this inner strength to make the self even stronger.[4]
Again, the Hutians and other magicians would embrace this type
of power since they value developing the will by working on
the self.

In Stage III, the individual seeks to experience power
by having an impact on others through controlling them or com-
peting successfully against them. In its most aggressive
mode, this type of power is expressed through giving orders
or physically or psychologically beating others down. But
it also can be expressed by giving information or assisting
others.[5] For Hutians and other magicians, this is an
important source of power since, within the group, higher-ups
exercise power over underlings, and all members use ritual
to try to control others.

Finally, in Stage IV, the individual's need for power
is altruistic, for he sees himself as an instrument for a
higher authority which directs him to influence or serve
others. By submitting to and acting in behalf of this higher
principle or being, he seeks to achieve an egoless state where
the self drops out. For example, the mystic seeks to merge
himself with a higher being, or more mundanely, an individual
might join an organization and experience power through serving the group.[6] In principle, Hutians and other magicians are
not attracted to this type of power since they want to expand
the self, not diminish it, and they want to gain benefits for
the self, not for a higher authority or organization. But in
practice, magicians exhibit this kind of power motivation, too,
since they may identify closely with a magical group and use
their best efforts to serve it, even though they may have
joined initially to advance their own power needs.

In outlining these four stages, McClelland suggests that
the way the individual seeks power is related to his level of

maturity. He claims that much psychotherapy is devoted to
helping individuals move from experiencing power coming from
outside themselves (Stage I) to developing the power within
(Stage II), so they can gain control over their own lives and
learn to exert their own will power. Also, he suggests that
it takes further maturity to move from Stage II to Stage III
and use inner power to relate to and compete successfully with
others. Then, it takes additional maturity to advance to
Stage IV and learn to subordinate self-interest to some
higher good without feeling one is losing oneself.

While McClelland's view that individuals achieving
Stage IV are most mature and self-actualized is questionable,
since the ideal of self-subordination to a higher good represents a value judgment, his four-way classification of power
is useful. For it suggests that the fully mature powerful
person is one who can use all four modes of a power as appropriate to the situation. Depending on circumstances, he
should look to others for help, depend on himself, assert
himself over others, or act in behalf of a larger organization or principle.[7]

Applying these four developmental stages to the Hutians
and other magicians indicates that they are primarily interested in mastering the first three stages, since they want
power primarily to benefit the self. So their concern with
power is ultimately selfish; for the most part they are not
interested in using power to benefit others, although members
may use their power for group ends.

This focus, in turn, has potential dangers which are
present in any group where members seek power primarily for
the self and are not interested in using it for the good of
the larger community. The problem is that if the benefits to
be gained for the self come in conflict with community needs,
there is always the risk that the individual may turn against
the community and direct his power against it.

Then, too, there are different dangers in seeking power
at each stage, for each has its own pathology. The Stage I
individual who looks to sources of power outside himself may
become overly dependent on them. The Stage II individual who
focuses on developing the self may exercise too much control
and become obsessive-compulsive in trying to control every
thought and action or in performing certain behaviors. The
Stage III individual may become overaggressive in seeking to
dominate others, using violence against them, or smothering
them with attention. Finally, the Stage IV individual might
come to think of himself as a direct instrument of the will

of God or another higher authority, so he can no longer
distinguish between what he and the higher authority wants.[8]
All of these dangers apply to the Hutians and other magicians.

    McClelland and other psychologists also distinguish
between a socialized and personal power motivation based on
the extent to which the individual controls or inhibits his
high motivation for power over others. They consider power-
motivated individuals with a high level of inhibition to have
a "socialized power motivation," because they are willing and
able at the Stage III level to discipline their expression of
power or use it for the benefit of others. By contrast, they
regard those with low inhibition as having a "personal power-
motivation," since these individuals see themselves engaged
in a struggle to win over others at all costs because they
see life as a zero-sum game, where one only wins if the other
loses.[9]

    In McClelland's view, this personal style of power,
characterized by dominance and submission, is more primitive,
since the child discovers the "I win/You lose" philosophy
early in life, before he learns more subtle modes of influence. Also, the personally motivated individual expresses
his power needs more simply and directly, such as by being
aggressive, drinking heavily, and acquiring prestige symbols.
Then, when he is in a leadership position, he treats others
like pawns, which often makes them passive. By contrast, the
individual who displays a socialized style of power is more
concerned with formulating and achieving group goals and
making group members feel competent and powerful, so they are
inspired to work hard and feel they can accomplish what they
want.[10]

    When the Hutians and other magicians are analyzed in
these terms, they fall squarely in the personalized power
category. By stated intention, they want this kind of power
for their own benefit, and find the idea of being dominant and
aggressive and acquiring prestige symbols appealing. Although
McClelland doubts such power-motivated leadership can be
effective because it makes underlings feel passive and helpless, this need not be the case for even in the most rigidly
controlled hierarchy, group members at each level can dominate
others under them. And even those on the bottom can look
forward to moving up the hierarchy and controlling others
below them. Additionally, even Hutians on the bottom can feel
or act superior to the humans outside, and so psychologically
have someone to dominate, too, as well as feeling the power
of being part of a power-oriented group.

The Reasons for Wanting Power

Certainly everyone wants some power, since no one wants to be totally dependent on others or the random forces of nature. Yet not everyone makes power a central focus of his life, as do those interested in magic. Why is it so important to them? Understanding the dynamics involved is important, because in certain key ways their search for power reflects the processes underlying the desire for power generally and points up why certain individuals are especially drawn to it. The processes include the need to feel in control, the innate drive for power, social and cultural factors, and individual psychological needs. I will discuss each of these in turn.

The Importance of Feeling in Control

The desire to feel in control is a key motivation for seeking all types of power since attaining a certain level of power provides this feeling.

In the last decade, psychologists have begun exploring This control concept and agree this feeling is important to the individual's well-being. As Lefcourt observes: the individual must "perceive himself as the determiner of his fate if he is to live comfortably with himself."[11]

Research supports this view, since it shows that the individual who feels in control is more likely to take initiative and be more effective in what he does.   For instance, David Glass, Jerome E. Singer, and colleagues found that subjects who experienced random noise but could turn it off had more control than those who couldn't, and they were more committed and effective in performing assigned tasks—solving an insoluble design problem and proofreading a manuscript. Other researchers have found that if an individual can predict when an aversive event, such as receiving a shock, will occur or can control its intensity or duration, he experiences less discomfort and can endure the bad experience longer.[12]

In a similar fashion, individuals who are better able to achieve desired values due to their position or group membership, experience more personal satisfaction and control.   By contrast, people who experience a lack of control, such as those living in poor circumstances they can't change or leave, often have feelings of hopelessness, helplessness, despair, and low self-worth.[13]

In short, having power gives one a feeling of control, and this feeling helps one function more effectively. Thus, it is not surprising that Hutians want this control and seek power to get it through developing the will to gain control over others and the self.

Power as an Innate Drive

Many psychologists consider the desire for power an innate drive; thus, it is natural for humans to seek power and express it by being aggressive, wanting to dominate others, and striving to improve their status or prestige. As numerous studies show, dominance relationships are prevalent in animal groups; and in all human societies, even the simplest, humans have sought prestige or status by accumulating material possessions, wives, or servants, being a good warrior or craftsman, or making decisions for the group. Further, war between groups has been part of the human condition.[14]

These strivings for power have occurred again and again because, as Freud and other psychologists have claimed, all individuals possess an instinctual will to power which drives them to seek mastery and control. Normally, the individual restrains his instinctual agression and behaves in response to the demands of his conscience or community sanctions, though his holding back causes him to experience guilt or other psychic tension. But then, once personal or community sanctions are withdrawn, he feels free to express his aggression again. In fact, Freud claimed wars and attacks on other groups were a form of psychic release for pent-up aggression.[15]

In Freud's view, this will to power goes very deep, for it represents a reaction to the child's experience of bondage and subservience to his parents, which continues as a striving to break free of the bonds tying the individual to his own psyche, parents, and society, as a whole.[16]

However, not all succeed in breaking free, for as Freud suggested, there are two types of people—those submitting to power and those seeking and achieving it for themselves. All struggle for it, and while the strong obtain power, the weak consciously or unconsciously envy them or hope to replace them. Meanwhile, all suffer from the experience of being weak relative to society or the environment and in response worship power; it is a reaction to the basic human condition. Thus, as Freud wrote in Civilization and Its Discontents,

humans are instinctually aggressive, and see others as objects
they can use to gratify their aggressive drives or subjugate
to their own purposes. Perhaps only the mother's love for
her son is exempt.[17]

Other psychologists following in Freud's footsteps
argued for the existence of this instinct, too. Melanie Klein
believed the drive for aggression was present in the infant
from the beginning of life. Alfred Adler postulated that the
dominant human motive was "striving for superiority"—a drive
linked to a primary aggressive instinct or will for power.
And some psychologists point out 'hat humans sometimes seek
out stimuli to provoke aggression or assert their will.[18]

Although this aggressive, power-oriented instinct may
be oriented destructively, psychologists recognize this need
not be the case. As the American analyst Clara Thompson
wrote:

> Aggression is not necessarily destructive at all.
> It springs from an innate tendency to grow and master
> life which seems to be characteristic of all living
> matter. Only when this life force is obstructed in
> its development do ingredients of anger, rage, or hate
> become connected with it.[19]

Psychologists are not the only ones to argue for this
power drive. Political philosophers and scientists have
claimed the will to power is always present in social relationships, because humans have always sought to provide for
their own security and welfare, and gaining power enables them
to better pursue them. In his classic argument, Hobbes proposed that men form states in response to this basic need for
security to protect themselves against the uncontrolled expression of this power drive. But then, this pent-up drive
for power eventually must find a release, and does on the
societal level through the state making war on other states.[20]

Darwin's writings on the survival of the fittest contributed support to the belief in humans' natural aggressiveness, too. Although Darwin didn't specifically say so, others
interpreted his writings to say that human society is based
on the same sort of struggle, hostility, unrestrained competi-
tion, and aggressiveness characterizing the animal world,
since humans are descended from animals. Also, these social
Darwinists argued, since society is a battleground for survival, the winners must be stronger and more powerful since
they are successful, whereas the losers must be inferior
weaklings and failures.[21]

Though these ideas about the drive for power do not

explain why the Hutians and others in magical groups should
be particularly interested in power, since these ideas apply
to everyone, Hutians and other magicians draw on these views
to reinforce and justify their own interest in power. If
society is based on a principle of self-interest or survival
of the fittest, they might as well do all they can to maximize
their self-interest, and they should be as strong as possible
to survive. Likewise, if humans are naturally aggressive and
naturally want power, then they are only expressing these
natural drives, though they are more open and uninhibited in
expressing them. Finally, if dominance hierarchies exist
everywhere in nature and if the more powerful subjugate the
less so, they are only doing what comes naturally: they are
acknowledging their drive for power and using it to dominate
and control as much as they can.

Conversely, those who believe they have this drive for
power must acknowledge that others do, too. Thus, a natural
outgrowth of this drive is the fear the other side will
acquire more power, so power-seekers must protect themselves
against the powers of others. This process occurs on all
levels of society. On the macrosocial level, it is reflected
in the international arms race and continual efforts of states
to assert themselves against one another. And on the micro-
social level of magical groups, this process is reflected in
the pervasive concern magicians have that someone else may
have more magical power and can therefore perform better
magic or turn their magic back against them. Thus, like
states struggling for political, military, or economic superiority, magicians are constantly seeking to increase their
power.

Social Learning

The importance an individual places on seeking personal
power is also affected by social learning. If he is in a
situation where he learns or observes certain kinds of behaviors or attitudes, he will be more likely to express them.
But if he doesn't have such an opportunity or is less exposed
to it, his drives, feelings, or impulses to seek or express
power may be inhibited.

For instance, a member of one cultural, ethnic, or class
group may respond to frustration by expressing aggression,
while another learns to hold those feelings in. Both behave
differently, since they have learned to behave in ways their

social group considers socially correct.[22]   According to
Ashley Montagu, this social learning represents a kind of
programming which influences the image we come to have of
ourselves. If we think of ourselves as aggressive and powerful we will act or become like that; if we think we are weak
we will act accordingly.[23]

     This social context of learning is so important that
even if an individual has developed certain power needs because of past experiences, he may not act on his feelings
until he encounters others who feel the same way, for only
then will he feel free to act. Or he may look to them for a
model for channeling his feelings into a specific social
form.

     Numerous laboratory studies on aggression with children
and adults support this social learning view, in that subjects
exposed to models who act aggressively are more likely to act
aggressively themselves, since seeing this model gives them
permission and an example to follow. For example, Albert
Bandura and his co-workers found that nursery school children
who saw an experimenter engage in aggressive acts were more
likely to behave aggressively when they performed a task or
played after being mildly frustrated than children not exposed.[24]   Leonard Berkowitz found that college men who viewed
a violent prize fight movie after trying to solve an insoluble
puzzle gave more intense shocks to the person who helped them
than those who saw a nonviolent track race movie.[25]

     The social learning process similarly affects the be-
havior of individuals drawn to magical groups. When first
attracted, they usually feel frustrated, alienated, or powerless, because they experience a lack of personal power in
some way. Then, in the group they can openly and with group
approval express their aggressive feelings and desire for
power through learning specific power techniques, such as
conducting rituals to get something they want or to harm someone they hate. Without group support, the individual might
be inhibited by feeling guilty or fearing punishment. But in
the group, his feelings are acceptable, and he learns how to
channel and direct them to achieve his goals. Thus, he feels
he has power, and his psychic tensions originally motivating
him to seek out the group are released.

     Being in such a group has both benefits and potential
dangers. On the one hand, an individual might find it bene-
ficial to express his hostility towards someone else symbolically through magic instead of directly, since a direct
act might result in someone stronger overpowering him or in

his punishment for an antisocial act. Also, he may believe he can achieve his goals through his magical prowess, and gain feelings of strength and confidence, so he becomes a more effective person.

On the other hand, being involved in magic may cause the individual to develop a paranoid outlook, because of the group's way of looking at events, and create other problems only the group can solve. For example, a person may be drawn into a magical group because he feels alienated from the world and wants to learn how to do rituals to get back at those he feels alienated from. But once in the group, he may learn that many more people are against him than he thought; so he has even more need to learn magic and work with other members.

A well-known example of this paranoia-building occurred in Nazi Germany. Through totalitarian control and propaganda, the Nazis increasingly created a limited learning environment, which undermined the individual's ability to test reality. As a result, the German people increasingly came to view things from the perspective of their paranoid leaders, who asserted Germans were superior, had access to special knowledge, had a manifest destiny to rule the world, and were persecuted by outsiders. As the Nazis became more and more aggressive and vindictive, most people simply went along.[26]

In the limited learning environment created in the small magical group, Hutians have similarly come to identify with the group perspective and its particular paranoias, such as the belief that all outsiders are mediocre fools and the world is in danger of imminent destruction.

Social Conditions and the Desire for Power

The social or cultural context also affects how individuals seek magical power and use it, since different cultures, societies, classes, and groups have different attitudes towards power of all types. Also, prevailing social conditions or changes in social norms influence the level of interest in seeking power. Although this social or cultural explanation will not explain why certain individuals are drawn to magic and others not, it does suggest why a particular culture should have more or less general interest in magic or why interest in it rises or falls over time. Within this cultural context, the individual learns to have a

certain type of interest and to express this in certain
culturally defined ways.
      Two major factors are involved:
      • cultural differences in attitudes towards power,
        including class and ethnic differences
      • social-structural conditions, such as social scale,
        economic conditions, and social change.

1. Cultural Differences

      In different cultures, attitudes towards power differ
broadly and these influence the extent to which members seek
out personal power through various means, including the use
of magic. Some cultures, such as those oriented around con-
quest, highly value gaining power by dominating others, and
their religious or magical system typically reinforces this
cultural focus. For example, the Roman generals consulted
augurs before going out to battle to be sure their timing
was auspicious. Conversely, some cultures are fundamentally
unaggressive, such as the Hopi Indians, the Tasaday tribe of
the Philippines, and the Pygmies of the Ituri Forest, and
their beliefs emphasize the idea of peace, balance, or har-
mony in nature.[27]
      These cultural attitudes toward power are, in turn,
passed on to the individual through social learning. In a
power-oriented society, his aggressive behavior is reinforced
through approval or prestige for performing an aggressive
act, and sometimes he gains this approbation through ceremony
or ritual. For instance, in the U.S., the cheer leaders
cheer on the football player as he charges to the goal. By
contrast, in societies which stress living together peace-
fully, aggressive behavior is consistently unrewarded, as it
is among Pueblo Indians.
      Thus, whether or not the power drive is instinctual,
culture influences how that drive will be expressed. Some
cultures encourage aggression; others inhibit it. Or a culture may be ambivalent about power, as is American society in
some ways, since the individual is encouraged to be powerful
to gain success and achieve. Yet, simultaneously, Americans
view seeking power over others as somewhat reprehensible,
since this idea contradicts another basic value—the ideal
of equality.
      Thus, both behavioral scientists and the general public
tend to characterize power relations in negative terms. For

instance, in The Authoritarian Personality, T. W. Adorno
describes people concerned with power as "harsh, sadistic,
fascist, Machiavellian, prejudiced, and neurotic," and
Americans generally hold the popular view that striving for
power too energetically can lead to a Nazi-type dictatorship, to political terror, to a police state, to brainwash-
ing, or to the exploitation of helpless people.[28]
     Under the circumstances, psychologists have found that
Americans generally don't like to be told they have a high
need for power or are manipulating others, although they may
like to exercise leadership through making friends and influencing people. They also tend to be suspicious of someone
who wants power, particularly if he expresses this desire
openly, rather than concealing it behind some guise, such
as doing good or helping others.[29]
     However, in different ethnic groups and classes, the
expression of aggression and power is more or less encouraged.
For example, lower class blacks value the image of being
tough, cool, and powerful; while Japanese Americans encourage gentleness, docility, and pursuing high achievement.
     These class and ethnic differences are relevant in
understanding magical groups like the Hutians, since members generally come from the white middle class, where
ambivalent feelings towards power are common. But the Hutians and other magicians have cast this ambivalence aside.
It is as if they have reversed the middle class dilemma of
wanting power yet trying to conceal its pursuit by being
forthright in their desire for it, while cutting loose from
the usual middle class commitment to achievement and success.

2. Social-Structural Conditions

     Social conditions within a society also influence the
extent to which its members seek power through magic. Three
major factors contribute: social scale, economic problems,
and the stresses due to social change.
     The large social scale in modern society has a major
impact, since it makes people feel small, helpless, and
insignificant. While a successful career or warm loving
family may protect some against feelings of powerlessness,
others may experience them intensely, and compensate by seeking a group which helps them feel they have power. While
some may seek this through political power, others find it
in magic. In both cases, devaluing others may add to the

feeling of power.

Viola Bernard, Perry Ottenberg, and Fritz Redl observed this process in studying what attracts people towards political demagoguery. As they found, the more inwardly frightened, lonely, and helpless people became, the more susceptible they were to the promises of demagoguery and the more they sought superiority and privilege by devaluing the full humanness of some other group.[30] The same dynamic appears to attract individuals to magical groups.

Hard times, whether resulting from war or failing economic conditions, also cause an upsurge in the desire for personal power, since under these conditions people feel threatened and fear for their survival. Thus, they tend to become more aggressive and more interested in having their own power or turning to someone else with power for protection. Politically, this tendency is reflected in the swing to the right and greater receptivity to stronger leadership in even liberal countries.[31] For instance, in Germany, the depression made people more responsive to Hitler's message of hate, and in the 1980's, as economic conditions have worsened, bigotry and hatred have increased in America, as reflected in the growth of groups like the Ku Klux Klan. Also, during difficult times, religious and magical cults tend to proliferate, some with apocalyptic visions, as people seek out alternate sources of power. Significantly, the Hutians and the C of E got their start in the mid-1970's, a period of diminishing economic resources; and the Hutians believe the world is heading into a period of crisis and annihilation.

Rapid social change also can contribute to a greater concern with personal power, because any change produces insecurity and social stress. Old institutions which once provided a grounding become modified or swept away, and when social change occurs during a time of economic difficulty, even more insecurity is produced. In response, to replace lost moorings, the individual looks for new sources of comfort, protection, and power—often in a religious or magical group.

In Nazi Germany, for example, the masses sought to escape the stresses of social change and economic turmoil by submitting to Hitler's protective leadership and authority. Then, when he trumpeted his fantasies of power and glory, the masses embraced these images, too.[32]

Similar dynamics occur among the Hutians and some other

magical groups. Much like Hitler offered the masses glorious
visions, Hutians offer members the promise of developing
unlimited personal power and becoming totally free. But to
obtain this desired vision and secure protection from outsiders and the coming annihilation, members must submit to a
small group at the top who make the rules.

The Search for Power in Response to
Frustration and Deprivation

While the power drive concept can explain why everyone
wants power, and while social and cultural factors can explain why individuals are more attracted to power under
certain conditions, these ideas do not explain why certain
individuals are more drawn to power than others. For this,
psychological concepts are necessary, and particularly those
dealing with frustration and deprivation. As psychologists
have discovered, individuals experiencing some sort of
frustration or deprivation tend to be more attracted than
others to seeking power and expressing aggression to compensate for their dissatisfaction or loss of esteem. I will
discuss each of these two pushes to power in turn.

1. The Role of Frustration

The idea that frustration leads to the expression of
aggression was first developed by John Dollard and then expanded upon by others. Dollard contended that a person will
experience frustration when blocked from achieving a desired
goal, and that this frustration will cause him inner tension,
which will lead him to express aggression to release the
tension. Accordingly, the more frequently or the more
strongly he experiences this blocking, the more frustrated
he will feel, and the more apt he will be to express aggression. However, the threat of punishment might inhibit him
from expressing it. Dollard also suggested that minor frustrations could combine together to produce an even greater
frustration, and hence an even more aggressive response. [33]
Once the individual experiences frustration, Dollard
argued, he will want to direct his aggression against the
responsible party. But, if he cannot do so directly, because
he fears punishment or for other reasons, he will deflect his
aggression onto another object or express it in modified
form, so his act is more socially acceptable or he is less

likely to be detected or punished. Presumably, the more
inhibited he feels in expressing aggression, the more likely
he will express it in less direct ways. At the same time,
this inhibition can contribute to the frustration he feels,
which can up his level of pent-up aggression. Then, when
his aggression is finally expressed in whatever way, he
experiences a catharsis.[34]

Leonard Berkowitz and others have argued this theory by
suggesting that frustration does not always lead to aggression and that aggressive behavior may occur without frustration, since learning affects whether the frustration reaction
is expressed or inhibited, as reflected in attitudes to the
expression of aggression in different cultures or groups.[35]
Yet, if one looks at why members join magical groups and how
they act as members, the frustration-aggression hypothesis
frequently applies. Over and over again at meetings, I
heard Hutians describe their everyday frustrations, which
led them to want power—such as problems with jobs and relationships. Then, once they joined the group, they often
used the practices they learned to counter these problems or
vent their frustration and anger. These practices in turn
provided them with a socially channelled form to express
these feelings. For the Hutian the advantage of this
approach is that he might hesitate to directly confront the
individual he feels wronged him because of repercussions.
But he can direct his anger and power against the wrongdoer
and "destroy" him through magical or symbolic acts.

2.   The Role of Deprivation and
the Loss of Self-Esteem

Individuals may also be drawn to seek power and express
aggression because they feel deprived or experience low self-
esteem and want to compensate for these feelings by obtaining
power. In a general statement of the dynamics involved,
Harold Lasswell suggests a person will feel deprived if he
lacks an important source of satisfaction, fears losing some
satisfaction, or encounters obstacles to gaining it.[36]

According to Lasswell, these satisfactions come from
eight major sources of experiencing power:
  • Acquiring power since one is already in a position of
    power, such as being born to a privileged status.
  • Receiving a great deal of respect, due to occupying
    a desirable social position.
  • Having or attaining wealth.

- Receiving affection and having the qualities needed
  to gain affection, such as a pleasing personality
  or being sexually attractive.
- Having a good reputation for honesty, reliability,
  or other favorable characteristic.
- Having knowledge in some area.
- Being very proficient in some skill.
- Having powerful physical characteristics, such as a
  large stature, high energy, good coordination, or
  other attributes of general well-being.

If the individual does not obtain satisfaction in one
or more of these ways, he feels deprived, which threatens
his sense of self-worth. But by seeking power through religion, magic, or other means, he hopes to overcome these
feelings of deprivation.

There are a number of reasons why a person may feel
unsatisfied and deprived. He may be in a marginal or low-
respect position. He may feel he lacks sufficient prestige.
He may have had career set-backs. He may have physical
limitations. He may have problems in his relationships and
experience a lack of love. He may have experienced an early
rejection from unloving parents. He may feel insufficient
acceptance and recognition. Or, for numerous other reasons,
he may feel inferior, humiliated, hopeless, or a failure.

Then, whatever the reason, he will typically seek ways
to counteract his feelings of low esteem by denying his
feelings, being hostile to others, seeking power over them,
or trying to prove himself to restore his sense of worth.

As Leon Saul summarizes it, a common route to hostility
and an excessive concern with power looks like this:

The child's emotional development is harmed.

His personality is crippled or impaired.

Conscious or unconscious feelings of inferiority develop.

The individual feels a sense of insecurity, anxiety, or
internal irritation.

The individual reacts against these feelings through
compensating by being overly egotistical, asserting power,
or expressing hostility or rage. [38]

When the Hutians and members of other magical groups
are considered in light of Lasswell's list of sources of
power, it becomes apparent that they lack power in a number
of ways. In general, they were not born to a position of
power, nor do they currently occupy a high status position
or have much wealth. Most are simply middle class. Many
also have trouble gaining affection for various reasons,
such as having an abrasive personality or not being attractive physically. And so on down the list. Not all Hutians
or other magicians have each of these lacks. But generally
they lack power in key areas. As noted, the Hutians regularly talked about subjects suggesting low self-esteem, such
as having problems getting good jobs, making enough money,
or feeling themselves different or weird. Seeking religious
or magical power, in turn, helps compensate for such lacks.

In analyzing this issue of deprivation and power in more
depth, Gregory Rochlin suggests that aggression represents a
response to the human need for self-love. Normally the self
strives to see a rewarding self-image by gaining social
support and reassurance from others, obtaining mastery over
the environment, and directing the natural will to power to
expand and improve himself. So Rochlin believes a person
can express the drive for power in a mature way by directing
it towards technological, productive, or artistic achievement, fulfilling social and community values, or protecting
himself against danger. [39]

But under certain conditions, the individual can become
overconcerned with the self and gaining power: when he
experiences some deprivation, such as losing someone he
loves, not receiving sufficient care and affection as a
child, or not obtaining the needed praise or feelings of
self-worth. These losses, according to Rochlin, injure the
self and lead to feelings of damaged worth and low esteem.
Then, to compensate, the individual turns to himself and
becomes less concerned with others. Or he feels hostile
towards those causing the injury or deflects this hostility
onto others or himself. Presumably, the greater the injury,
the more aggressive he becomes and the harder it is for him
to socially adapt.

Regardless of the source of this injury, once he has
these feelings of low esteem, the individual can express his
will to power in a variety of ways, acting alone or as the
leader or member of a group. As one strategy, he can try to
get rid of his feelings of inferiority by attributing them
to others, particularly to those in a lower socio-economic

status or in a minority group; then he can blame a scapegoat
instead of himself.[40]   He can try to compensate by seeking
power through muscular prowess, sexual potency, asserting
physical control over others, or demanding obedience. He can
act out against others in antisocial or violent ways. Or if
he conforms to the law, he can express his hostility to
others through subtle means, such as putting others down.

Then, too, he can deflect aggressive impulses he cannot
otherwise express through the use of fantasy and imagination;
say by imagining a hated person's death or performing a
ritual to destroy him. Similarly, he can retreat into himself and deny his social need, turn to infantile behavior,
or believe he can gain instant gratification just by wishing
it were so. Or more constructively, he can strive for new
goals which build up the self, like achieving competence in
some field.[41]

Yet in spite of these efforts to compensate and exhibit
outward signs of power, his underlying feelings of inferiority may still remain to some degree, especially since his
efforts to restore the self by focusing on it or expressing
aggression may lead to poor social relationships. Then,
these poor relationships lead to even lower self-esteem,
which results in more concern with the self and additional
efforts to compensate by gaining power.[42]   So the process of
power-seeking to compensate can become something of a never-
ending spiral.

The type of magical practices employed by the Hutians
and other magical groups might be viewed as a form of com-
pensatory behavior, too, in that the belief one can influence fate, transcend limitations, and summon superhuman
powers from within may represent another type of defense
against the loss of self-esteem. According to Rochlin,
children think they can do such things when they are
threatened in childhood, and among some adults, these infantile patterns of thinking continue, because the individual
hopes he can gain otherwise denied gratifications by merely
wishing or willing he can have them.[43]

The presumption underlying this analysis, of course, is
that magical thinking isn't valid. Yet believers and some
social scientists, notably symbolic anthropologists, would
argue that it is, for thinking this way changes the perceived
reality, and thereby produces an effect. This argument,
however, becomes a metaphysical problem, not easily resolved.
Yet whether this style of thinking does have this effect or
not, the fact that an individual turns to it may still be a

way of compensating for the deprivations discussed, since
magical thinking represents an alternate, and not fully
accepted, way of viewing the world.

Unfortunately, according to Rochlin and others, any
individual effort is doomed to failure, since a person can
only raise his esteem and keep it up through successful
relationships with others, since the attitudes and actions
of others are what determine social worth. Thus, retreats
into fantasy and personal efforts to achieve mastery won't
work by themselves, for the basic social need to gain esteem
through others still remains.

Unfortunately, the individual with lowered self-esteem
has difficulty resolving the problem, because his need to
compensate through seeking power and expressing aggression
continually get in the way. For example, to avoid self
blame, he may deny his hostility springs from within by
believing he is the victim of someone else's aggression; he
may want a close relationship, yet shies away because his
lowered self-esteem makes him suspicious of others; or he
may try to deny his need for a relationship by being hostile
to others, which only increases his feelings of low esteem.[44]

Thus, he becomes enmeshed in an inescapable spiral.
Alienated from others, he loses esteem and behaves to compensate for this loss. Then his behavior further alienates
him from others, which additionally reduces his esteem.
Though he may seek to conceal his feelings through an outward show of power, inwardly, he still feels these lacks,
since at base, a true feeling of self-esteem and inner power
is based on one's social connections with others.

Thus, as Rochlin proposes, the individual's only way to
increase his esteem is becoming involved in a group where he
can express his desires for power and aggression. Then,
through identifying with the group, he can overcome his feelings of being helpless, weak, and dependent, just like the
child feels power by identifying with his more powerful
parents. Alone, he is isolated; but in the group, he gains
the social support he needs to build his esteem. Then, when
he acts aggressively towards others with group support, he
gains relief from his feelings of oppression and experiences
an expanded sense of self.[45]

History provides numerous supports for this argument
that deprivation leads to lowered esteem and then to efforts
to compensate through seeking power or expressing aggression.
For example, students and the unemployed are frequently involved in political protest movements. And many noted people

who have actively sought power have been socially marginal,
had physical limitations, or suffered major disappointments.
As a case in point: Karl Marx could never get a Ph.D. at a
Prussian University; Adolph Hitler failed many times in his
early career; and Napoleon always felt slighted by his short
stature.[46]

Research studies indicate that deprivation leads to
aggression, too. For example, in a 20-year study of 900
children under four years old, Katherine Baham found they
were naturally affectionate but became hostile when rebuffed,
ignored, or neglected.[47]

The background of the Hutians shows this pattern of
deprivation, too. As described, many experienced serious
humiliation or other hurts from others. But in the group
they can symbolically express the hatreds they feel towards
those who have wronged them or towards humans as a whole.
Furthermore, by seeing others as inferior, they can claim
they are superior and thereby build up their esteem.

Summing Up

In summary, the experience of the Hutians in seeking
power supports the thinking of many psychologists about the
need for power and the reasons individuals seek it. As
illustrated, the Hutians strive for power in its various
forms—aggression, control, domination, and expressing
feelings of hostility and hatred. They seek power by looking to outside sources, making efforts to strengthen the
self, trying to have an impact on others, and to an extent
acting in behalf of a higher authority vested in the group.
In turn, they seek power for various reasons: because they
have experienced some sort of frustration or aggression;
because they have learned to want power from the larger
culture and the group; and because they have experienced a
number of social conditions which have contributed to a
growing interest in personal power generally—the increase
in social scale, serious economic problems, and various
forms of social stress.

13

The Expression of Power

Regardless of why individuals seek power through joining
groups like the Hutians, they express power and justify
using it in different ways. Employing power in turn has
major effects on the personality. This chapter explores
these issues.

The Expression of Power
Through the Group

When a person is attracted to power, the group can
become an important arena for expressing power, and it can
give him a rationale for using power as he does. Also, the
group gives the power-seeker a sense of identity and a new,
more powerful self-image. Outside the group he may wonder
about his worth. But as a member his new identity gives him
power.

This process of affirming identity in the group is
especially valuable for the individual who is insecure or
feels hostile to society, since, according to psychologist
Anthony Storr, hostility frequently respresents a reaction
to inner securities, and the more insecure we are, the more
we seek to affirm our own identity in a group. Then, as
part of a group, the individual can feel a closeness with
others and a sense of support and belonging. This is
particularly true of a group oriented around a religious
belief, since these beliefs touch the deepest human needs.[1]

The group also gives the power-motivated individual a
way to express inner feelings without normal inhibitions,
since the group offers social approval, and often other members will act with him. This approval and group participation in turn helps him feel better about expressing his drive

for power and aggression.[2] Moreover, when he is a member
of a group that isolates itself from outsiders, such as the
Hutians, this draws him away from others and makes him see
them as even more different from himself. So he feels even
freer to vent his hostility against them and thereby feels
more power.

They myths and symbols of the group also contribute
to the power-building process by making the group seem more
important or special, increasing its distance from others,
and making hostility to outsiders more acceptable through
group-developed justifications. For example, because of
their membership, members may believe they are chosen and
others correspondingly rejected, unclean, untouchable, or
otherwise undesirable. Such ideas help bind members together and to the group. Then if anything threatens, members
are even more ready to mobilize to protect the group and
through it their own identity and self-esteem.

The leader plays an important role in a power-oriented
group, too, since his image can contribute to members' feelings of power, in that people feel more powerful when exposed
to a powerful charismatic leader. Even though they may be
submissive to him, their identification with him gives them
a psychological lift, for they bask in the glow of his power
and are expanded by it. Also, the leader inspires their
confidence so they feel more motivated and better able to
accomplish shared goals.[3]

Some psychological research shows this. For example,
D. G. Winter found that students who saw a film on John
Kennedy, as president, expressed more power themes in the
stories they wrote after the film than those who saw a film
on modern architecture. He concluded that seeing the film
of a powerful leader made those students feel more powerful.[3]

Among Hutians the group provides numerous opportunities
for experiencing and expressing power. First, numerous
activities increase feelings of power and self-esteem: having secret knowledge, ascending a hierarchy, thinking oneself
as above and outside the natural order, believing oneself
part of an elect, viewing others as mere humans, and believing one can transform oneself through growth to outwit death,
become immortal, and attain perfect freedom. Secondly, the
Hutian gains social approval for who he is and his behavior.
Thirdly, within the group, he can release his inhibitions,
express his will to power, and direct his hostility towards

outsiders in various ways: performing group rituals paro-
dying established religion, or shocking others by doing
something sacrilegious, such as confronting a fervent Christian with a Satanic Bible. In addition, Hutians can express
their hostility towards a rejecting world by believing the
whole world is about to be destroyed, and pointing to world
turmoil as a sign of the coming apocalypse. According to
Storr, this kind of transformation of real problems into
massive disasters occurs when feelings of hatred and paranoia
become particularly intense.[4]

Finally, the power of the High Priest increases the
power group members feel. He derives much of his power from
the members' belief that he is better able to communicate
with and manifest Hu through his being. Also, when members
honor him with salutes and hails, he appears that much more
powerful. His power, in turn, reflects back on the group.

However, by providing an arena where the member can
express power, the group is subject to certain dangers, for
once group members feel free to release their feelings of
hostility and aggression and seek power, these feelings may
not be easily contained. Instead, once released, they may
spill out on other members of the group, particularly when
one member does something to arouse another's anger or make
him fear his esteem is being attacked. Similarly, the
suspiciousness of outsiders breeds a climate of distrust
which can swing back on the group. And the belief that the
outside world is inferior and about to be destroyed adds to
the climate of suspicion and paranoia.

Among the Hutians, this swing-back pattern is reflected
in the highly critical attitude members have towards each
other, and in their propensity to cast others out who have
difficulty adjusting to group guidelines or managing the
split between the magical and mundane worlds.

Justifying the Expression of Power

Although power-seekers may see the expression of power
as its own justification or feel it sufficient that expressing power satisfies their own needs, often they seek some
broader justification. For example, when group members
direct feelings of hostility and aggression outside the group,
they may justify doing so by seeing the victim as somehow
evil, inferior, or in the wrong, or find other reasons for
exercising power.

This justification becomes necessary because the blatant
pursuit of power to serve the self, even in response to deep
psychological needs, can create value conflicts for the individual. This may occur since the group's way of expressing
power may conflict with other values he has learned and may
still espouse, particularly when he first joins the group.
Or he may find the group's power-oriented values, as much as
they appeal to him, are in opposition to the values of the
larger society, which are based on the ideals of equality
and fair-dealing.

In response, he may seek to employ strategies which reinforce group values and defend him against alternate ideas.
These strategies may involve a number of psychological
mechanisms: rationalizing ulterior motives; disowning guilt
feelings by projecting them; identifying with the symbols
and values of the group; limiting social contacts to the
group; avoiding people, places, and activities in conflict
with group values; confining oneself to selected sources of
information which reinforces group ideas; following group
rules; and keeping too busy to think about troubling issues.
G. M. Gilbert calls these avoidance-suppression strategies,
and observes that a person can use these on his own or the
group may adopt them in requiring members to behave in a way
that maintains their loyalty to the group.[5]

One of the most compelling strategies is seeing the
outsider as an inferior or dehumanizing him and then rejecting him or expressing aggression against him for this reason.
This strategy has a long history, since humans have long
been cruel to small minority groups, and the aggressor or
conqueror has typically viewed his actions to exploit, de-
mean, or scapegoat the conquered as fully just on the basis
that the other group is inferior, different, less human, has
wronged his side, or because the prevailing god or gods "are
on our side." These racial, religious, and social justifications are common for, according to Samuel Tenenbaum, the
individual must explain his inhumanity to others to himself
because he has a conscience.

On the other hand, a person can feel free to maltreat
or destroy others without his conscience or feelings of
brotherhood restraining him if he views them as subhumans,
bad humans, or non-humans. He gains this freedom because in
dehumanizing others he stops identifying with them, distances
himself from them emotionally, blocks out their basic human
qualities, ceases to have concern for them, and feels less
personally responsible for the consequences of his acts,

since his feelings of guilt, shame, or horror diminish or
disappear.[7]

According to psychologists Viola Bernard, Perry
Ottenberg, and Fritz Redl, people use a variety of defense
mechanisms to dehumanize, including unconscious denial, repression, depersonalization, isolation of affect, and com-
partmentalization. Or, expressed in non-psychological terms,
they deny others are like themselves, repress their feelings
of empathy, see outsiders as abstract entities or non-humans,
eliminate their emotions, and partition themselves mentally,
so that they can engage in action towards outsiders they
would consider wrong if directed towards members of their
own group. In turn, modern social conditions facilitate
using this strategy, since daily life is characterized by
anonymity, impersonality, and the fragmentation of social
roles, which encourage the individual to become emotionally
detached.[8]

However, while dehuminization may be an effective way
to gain the freedom to attack others, the strategy can have
negative personal consequences since a person impoverishes
himself by reducing his ability to identify, feel, and love
generally. Also, he becomes less able to relate to others,
since dehumanizing others diminishes his own sense of humanity and thus makes him a less "human" being.[9]

Another negative consequence is that this attitude
towards the out-group can spill over into in-group relationships, so they become less satisfying, too. Furthermore, as
a person becomes more and more alienated from mass society
by dehumanizing others, he may find it more and more difficult to see himself as an individual apart from the group.[10]

Seeing outsiders as aggressive or evil is another type
of justification, which may accompany dehumanization or be
used alone. In this approach, the individual claims others
are dangerous or about to perform some evil or aggressive
act, so he can justify taking some action against them or
even destroying them. According to sociologist Neil Smelser,
the individual who believes in outside evil typically believes in his own omnipotence and moral superiority as well,
which makes it even easier for him to wreak destruction on
others. After all, he is morally justified and all-power-
ful.[11] The history books are full of such crusaders—
Christians, Moslems, Nazis, and others—who have gone after
forces of "evil" to advance their own cause.

Finally, group members may justify their aggression on
the grounds they are acting in concert with others in the

group, are responding to their leader's command, or have the
permission of their peers. They feel free to act because
they have given up their sense of responsibility and conscience to the group. Fritz Redl suggests this sense of
giving up or release occurs because the individual merges
his own ego with the collective ego when he puts on a group
uniform or participates in a group ritual or activity. Then
he feels free to act because he has merged his self into a
group where his behavior is acceptable, or where he has a
license to act a certain way for a limited time. As a result, behavior that might otherwise cause him guilt feelings
becomes suddenly "okay."[12]

For example, where a person may resist killing someone
when acting alone, when he puts on a uniform and goes to war,
he now feels it permissible to kill; he may even consider it
a duty. But even though he gains group permission to act
against outsiders, he still may not harm members of the
group. For doing so would chip away at his own identity and
attack his own source of power which flows from the group.

Hutians employ all of these justifications. For example, they use many, if not all, of the avoidance suppression
strategies: they stick very much to themselves to avoid
outside challenges to their values; they dehumanize others
by classifying them as mere humans; and they accuse outsiders of wrongdoing, such as making the world a mess. At
the same time, they regard their actions as righteous, since
as an elect, they can become of the gods and transcend human
limitations and feelings. Finally, they gain emotional support by performing rituals with others, and they agree that
members may not attack others in ritual. Destruction is
justified for outsiders alone.

The Relationship Between
Personality and Power

Regardless of how the member of a power-oriented group
expresses power or justifies its use, he tends to have certain personality characteristics, partly because individuals
with certain traits or needs are attracted to the group, and
partly because being in the group shapes his personality.
As in any group, the personality traits of members come to
reflect group cultural values. Those who fit those values
tend to stay; those that don't, drop out.

Since the Hutians are a power-oriented group, members

tend to have the personal qualities associated with high
power motivation, such as an aggressive or authoritarian
style of relating to others and a concern with the self.
They also tend to develop a paranoid outlook. Psychologists have characterized these styles of relating as personality types and have written extensively about the traits
associated with each type. The following section describes
the traits associated with these types and considers how well
the Hutians seem to fit these models, based on my impressions
of their character.

The Authoritarian Personality

The characteristics of the authoritarian personality
were first outlined by T. W. Adorno in The Authoritarian
Personality, and subsequently researched by other psychologists. From these studies, Adorno and the others found that
individuals scoring high on the F Scale (for fascism) shared
a number of traits which formed a distinct personality com-
plex and were correlated with a high level of prejudice.
They called this the "fascistic" or "authoritarian personality," and identified nine major traits:
- a rigid adherence to conventional middle class
  values;
- a submissive, uncritical attitude towards moral
  authorities in the in-group;
- a readiness to condemn and punish the slightest
  violation of conventional values;
- an opposition to the subjective, imaginative, or
  soft-minded;
- a belief in the mystical determination of the individual's fate;
- a tendency to think in rigid categories and an
  inability or unwillingness to deal with the indefi-
  nite, ambiguous, or probable;
- a preoccupation with dominance and submission and
  with strength and weakness in human relationships;
  an identification with power figures, and an exag-
  gerated expression of strength and toughness;
- a cynicism about human nature, combined with a
  generalized hostility toward human beings;
- a disposition to ascribe evil motives to people, and
  to believe that evil or dangerous things go on in
  the world; a tendency to project unconscious emotional
  impulses onto others. [13]

Many researchers also found a close relationship between authoritarianism and high scores on ethnocentrism, rigidity, misanthropy, dogmatism, and restrictive attitudes towards using alcohol. Some found that people high in authoritarianism tend to exhibit power-related characteristics in certain social roles. For example, mothers tend to be dominant and possessive; teachers autocratic and totalitarian.[14]

Nevitt Sanford observed a relationship between authoritarianism and social destructiveness, too. When he studied the social attitudes of over 2500 Americans of varied backgrounds, he noticed that authoritarian individuals tend to be highly prejudiced and that the prejudiced person tends to divide all people into homogeneous groups or classes, infer what a person is like from his memberships, and arrange all groups into hierarchies ranging from the strong on top to the weak on the bottom. Also, he tends to generalize his prejudice, so he is not only hostile towards specific racial and ethnic groups, but towards any group—social, economic, national, religious, or ideological—which he sees as different, and hence inferior, to his own. Conversely, he tends to be biased toward seeing his own group in a favorable light.[15]

According to Sanford and other psychologists, a major reason the individual responds this way is to overcome a sense of inner weakness. He sees weakness as contemptible, cannot admit he is weak, will not tolerate it in others, and therefore presents himself as a strong, tough-minded person and claims to be superior. When he perceives weakness in others, this reminds him of his own; so he lashes out against his victim or projects onto him the inner weakness he cannot admit in himself.[16]

In most respects, the Hutians appear to have these characteristics. Although they do not adhere to all conventional middle class values and do not condemn people for violating them, they rigidly uphold their own set of values, centered around the image of being a disciplined, controlled, powerful, and outwardly conforming person, and in other respects appear to possess characteristic authoritarian traits. Most notably, they are concerned with dominance and submission and strength and weakness, are cynical about human nature, tend to see evil in others and in the world, and believe in submitting to higher-ups in the group. Moreover, they are highly ethnocentric in that they perceive themselves as a superior elite, often put down others, and reject the liberal philosophy of helping the weak and needy,

since they see them as a lesser breed of humans who deserve
no help.

The Aggressive Personality

The characteristics of the aggressive personality are
also common among the Hutians. After reviewing the research
on this personality type, Roger Johnson suggests there are
two kinds: the inwardly aggressive, normally overcontrolled
person, who usually keeps his feelings of aggression in
check and inhibits his behavior; and the brusque, argumenta-
tive, sometimes abrasive person, who lets his feelings out.
Typically, the first type is very guarded in his behavior
and holds back in expressing the softer emotions. When
matters go smoothly, he can be outwardly very gracious and
cheerful, but when things go against him, he tends to have
a low frustration tolerance and can readily be provoked to
retaliate. By contrast, the second type is often sharp and
snappish when he talks with others and is quick to arouse.[17]
Among the Hutians, I observed both types. I saw the
most dramatic example of the first just before I was uncere-
moniously asked to leave. Outwardly, people were extremely
polite and friendly and gave no clue to their real feelings.
But then, without warning, the hostility they quietly re-
strained suddenly erupted when they announced they were
kicking me out. Also, I observed them keep their emotions in
check in many other instances, despite serious difficulties
(such as the loss of a job or death of a friend). Then when
they released those emotions in response to mounting frustrations, they did so in a highly controlled way, such as
through a ritual. I also found many Hutians who fit the
brusque, abrasive portrait and were almost military-like in
bearing.
The aggressive personality also has some of the traits
of the person with an "active-independent" behavior pattern,
according to Johnson, which includes seeing oneself as
assertive, energetic, self-reliant, strong, honest, and
realistic. Hutians try to present themselves as such, and
they work on developing this active-independent way of
being.[18]

The Egocentric Personality

Psychologists have also found a high concern with self-

interest among those seeking personal power. According to
Harold Lasswell, the highly self-concerned person or "ego-
centric personality" type is entirely absorbed with advancing
his own interests and is willing to sacrifice anyone and
everyone to increase his own power. However, he is not
particularly concerned with using power to advance the
interests of his family, neighborhood, nation, or other
group, unless he gains his identity from that group.[19]

Outwardly such self-interested types may be deceiving,
since they may be able to fake affectionate warmth at one
moment and turn off at another, as it suits their ends.
Likewise, they can engage in destructive conduct calmly,
showing no pity for those they hurt.

Again, the Hutians seem to fit this model, and the
group encourages this kind of behavior, since they believe
self-growth is the key to becoming of the gods and transcending human limitations. Thus, they urge each member to
promote his own self-interest through better understanding
himself and developing his will.

The Problem of Paranoia

The problem with seeking power through being aggressive,
dominant, and building up the self while being hostile to
others, is the individual can develop a paranoid outlook,
since this power-seeking orientation tends to make him dis-
trustful of outsiders or anything which threatens his will
to power. At the same time, he must have reasons to justify
his hostility to others. Thus, he readily sees sinister or
ulterior motives in everyday behavior and relates to others
with suspicion and reserve. For example, he may believe an
innocent smile masks someone's inner dislike, think a passing
remark is an innuendo, or see a normal interaction as devious.
So his world may become "a giant conspiracy" where everyone
is potentially conniving and plotting, just as he may himself
to counter the threats he imagines "out there."[20]

A key disadvantage of having this outlook is it tends
to provide its own confirmation, which further intensifies
the paranoia. This occurs because this view tends to narrow
down the individual's thoughts, feelings, and imagination,
so he comes to see the world as a place of hostile sinister
forces and potentially harmful individuals. Since he believes these forces and people exist, they do. Unfortunately,
as the individual's view narrows, his imagination increasingly

exaggerates and distorts what he experiences to further con-
vince him the world is sinister and hostile, thereby justifying his suspicions. Thus, he continues to suspect and
hate, for everyone outside his group—and perhaps even some
within it—may be a potential source of danger. Even if he
considers outsiders inferior, he believes there is always
the chance they may organize and turn against him, and he
fears members of his group may turn out to be false, too.
So he must always be on his guard.

Many Hutians have this outlook, which is stimulated by
the group itself. For example, discussions and newsletter
articles continually gear up the Hutian's hatred towards
outsiders by describing them as pitiful, mediocre creatures
who are wreaking destruction on the planet and deserve to be
destroyed. But, even as they attack these inferior beings,
Hutians fear they may retaliate back if the group has too
high a profile. Additionally, they become suspicious when
members stray too far from the group line.

The Implications of the Hutian's
Search for Power

In conclusion, the Hutian's search for power arises out
of a variety of sources, and is expressed through a group
ideology and activities which attract and mold a certain
type of individual, as in power-oriented groups generally.
To a degree, the Hutian's search for power reflects a general
social striving for power, expressed through aggression,
dominance over others, and efforts to attain status and
prestige. However, more than typical, the Hutians and other
magical groups are oriented around power in response to
deeper needs which draw certain types of people to the group
and shape them in the group image. Such individuals appear
to have more than an average need for power for various
reasons, including thwarted needs for love, feelings of inferiority, and personal frustrations.

By participating in the group, the Hutian, like members
of similar groups, may find many needs fulfilled, and he
may be pleased he is one of an elite and is developing a
personal style characterized by self-reliance, toughness,
and strength. However, in the process, he may develop other
traits which have negative consequences for himself and his
relationships—such as a pervasive attitude of hostility,
suspiciousness, and criticalness to others. Moreover, his

extreme focus on self may slip from self-improvement into
selfishness, isolation, and alienation—a development which
has its dangers. Ironically, the Hutians focus on the self
to strengthen the will because they believe the outside
world is a place of mediocrity doomed to destruction. But
this selfishness contributes to this destruction process,
for as Ashley Montagu warns:

> When for any reason the members of a society
> become concerned exclusively with their own selfish
> interests, so alienated from the rest of the group
> that they lose all sense of involvement in them,
> and live entirely for themselves, such a society
> is doomed to extinction.[21]

To be sure, the Hutians and other magical groups focusing on self-development are small. But they highlight a
larger social problem—the proliferation of groups and individuals bent on their own self-interest. No society can
exist this way. Ultimately, when the sense of community
breaks down, people grow suspicious of others. They see
others as potentially exploitable outsiders, and cut off
their feelings and needs for love.

Thus, groups like the Hutians represent a potentially
growing threat to society. They are a response to social
problems, but they exacerbate these problems by adding to
the growing climate of hatred and fear. Although individuals
may find personal solutions to their difficulties in these
groups, ultimately these solutions will not be satisfactory,
since they do not address the problems of society as a whole.

Moreover, the mind-transforming processes employed in
the groups can trap members into a belief system they cannot
easily escape. They believe in the magical teachings; they
have taken on a new magical persona; they think they have
grown spiritually; and are convinced they are part of an
elect. So to them survival and salvation lie within the
group, and these ideas bind them to it and its antisocial
message.

Currently, these groups represent a small enclave for
individuals who see themselves as outsiders in society and
gain a feeling of belonging and personal empowerment in the
group. But should such groups grow larger, they could pose
a major threat, for they represent a model of intolerance,
hate, and fear oriented around self-love and a dislike of
outsiders.

No society can exist for long with this kind of model,
since the members of a power-oriented group can readily

become hostile to one another as well as to others, so
hostility can run rampant. This can happen because once the
expression of hostility, aggression, and status striving is
freed from the usual social inhibitions, individuals feel
freer to express all of their anti-social power-related needs
in a general explosion of hate—towards outsiders, other
group members, even themselves. Thus, the intensive search
for power to aggrandize the self contains the seeds of its
own destruction. Ultimately, hate will consume itself. But
in the meantime, the group can present many dangers to both
its own members and outsiders, as this study of the Hutians
shows.

APPENDIX

Notes

Introduction

1. The growing interest in magic is reflected by a number of indicators—the continued growth of the Pagan movement since the mid-1960's, now estimated at about 40,000 members by J. Gordon Melton, Director of the Institute for the Study of American Religion; the publication of new books on this topic directed to believers; the popularity of spiritual programs, like the *Course in Miracles;* and the proliferation of groups designed to develop the will, such as groups oriented around the teachings of Gurdjieff. Also, this growing interest is reflected in the introduction of courses in astrology, mysticism, and magic in several dozen established colleges, and the recent efforts of scientists to combat what they perceive as a growth of irrational modes of thinking by forming the Committee for the Scientific Investigation of Claims of the Paranormal and a few other small ad hoc groups, such as a group to study psychics, founded by Marcello Truzzi.

2. Rosinski, 1965, 9-11.

3. The distinction between magic and religion has long been debated by social scientists and theologians, and there is still some dispute about the differences, since the terms refer to closely related behaviors or beliefs. However, at the risk of oversimplification, the basic difference is that magic refers to the manipulation of spiritual power for goal-directed purposes; while religion refers to the expression of spiritual feelings, the worship of higher beings, the use of prayer and supplication to gain help from these

beings, and the participation in expressive rituals to
appeal to these beings or experience belongingness with
other believers. However, in any given religious or magical
system, it is often difficult to distinguish between these
two elements, since religious ceremonies can incorporate
elements of magical manipulation, while magical rites can
have a communal and social function. The differences between magic and religion have generated much quibbling
among social scientists, but after much debate, modern
writers have recognized that the two ideas are difficult to
separate in practice and often refer to religion and magic
as two poles of a continuum of belief or talk about magico-
religious systems (Comstock, 1972, 53-54).

    4. O'Dea, 1966, 5.

    5. Fallding, 1973, 83, 211.

Chapter 1: Magic and Religion as a
Source of Power in Primitive
and Modern Society

    1. Some of the authors who have studied magic from
this perspective include Douglas (1966, 1973, 1975), Geertz
(1966), Levi-Strauss (1967, 1978), Peacock (1968, 1975,
1980), Tambiah (1970), and Turner (1967, 1968, 1969, 1975,
1978).

    2. Frazer, 1958, 56.

    3. Norbeck, 1961, 33.

    4. Phenomenologically-oriented anthropologists and
sociologists may take a different view of magical belief,
since they focus on the way having such beliefs changes the
actor's view of reality, and they make no judgment of the
validity of this view. In fact, some accept this new
reality as true. On the other hand, empirically-oriented
social scientists tend to be appalled by magical beliefs.
An example of this concern is reflected in the creation of
the Committee for the Scientific Investigation of Claims of
the Paranormal, which publishes the *Skeptical Inquirer* and
the publication of the *Zetetic Scholar*. Through these publications, several dozen social scientists and other types
of scientists have been involved investigating, and so far
mostly discrediting, false claims that magical thinking and
willing works.

    5. Devos, 1981. Personal communication.

    6. Durkheim, 1965.

7. Frazer, 1958, 56.
8. O'Dea, 1966, 8.
9. Malinowski, 1954, 29-31.
10. Middleton, 1967, 3.
11. Comstock, 1972, 44.
12. O'Dea, 1966, 10.
13. Yinger, 1961, 46.
14. Johnstone, 1975, 23.
15. Gluckman, 1972, 6.
16. Durkheim, 1965.
17. Berger, 1967, 50-51.
18. Comstock, 1973, 45-47.
19. Freud, 1961, 45, 88.
20. Adler, 1970.
21. Glock, 1970, 24-32.
22. Norbeck, 1961, 49.
23. Levy-Bruhl, 1971, 17.
24. Malefijt, 1968, 147.
25. Eliade, 1967, 21.
26. Malefijt, 1968, 148.
27. Norbeck, 1974, 36.
28. Scott, 1980.
29. Scott, 1980.
30. Vernon, 1962, 63.
31. Norbeck, 1974, 77-79.
32. Malefijt, 1968, 25.
33. Norbeck, 1974, 46.
34. Eliade, 1974.
35. Norbeck, 1974, 45.
36. Norbeck, 1974, 68.
37. Middleton, 1967, 14-15.
38. Vernon, 1962, 68-69.
39. Vernon, 1962, 71-72.
40. Goode, 1951, 53.

Chapter 2: The Pervasiveness of
Magical Thinking

1. Burland, 1966, 10-11.
2. Childe, 1936, 115-116.
3. Contrell, 1956, 22-57.
4. Seligmann, 1974, 34-35.
5. Alleau, 1966, 77.
6. Seligmann, 1974, 145.

7.   Redgrove, 1973, 134.
8.   Wilson, 1973, 261.
9.   Woods, 1976, 21.
10. Woods, 1973, 159; Glock and Bellah, 1976, 341.
11. Woods, 1973, 10.
12. Peale, 1956, 55, 59.
13. Bristol & Sherman, 1954, 25, 39.
14. Schwartz, 1965, 55.
15. Manning, 1974, 21.
16. Murphy, 1971.
17. Ouspensky, 1973, 20-35, 54-55.
18. Wilson, 1971, 58-59.
19. King & Skinner, 1976, 14.
20. Conway, 1972, 96-101.
21. Conway, 1972, 102-103.
22. Cavendish, 1967, 150-155.
23. Gray, 1978, 196.
24. Adler, 1979, 19.
25. Rhine, 1962.
26. Mishlove, 1975, 161.
27. Moss, 1974, 43.
28. Mishlove, 1975, 112, 118.
29. Mishlove, 1975, 134.
30. Moss, 1974, 53.
31. Mishlove, 1975, 163.
32. Tart, 1975, 137.

Chapter 12: The Importance of
Personal Power

1.   McClelland, 1975, 7-8.
2.   McClelland, 1975, 9-11.
3.   McClelland, 1975, 13.
4.   McClelland, 1975, 15.
5.   McClelland, 1975, 17-19.
6.   McClelland, 1975, 20-21.
7.   McClelland, 1975, 23-24.
8.   McClelland, 1975, 16-21.
9.   McClelland, 1975, 258, 264.
10. McClelland, 1975, 263.
11. Lefcourt, 1976, 3.
12. Lefcourt, 1976, 4-6.
13. Lefcourt, 1976, 21-25.
14. Johnson, 1972, 53-57.

15. Sampson, 1966, 36–37, 41.
16. Sampson, 1966, 26–30.
17. Sampson, 1966, 30–31.
18. Storr, 1968, 5, 9, 21.
19. Storr, 1968, 47.
20. Sampson, 1966, 179.
21. Montagu, 1976, 40, 46.
22. Bandura & Walters, 1970, 30.
23. Montagu, 1976, 294–295.
24. Walters, 1970, 126–127.
25. Berkowitz, 1968, 8–9.
26. Gilbert, 1950, 270–271.
27. Montagu, 1976, 317.
28. McClelland, 1975, 255.
29. McClelland, 1975, 255–256.
30. Bernard, Ottenberg, Fredl, 1971, 116.
31. Storr, 1968, 31.
32. Gilbert, 1950, 267–270.
33. Dollard, 1939, 26, 37.
34. Dollard, 1939, 30, 53.
35. Berkowitz, 1969, 2; Bandura & Walters, 1970, 36–37.
36. Lasswell, 1948, 39–40.
37. Lasswell, 1948, 27–30.
38. Saul, 1956, 33–44.
39. Rochlin, 1973, 5; 19–20.
40. Saul, 1956, 55.
41. Rochlin, 1973, 34–35; 92.
42. Rochlin, 1973, 84.
43. Rochlin, 1973, 93.
44. Rochlin, 1973, 119.
45. Rochlin, 1973, 252–255.
46. Lasswell, 1948, 50–52.
47. Montagu, 1976, 99.

Chapter 13:   The Expression of Power

1. Storr, 1968, 60–61.
2. Rochlin, 1973, 258.
3. McClelland, 1975, 259.
4. Storr, 1968, 110.
5. Gilbert, 1950, 275–277.
6. Tenenbaum, 1947, 13–20.
7. Bernard, Ottenberg, Redl, 1971, 102, 112–121.
8. Bernard, Ottenberg, Redl, 1971, 103–104.

 9. Bernard, Ottenberg, Redl, 1971, 104.
10. Redl, 1971, 14-15.
11. Smelser, 1971, 17-19.
12. Redl, 1971, 95.
13. Gelbmann, 1958, 48.
14. Sanford, 1971, 142.
15. Sanford, 1971, 140-141.
16. Sanford, 1971, 144.
17. Johnson, 1972, 127.
18. Johnson, 1972, 127.
19. Lasswell, 1948, 56.
20. Tenenbaum, 1947, 147-149.
21. Montagu, 1976, 307.

BIBLIOGRAPHY

Adler, Alfred
1970   *Superiority and Social Interest: A Collection of
         Later Writings.* Evanston, Illinois: Northwestern
         University Press.

Adler, Margot
1979   *Drawing Down the Moon.* New York: The Viking Press.

Alleau, Rene
1966   *History of Occult Sciences.* London: Leisure Arts,
         Ltd.

Bandura, Albert and Walters, Richard H.
1970   "Reinforcement Patterns and Social Behavior:
         Aggression," in Edwin I. Megargee and Jack E.
         Hokanson (eds.), *The Dynamics of Aggression.*
         New York: Harper & Row.

Berger, Peter L.
1967   *The Sacred Canopy.* Garden City, New York: Double-
         day & Company.

Berkowitz, Leonard.
1969   *Roots of Aggression.* New York: Atherton Press.

Bernard, Viola W.; Ottenberg, Perry; and Redl, Fritz.
1971   "Dehumanization," in Nevitt Sanford and Craig
         Comstock (eds.) *Sanctions for Evil.* San Francisco:
         Jossey-Bass.

Bharati, Agehananda.
1976   *The Realm of the Extra-Human.*   The Hague: Mouton
          Publishers.

Bonewits, P.E.I.
1979   *Real Magic.*   Berkeley, California: Creative Arts
          Book Company.

Bourguignon, Erika.
1973   *Religion, Altered States of Consciousness, and
          Social Change.*   Columbus, Ohio: Ohio State Univer-
          sity Press.

Bristol, Claude M. and Sherman, Harold.
1954   *TNT: The Power Within You.*   Englewood Cliffs, New
          Jersey: Prentice-Hall.

Burland, C. A.
1966   *The Magical Arts.*   London: Arthur Baker, Ltd.

Butler, E. M.
1971   *Ritual Magic.*   Hollywood: Newcastle Publishing
          Company.

Castenada, Carlos.
1971   *The Teachings of Don Juan: a Yaqui Way of Knowledge.*
          New York: Bantam Books.
1972   *Journey to Ixtlan: The Lessons of Don Juan.*   New
          York: Simon and Schuster.
1972   *A Separate Reality.*   New York: Pocket Books.

Cavendish, Richard.
1967   *The Black Arts.*   London: Pan Books.

Childe, Gordon
1936   *Man Makes Himself.*   London: Watts & Co.

Christopher, Milbourne.
1970   *ESP, Seers, and Psychics: What the Occult Really Is.*
          New York: Thomas Y. Crowell.

Comstock, W. Richard.
1972   *The Study of Religion and Primitive Religions.*   New
          York: Harper and Row.

Contrell, Leonard
1957   *The Anvil of Civilization.*   New York: The New
        American Library.

Conway, David.
1973   *Magic: An Occult Primer.*   New York: Bantam Books.

Crow, W. B.
1973   *A History of Magic, Witchcraft and Occultism.*
        London: Abacus Books.

DeVos, George.
1971   "Conflict, Dominance, and Exploitation," in Nevitt
        Sanford and Craig Comstock (eds.), *Sanctions for
        Evil.*   San Francisco: Jossey-Bass.
1981   Personal communication.

Dollard, John et al.
1970   "Frustration and Aggression," in Edwin I. Megargee
        and Jack E. Hokanson (eds.), *The Dynamics of
        Aggression.*   New York: Harper and Row.

Douglas, Mary.
1966   *Purity and Danger.*   London: Routledge & Kegan Paul.
1973   *Natural Symbols.*   New York: Vintage Books.
1973   *Rules and Meaning.*   Baltimore: Penguin Books.
1975   *Implicit Meanings.*   Boston: Routledge & Kegan Paul.

Drury, Nevill.
1978   *Don Juan, Mescalito, and Modern Magic.*   Boston:
        Routledge & Kegan Paul.

Durkheim, Emile.
1965   *The Elementary Forms of Religious Life.*   New York:
        Free Press.
1973   *On Morality and Society.*   Chicago: University of
        Chicago Press.

El Guindi, Fadwa.
1977   *Religion in Culture.*   Dubuque, Iowa: William C.
        Brown Company.

Eliade, Mircea.
1967   *Patterns in Comparative Religion.*   New York: Meri-
        dian Books.
1974   *Shamanism.*   Princeton: Princeton University Press.

Fallding, Harold.
1973   *The Sociology of Religion*.   New York: McGraw Hill.

Frazer, Sir James George.
1958   *The Golden Bough*.   New York: The Macmillan Company.

Freud, Sigmund.
1961   *The Future of an Illusion*.   New York: W.W. Norton &
        Company.

Gardner, Martin.
1957   *Fads and Fallacies in the Name of Science*.   New
        York: Dover Publications.

Gelbmann, Frederick John.
1958   *Authoritarianism and Temperament*.   Washington, D.C.:
        Catholic University of America Press.

Gilbert, G. M.
1950   *The Psychology of Dictatorship*.   New York: The
        Ronald Press Company

Glock, Charles Y.
1970   *The Role of Deprivation in the Origin and Evolution
        of Religious Groups*.   Berkeley, California: Survey
        Research Center, University of California.

Glock, Charles Y. and Bellah, Robert N.
1976   *The New Religious Consciousness*.   Berkeley, Califor-
        nia: University of California Press.

Gluckman, Max.
1972   *The Allocation of Responsibility*.   Manchester,
        England: Manchester University Press.

Goode, William J.
1951   *Religion Among the Primitives*.   New York: The Free
        Press.

Gray, William G.
1978   *Inner Traditions of Magic*.   New York: Samuel Weiser.

Halifax, Joan.
1979   *Shamanic Voices*.   New York: E. P. Dutton.

Hammel, Eugene A. and Simmons, William S.
1970   *Man Makes Sense*. Boston: Little, Brown and Company.

Hollander, E. P.
1962   *Leaders, Groups, and Influence*. New York: Oxford
         University Press.

Jahoda, Gustav.
1971   *The Psychology of Superstition*. Baltimore: Penguin
         Books.

James, William.
1929   *The Varieties of Religious Experience*. New York:
         The Modern Library.

Johnson, Roger N.
1972   *Aggression in Man and Animals*. Philadelphia: W. B.
         Saunders Company.

Johnstone, Ronald L.
1975   *Religion and Society in Interaction*. Englewood
         Cliffs, New Jersey: Prentice-Hall.

King, Francis and Skinner, Stephen.
1976   *Techniques of High Magic*. New York: Destiny Books.

Korda, Michael.
1976   *Power: How to Get It, How to Use It*. New York:
         Ballantine Books.

Lasswell, Harold Dwight.
1948   *Power and Personality*. New York: W. W. Norton and
         Company.

Lefcourt, Herbert M.
1976   *Locus of Control*. Hillsdale, New Jersey: Lawrence
         Erlbaum Associates.

Lessa, William A. and Vogt, Evon Z.
1972   *Reader in Comparative Religion*. New York: Harper &
         Row.

Levi-Strauss, Claude.
1967   *Structural Anthropology*. Garden City, New York:
         Anchor Books.
1978   *Myth and Meaning*. Toronto: University of Toronto
         Press.

214   BIBLIOGRAPHY

Levy-Bruhl, Lucien.
1971   *The "Soul" of the Primitive*. Chicago: Henry Regnery
        Company.

Lewis, I. M.
1978   *Ecstatic Religion*. New York: Penguin Books.

Malefijt, Annemarie de Waal.
1968   *Religion and Culture*. New York: The Macmillan
        Company.

Malinowski; Bronislaw.
1954   *Magic, Science and Religion*. Garden City, New York:
        Doubleday Anchor Books.

Manning, Al G.
1974   *The Miracle of Universal Psychic Power*. West Nyack,
        New York: Parker Publishing Company.

Maslow, Abraham H.
1970   *Religion, Values, and Peak-Experiences*. New York:
        The Viking Press.

McClelland, David C.
1975   *Power: The Inner Experience*. New York: Irvington
        Publishers.

Middleton, John.
1967   *Magic, Witchcraft, and Curing*. Garden City, New
        York: The Natural History Press.

Mishlove, Jeffrey.
1975   *The Roots of Consciousness*. New York: Random House.

Montagu, Ashley.
1976   *The Nature of Human Aggression*. New York: Oxford
        University Press.

Moss, Thelma.
1974.   *The Probability of the Impossible*. New York: The
        New American Library.

Murphy, Joseph
1971   *Psychic Perception: The Magic of Extrasensory Power*.
        West Nyack, New York: Parker Publishing Company.

Needleman, Jacob.
1974   *The New Religions*. New York: Pocket Books.

Norbeck, Edward.
1961   *Religion in Primitive Society*. New York: Harper and Brothers.
1974   *Religion in Human Life*. New York: Holt, Rinehart and Winston.

O'Dea, Thomas F.
1966   *The Sociology of Religion*. Englewood Cliffs, New Jersey: Prentice-Hall.

Ostrander, Sheila and Schroeder, Lynn.
1971   *Psychic Discoveries Behind the Iron Curtain*. New York: Bantam Books.
1974   *Handbook of Psychic Discoveries*. New York: Berkley Publishing Corporation.

Ouspensky, P. D.
1974   *The Psychology of Man's Possible Evolution*. New York: Vintage Books.

Peacock, James L.
1968   *Rites of Modernization*. Chicago: University of Chicago Press.
1975   *Consciousness and Change: Symbolic Anthropology in Evolutionary Perspective*. New York: Halstead Press.

Peacock, James L. and Kirsch, A. Thomas.
1980   *The Human Direction*. Englewood Cliffs, New Jersey: Prentice-Hall.

Peale, Norman Vincent.
1956   *The Power of Positive Thinking*. Greenwich, Connecticut: Fawcett Publications.
1959   *The Amazing Results of Positive Thinking*. Greenwich, Connecticut: Fawcett Publications.

Rawcliffe, D. H.
1959   *Illusions and Delusions of the Supernatural*. New York: Dover Publications.

Redgrove, H. Stanley.
1972   *Magic and Mysticism*. Secaucus, New Jersey: The
         Citadel Press.

Redl, Fritz.
1971   "The Superego in Uniform," in Nevitt Sanford and
         Craig Comstock (eds.), *Sanctions of Evil*. San
         Francisco: Jossey-Bass.

Rhine, J.B.
1962   *The Reach of the Mind*. New York: William Sloane
         Associates.

Richardson, James T.
1977   "Types of Conversion and 'Conversion Careers' in
         New Religious Movements," paper read at the Ameri-
         can Association for the Advancement of Science
         annual meeting in Denver.

Ringer, Robert J.
1974   *Winning Through Intimidation*. New York: Fawcett
         Crest.
1977   *Looking Out for #1*. New York: Fawcett Crest.

Robbins, Thomas; Anthony, Dick; and Richardson, James.
1978   "Theory and Research on Today's 'New Religions,'"
         Sociological Analysis, 39, 2:95-122.

Rochlin, Gregory.
1973   *Man's Aggression*. Boston: Gambit.

Rogo, D. Scott.
1976   *Parapsychology: A Century of Inquiry*. New York:
         Dell Publishing Company.

Rosinski, Herbert.
1965   *Power and Human Destiny*. New York: Frederick A.
         Praeger.

Sampson, Ronald V.
1966   *The Psychology of Power*. New York: Pantheon Books.

Sanford, Nevitt.
1971   "Authoritarianism and Social Destructiveness," in
         Nevitt Sanford and Craig Comstock (eds.), *Sanctions
         for Evil*. San Francisco: Jossey-Bass.

Sanford, Nevitt and Comstock, Craig.
1971   "Sanctions for Evil," in Nevitt Sanford and Craig
        Comstock (eds.), *Sanctions for Evil*. San Francisco:
        Jossey-Bass.

Saul, Leon J.
1956   *The Hostile Mind*. New York: Random House.

Schwartz, David J.
1965   *The Magic of Thinking Big*. New York: Cornerstone
        Library.

Scott, Gini Graham.
1980   *Cult and Countercult*. Westport, Connecticut:
        Greenwood Press.

Seligmann, Kurt.
1974   *Magic, Supernaturalism and Religion*. New York:
        Pantheon Books.

Smelser, Neil J.
1971   "Some Determinants of Destructive Behavior," in
        Nevitt Sanford and Craig Comstock (eds.), *Sanctions
        for Evil*. San Francisco: Jossey-Bass.

Speeth, Kathleen Riordan.
1976   *The Gurdjieff Work*. New York: Pocket Books.

Storr, Anthony.
1968   *Human Aggression*. New York: Bantam Books.

Tambiah, S. J.
1970   *Buddhism and the Spirit Cults in North-East Thai-
        land*. New York: Cambridge University Press.

Tart, Charles T.
1972   *Altered States of Consciousness*. Garden City,
        New York: Anchor Books.
1975   *States of Consciousness*. New York: E. P. Dutton &
        Company.
1977   *Transpersonal Psychologies*. New York: Harper &
        Row.

Tenenbaum, Samuel.
1947   *Why Men Hate*. Philadelphia: Ruttle, Shaw &
        Wetherill.

Turner, Victor W.
1967   *The Forest of Symbols*.   Ithaca, New York: Cornell
         University Press.
1968   *The Drums of Affliction*.   Oxford: Clarendon Press.
1969   *The Ritual Process*.   Chicago: Aldine Publishing Co.
1975   *Revelation and Divination in Ndembu Ritual*.   Ithaca,
         New York: Cornell University Press.
1978   *Image and Pilgrimage*.   New York: Columbia University
         Press.

Tylor, Edward Burnett.
1958   *Religion in Primitive Culture*.   New York: Harper &
         Row.

Van Beek, W.E.A. and Scherer, J.H.
1975   *Explorations in the Anthropology of Religion*.
         The Hague: Martinus Nijhoff.

Vernon, Glenn M.
1962   *Sociology of Religion*.   New York: McGraw-Hill Book
         Company.

Walters, Richard H.
1970   "Implications of Laboratory Studies of Aggression
         for the Control and Regulation of Violence," in
         Edwin I. Megargee and Jack E. Hokanson (eds.),
         The Dynamics of Aggression.   New York: Harper & Row.

Webb, James.
1974   *The Occult Underground*.   La Salle, Illinois: Open
         Court Publishing Company.

White, John.
1974   *Psychic Exploration*.   New York: G.P. Putnam's Sons.

Wilson, Colin.
1973   *The Occult*.   New York: Vintage Books.

Woods, Richard.
1971   *The Occult Revolution*.   New York: The Seabury Press.

Yinger, J. Milton.
1961   *Religion, Society, and the Individual*.   New York:
         The Macmillan Company.

Zaretsky, Irving I. and Leone, Mark P.
1974   *Religious Movements in Contemporary America.*
         Princeton: Princeton University Press.

978-0-595-43362-9
0-595-43362-6

Printed in Dunstable, United Kingdom